*Prais...*

# FREEMASONRY

"Like a drowsy lion, Freemasonry arouses in the outsider both curiosity and mistrust. This landmark book anatomizes the creature without apology or mystification. At the same time, it summons insiders to revive their moribund craft in all the grandeur of its original mission to humanity. Mark Stavish, whose work is informed by a profound knowledge of esoteric traditions, has earned gratitude from both sides."

—Joscelyn Godwin, Professor of Music and
Medieval & Renaissance Studies, Colgate University,
author of *The Theosophical Enlightenment, The Pagan
Dream of the Renaissance,* and other works

"*Freemasonry* is one of the most comprehensive studies written on the esoteric aspects of Freemasonry in the past half-century. The author is a recognized leader in the field of Western magic traditions and approaches the analysis of Freemasonry from a fresh, nontraditional viewpoint."

—Charles S. Canning, M.Ed.,
Director, Harry C. Trexler Masonic Library

"This is a book written with intelligence, wit, and critical irony on the complex topic of Freemasonry in relationship to the history of Western esotericism. The historic mirror of Freemasonry has never reflected so brightly the vast range of its cultural influences. The author explicitly addresses the occult, esoteric, and, particularly, Hermetic influences that have shaped the teachings and values of Freemasonry. This is not a typical history, but an integrative analysis that explores Masonic organizations, various rites, symbols, ethical and secret teachings in relation to a wider context of concurrent movements. With excellent references, many historic examples, and a rich plethora of influences and cross-currents, this work is an informative contribution to the field of esoteric studies, occult history, and a genuinely needed overview of the deep pluralism inherent to Masonic history."

—Lee Irwin, College of Charleston,
author of *Alchemy of Soul*

## About the Author

Mark Stavish has over a quarter-century of experience in traditional spirituality and is an internationally respected authority in the study and practical application of alchemy, Qabala, and astrology. Stavish has published several hundred articles, book reviews, and interviews on the traditions of Western esotericism, many of which have been translated into numerous languages. He has also been a consultant to print and broadcast media as well as several documentaries.

In 1998, Stavish established the Institute for Hermetic Studies. In 2001, to further the advancement of nonsectarian and academic approaches to Western esotericism, he established the Louis Claude de Saint Martin Fund, thereby creating the only widely known tax-deductible, nonprofit fund dedicated exclusively to advancing the study and practice of Western esotericism.

Stavish's education includes two undergraduate degrees, in theology and communications, and a master's degree in counseling. He has also been a member and officer in several traditional initiatic organizations focusing on Rosicrucianism, Martinism, and regular Freemasonry.

For more information on the Institute for Hermetic Studies and its program of activities and to receive its free electronic newsletter, *VOXHERMES*, visit its website at www.hermeticinstitute.org.

# FREEMASONRY

*Rituals, Symbols & History
of the Secret Society*

MARK STAVISH

Llewellyn Publications
Woodbury, Minnesota

First Edition
First Printing, 2007

Book design and layout by Joanna Willis
Cover design by Ellen Dahl
Cover image © Steve Gottlieb / UpperCut Images / PunchStock
Illustrations on pages 54 and 57 from *Magic and the Western Mind* by Gareth Knight
    (Llewellyn Publications)
Illustrations on pages 14, 27, 49, 52–53, 56, 58–61, 63, 99, 215–16, 218
"Sacred Geometry and the Masonic Tradition" © 2004 by John Michael Greer. All
    rights reserved.

Excerpt from *The Fundamentals of Esoteric Knowledge* by Jean Dubuis reprinted with permission from Triad Publishing.

**Library of Congress Cataloging-in-Publication Data**
The Cataloging-in-Publication Data for *Freemasonry: Rituals, Symbols & History of the Secret Society* is on file at the Library of Congress.
ISBN: 978-0-7387-1148-5

Llewellyn Publications
A Division of Llewellyn Worldwide, Ltd.
2143 Wooddale Drive, Dept. 978-0-7387-1148-5
Woodbury, MN 55125-2989, U.S.A.
www.llewellyn.com

Printed in the United States of America

This book is dedicated to my wife, Andrea,
and our two sons, Luke and Nathaniel.
They are the cornerstone upon which
all my good works have been built,
and the capstone of my life.

# Also by Mark Stavish

*Kabbalah for Health & Wellness*

*The Path of Alchemy*

# Contents

# Acknowledgments

Special thanks are in order to Carl Weschcke, for asking me to write this book, and to Bill Krause, the publisher at Llewellyn, and Wade Ostrowski, my editor. Bill and Wade exhibited exceptional patience and understanding with me as the project spilled months past its initial deadline. However, as I told them, great projects often encounter great obstacles, and I really believe that this is a book that can help many Masons better understand the Craft and help non-Masons develop a "Masonic" philosophy even if they never join a lodge.

I am indebted to Brother Lon Milo DuQuette for writing such a touching and deeply personal foreword, and to occultist and Masonic scholar extraordinaire Brother John Michael Greer for allowing me to reprint his essay on sacred geometry.

I am grateful to Brother Charles S. Canning, director of the Harry C. Trexler Masonic Library (Allentown, Pennsylvania), for his enthusiasm for this book and his assistance in making it more appealing to our Masonic brethren. Brother Canning is a tireless worker in the area of Masonic research and education, and he generously took time out of his schedule to spend many hours researching materials in the Trexler Library as well as reviewing the manuscript with me to clarify points for both Masonic and non-Masonic readers. His approval of the general theme and content has meant a great deal to me from the standpoint of contemporary Masonic scholarship.

Thank you to Joscelyn Godwin, a true scholar and gentleman who has been supportive of my writing for many years now and whose friendship has changed my life in many ways, and to Paul Bowersox of the Writing Studio for his assistance with yet another book.

# Foreword

Masonry is a progressive moral science, divided into different degrees; and, as its principles and mystic ceremonies are regularly developed and illustrated, it is intended and hoped that they will make a deep and lasting impression upon your mind.

—FROM THE FELLOWCRAFT DEGREE,
FREE & ACCEPTED MASONS[1]

It's four o'clock a.m. I creep quietly past the rooms of my sleeping Brothers and out to the darkened hallway that leads to the staircase to the atrium. The atrium is a cavernous space, nearly two hundred feet long and over fifty feet wide, built in the style of the Roman Empire. The marble floor is adorned with Masonic symbols inlaid in brass and stone of contrasting colors. The Doric and Ionic columns that flank the great hall and support the second-story walkways and chambers are dwarfed by towering Corinthian columns that buttress the vaulted ceiling, three stories high, whose centerpiece stained-glass skylight now bathes the room in iridescent moonlight.

There are five statues here whose bronze presences I am moved to honor. Four are the goddess figures of the cardinal virtues: Temperance, Prudence, Fortitude, and Justice. They are positioned at the corners of

---

1  Grand Lodge of California, Free & Accepted Masons, *California Cipher* (Richmond, VA: Allen Publishing Company, 1990).

the room, which I slowly circumambulate as I move from pedestal to pedestal. The fifth goddess stands in the very center of the hall and bears no inscription or emblem. She simply holds her forefinger to her lips as if to hush the universe. It is here at the feet of silence that I sit down on the cool floor and close my eyes. Only a moment, it seems, passes before I hear the warm ring of a temple bowl. The others are awake, and we are being called to dawn meditation.

I slip off my shoes outside the door of the lodge room, tiptoe inside, and take my seat. The room is dark save for a single candle on the central altar. After a few quiet words of introduction and instruction, we close our eyes and enter our inner temples. Forty minutes later, the sun has risen. We open our eyes and see the room brilliantly illuminated by three large Italian stained-glass panels, which we now see form the entire southern wall of the lodge room. Each window dramatically depicts one of the three ages of man: youth, manhood, and old age. My eyes linger on each scene in turn as I weigh the well-lived episodes of my life against those of time misspent.

After breakfast, we gather beneath chandeliers of Czechoslovakian crystal in the spacious reception room and, for the first time, see who has come this year. I immediately recognize some of the brightest stars in the firmament of modern Masonry. I also see friends and colleagues from years past—writers, scholars, teachers, and students. As always, there are several Brothers who have been invited for the first time to present papers and lecture.

We are met for three days of presentations and discussions of issues and subjects relating to esoteric aspects of the Craft of Freemasonry. We have gathered secretly and informally, under no official warrant, charter, or auspices, to explore the Craft as a self-transformational art and science—gathered to labor and strategize how best to proceed to protect, preserve, and advance the esoteric soul of Freemasonry.

Appropriately, the venue for this gathering is one of the largest and most architecturally magnificent Masonic edifices in the world, inexplicably abandoned by its usual team of custodial stewards for the duration of our meetings. The building itself is intoxicating. We are all humbled by its beauty and perfect proportions. One cannot resist being tangibly elevated as we each intuitively attempt to adjust our inner imperfections to reflect the outer perfections of the sacred geometry around us. As we walk the sacred labyrinth, sit quietly studying in the Gothic library, or muse about alchemy at the feet of Assyrian sphinxes, we find ourselves pausing and asking each other, "Is this really happening?"

Yes. It really happens, and *this* is how I always dreamed Masonry would be.

*This*, however, is not what all Masons think the Craft should be. As a matter of fact, there are a great many who now feel that the esoteric roots of our ancient institution are an embarrassment—queer and unwholesome links to paganism, the occult, and perhaps even Satanism. You might be surprised to learn that there is a concerted effort now taking place within Masonry to once and for all divorce the Craft from its esoteric heritage and make it an organization open only to men professing certain specific religious convictions. Even though Masonic tradition dictates that a candidate need only profess a belief in a Supreme Being and a form of afterlife, today there are jurisdictions and lodges around the world that will not consider the application of a man if they believe his religion to be not "mainstream" enough or his interest in the esoteric nature of the Craft suspiciously intense.

This is why, sadly, I cannot tell you in what country our gathering takes place. Neither can I tell you the names of the participants, the circumstances that bring us together, or the details of our activities and goals. By necessity, Masonry has for us again become a secret society.

What makes this anti-esoteric movement so ill-timed and suicidal is the fact that Masonry's membership numbers are plunging precipitously. Lodges are closing or merging with other lodges for lack of members. Freemasonry as we've known it for the last three hundred years will be dead in just a few years' time if something isn't done. Ironically (and much to the terror of the anti-esoterics), the *only* demographic group that is applying for membership in significant numbers is composed of young men who are passionately interested in the esoteric mysteries of the Craft.

Fortunately, at least for the time being, exoteric Masonry is still, for the most part, a very big tent. Even in the most conservative quarters, leadership still pays lip service to the concept that Masonry opens her doors to upstanding men[2] of all races, religions, political persuasions, and social and economic circumstances. Aside from the obligatory duties required to advance through the degrees, the individual Mason is free to be as interested or disinterested as he likes in matters that concern the history, rituals, traditions, and mysteries of the Craft. As it is (much to the relief of the anti-esoterics), most Masons, once they are raised to the Sublime Degree of Master Mason (and, if they so choose, go on to complete the degrees in one or more concordant rites), are happy to put the "quaint and curious" stuff behind them and simply enjoy being part of one of the most active and generous service organizations in the world.

This is as it should be, and please don't think that I am denigrating the contributions and efforts of a Brother who wishes to participate at any level. The world needs a generous service organization to sponsor hospitals and clinics and scholarships. Some men need a relatively wholesome place to meet socially once or twice a month with other relatively wholesome men. Add to this the possibility that some men might actually have a psychological need to put on clown makeup and drive tiny cars in parades.

Without men like this, Masonry would not be (for the time being at least) the largest and wealthiest fraternal organization in the world. These are good men who *are* made better by their involvement in the Craft. But there are also those among them who would like to be spiritually transformed by Masonry's deeper secrets—and currently, these are the only men applying in any significant numbers. (Still, I'd wager that even some of the clowns in the tiny cars, if properly educated, might be fascinated by the esoteric side of things.)

The sad fact is, most Masons are never adequately exposed to knowledgeable Brothers or material that might excite their curiosity beyond wondering, "What's for Stated Meeting dinner?" It's not that the information is not available. Plenty of fine books have been written over the centuries, some of which might be found in the libraries of local lodges all around the world. But many of these books were written in the 1800s, at

---

2  Although there are several organizations, such as Co-Masonry, that accept both men and women, and other rites that are exclusive to women, "regular" Masonry remains at present a men's fraternity.

a time when interest in esoteric Masonry was at its zenith and when even a high school diploma meant a familiarity with Greek and Latin and a smattering of philosophy, world religions, and history. Anyone who has ever started to read Albert Pike's *Morals and Dogma* will know exactly what I'm talking about.

What has been lacking for the modern Mason, and what Brother Stavish now mercifully presents us, is a straightforward and step-by-step study of Freemasonry and the myriad movements and ideas that gave birth to the Craft in all its manifestations. Moreover, he sets it all vis-à-vis twenty-first-century science, philosophy, and mysticism and challenges the reader to do the same. This book is a one-volume liberal-arts education in Freemasonry, and never before in the history of the Craft has it been more important for individual Masons to be so educated. I wish I could put Brother Stavish's book in the hands of every new-raised Brother, not simply for his own benefit, but for the benefit of those individuals throughout his life who will look to him as a worthy example of a knowledgeable and enlightened member of the Fraternity.

> May the blessing of Heaven rest upon us and all regular Masons! May Brotherly Love prevail, and every moral and social virtue cement us! Amen.
>
> —THE MASTER'S CLOSING PRAYER,
> FREE & ACCEPTED MASONS[3]

Lon Milo DuQuette, 32°
Author of *The Key to Solomon's Key: Secrets of Magic and Masonry*

---

3 Grand Lodge of California, *California Cipher*.

# Introduction

## What Is the Secret of Freemasonry?

When asked if Freemasonry is a secret society, many Masons will simply reply that it is a "society with secrets." That is, there are things within Masonry that are only, or should only, be known to members. A true secret society is just that: a secret. It hides its existence and conceals its motives from the public at large—and sometimes from its own members. As such, if Freemasonry is a secret society, it is a pretty poor one. Masonic halls, with their lodges and banquet rooms, dot most urban landscapes. Massive and ornate variations, often called "temples," in that they are temples of learning, can be seen in almost every major city in the oldest and most established sections of town. Thousands of books have been written about Freemasonry, many by Masons (such as this one), and hundreds of websites devoted to Freemasonry in all of its forms and varieties exist. Masons march in parades and support charities, and they wear distinctive jewelry and ties and even put bumper stickers on their vehicles to recognize one another when traveling. Despite this, many people often think of Masonry as something other than what is described in this book—something to be feared.

It has always been stated that Freemasonry jealously conceals its secrets from the profane and extracts oaths to maintain that secrecy under pain of the most horrific penalties for oath breakers who violate them.[1] While this is true, it still raises the question of what exactly Freemasonry's secret is, or at least is about. Many authors have turned Masonry into their own personal publishing industry, writing an endless array of speculations about "the secret." For some, it is literally a buried treasure to be found somewhere underneath the Temple Mount in Jerusalem, Rosslyn Chapel in Scotland, or the famed Money Pit of Oak Island, Nova Scotia. For others, it is an esoteric secret, a form or style of initiation, possibly obtained by the Knights Templar during their stay in the Middle East and symbolized by their mysterious head of Baphomet. Others will say there are no secrets, except as you are able to find them, thereby making it the personal decision of each Freemason. Of late, many Grand Masters of various jurisdictions have pointed out that most of the Masonic rituals have been published in some form that is more or less accurate, and as such, the only real secrets modern Masonry has are the signs of recognition between its members—funny handshakes, passwords, and other relics of bygone days when dues cards were not issued and membership was outlawed by princes fearing possible democratic challenges to their power, and even considered heresy by the Roman Catholic Church.

When Carl Weschcke first brought up the idea of my writing a book on Freemasonry, I was both pleased and somewhat taken aback. It was no secret that within months Dan Brown's runaway bestseller *The Da Vinci Code* would be released as a movie with a top-of-the-line cast, and everyone wanted to get a piece of the action once Freemasonry became the hot topic of the season. The real question in my mind was how to write a book on Freemasonry that addressed the needs of the various readers, of whom some would be Freemasons, some potential Masons, and others simply interested in the topic. The more I thought about it, reflected on my own Masonic experiences, talked to other members of the Craft—their expectations from Freemasonry, their experiences, what they would like to see more of—and then began outlining the chapters

---

1  It is interesting to note that the Old English word for "oath breaker," *warlock*, became associated during the eighteenth century with a male practitioner of magic. This was a period when magic and esotericism were deeply entrenched in the proliferation of Masonic rites.

for the project, the more it became clear that the message of this book extends well beyond the limits of a single movement, no matter how large or significant it may be.

Above all, it is important for each reader to know that there is no such thing as "*the* book" on Freemasonry. Masonry is defined as a system of "moral teachings veiled in symbolism." This means that each Freemason is free to interpret his ritualistic experience in any manner he sees fit and that no one can tell him he is wrong. This places Freemasonry in a peculiar situation, but one that clearly reflects the attitude of the ages in which it came about. It provides an intellectually liberal framework in which one can meet with others while protecting the organization and its members to some degree from being an established challenger to the powers that be. If there is no creed of beliefs, other than belief in a Supreme Being, then it surely cannot be a religion, and as such is not competing with the religious establishment of the day.

Even so, those symbols used by Freemasonry that have their roots in religious and mystical practices—primarily those of the Jewish and Christian experience—also include elements that, while not identified, are clearly not biblical. The fundamental notion of building, or creating, is the centerpiece of Freemasonry, and it was said for generations that the origin of the Fraternity was to be found in the medieval building guilds. Oral tradition stated that Freemasons, or their predecessors, were said to have possessed some occult secret carried back from Jerusalem or elsewhere and had encapsulated it into the iconography of the great Gothic cathedrals. This theme was particularly expounded upon by the mysterious twentieth-century French alchemist Fulcanelli in *The Mystery of the Cathedrals*, wherein he states that the entire alchemical corpus can be found in the stonework of cathedrals such as Notre Dame and Chartres.

It is easy to see why this could be believed by modern minds. Even as I write this, I am listening to a CD of music that was composed in the twelfth century yet is hauntingly timeless: *Vision: The Music of Hildegard Von Bingen*, performed by Richard Souther, with Emily Van Evera and Sister Germaine Fritz, OSB, as the featured vocalists. I first heard Hildegard's music when it was used on the soundtrack for the documentary *Cathedral:*

*The Story of Its Construction*, based on the book by David Macaulay and narrated by him. The documentary, a mix of animation and live presenters, tells the story of the multigenerational construction of the cathedral of Notre Dame de Beaulieu in 1214. I first saw the movie in the early 1990s, when employed as a case-records manager for the J. Arthur Trudeau Center in Warwick, Rhode Island. As part of my duties, I had to arrange for and supervise activities for the developmentally disabled adults who were employed in the multisite facility. At that time, it became clear to me what the difference was between worship in the High Middle Ages and today, and why so many men and women longed for a sort of Middle Ages that never was—Masonic and Rosicrucian scholar A. E. Waite among them. Depicted in the images of the tarot deck created under his direction, we see an idyllic rural Gothic world in which the quest for the Holy Grail is all-encompassing and a seamless connection links the daily quasi-pagan/ shamanic beliefs of the peasantry with communal church worship and initiatic mysticism.

The beauty, charm, and inspiration of what our forebears built in the name of "Our Lady" can be seen in every European city and town. The last vestiges of Celtic, Roman, Egyptian, and Germanic paganism were enshrined in the Catholic cathedrals—the Prince's Seat—in the marble and wood statues of Mary, the mother of Jesus, the Child of the Sun, sending their silent message to future generations. It was about these fabulous structures and the men who built them that Joseph Fort Newton wrote *The Builders: A Story and Study of Freemasonry*, in which he states:

> Man was not meant to be a cringing being, eaten up by anxiety, shut up a prisoner in silent loneliness, living in blind cruelty. He was meant for great adventures, if he has the insight to see the laws of life and the key of kindness to unlock the doors; and in his quest for the best in others he will discover something in himself not guessed before. For each of us, though we may not be clever or commanding, but only average and unknown, life can be winged and wonderful, full of meaning and music, if we have the faith to trust the God who made us, and the wisdom to live, love, and learn.[2]

---

2 Joseph Fort Newton, *The Builders: A Story and Study of Freemasonry* (Cedar Rapids, IA: Torch Press, 1915). Also available online at http://www.gutenberg.org/etext/19049.

Building is what Masonry is all about: building a better person, a better community, a better society, and a better world—all in that order.

We know what a community values based on what it builds and what it allows to languish or decay. In the High Middle Ages, during the Gothic period, temples of stone and light were created to give praise to the Mother of God. These were once the central structures of a town or city, dominating the landscape, and often were the tallest building, visible for miles away. Now we build skyscrapers of poured concrete to warehouse human beings as they move invisible money and information (as no one wants to dirty themselves with actual material labor anymore) from one computer to another. These buildings belong to both the private interests that own them and the bloated social services system that has drained creativity and responsibility from people for over two generations now. One need only look at the size of the Department of Social Services building in Center City Philadelphia and compare it to the Grand Lodge of Pennsylvania (directly across the street from it), the neighboring Trinity Church, Philadelphia City Hall, or any one of a dozen office buildings to understand the message being sent about what is understood to be of value.

John Anthony West writes in the foreword to *The Return of Sacred Architecture: The Golden Ratio and the End of Modernism,* by Herbert Bangs, M.Arch.,

> Not so long ago, architecture was typically the highest and most complete artistic expression of a sophisticated civilization. It provided the framework within which the other art forms manifested. It was where the lion's share of any given society's creativity was directed; the architecture expressed and enshrined the soul. In fact, if we had no written history at all, we would be able to get a very good idea of the living essence of any given civilization simply by looking closely at where its creative energy is expended: Ancient Egypt's creative energy went into its temples, pyramids, and tombs; Rome's went into its roads, massive civic projects, and coliseums; ours today goes into an elaborate missile defense system and disposable products designed to feed our materialistic, consumer-driven culture.[3]

---

3 Herbert Bangs, *The Return of Sacred Architecture: The Golden Ratio and the End of Modernism* (Rochester, VT: Inner Traditions, 2006), x.

Each building represents the ideals of the age in which it was built. The raw functionalism of modern architecture is enough to destroy any sense of the divine—and in turn, destroy any sense of the individual as something other than a walking bag of bones. What inspires us in the United States is the churches and cathedrals, and even the civic facilities such as museums, and, of course, the Masonic temples—all of which were built before the Second World War, and many in the nineteenth century. While we are still young by European standards, Continental snobbery should not be too proud, in that two world wars and a collapsed sense of national identity, along with the moral and ethical values of rampant social materialism, has done significant harm to them as well.

Through all of this, one of the single constants has been Freemasonry.

At the risk of redundancy later on in this book, it is important to keep in mind that the lessons of Freemasonry are universal, in that they deal with human strivings and aspirations for improvement and the search for Light. Masonry also demonstrates the importance of commitment to a single ideal and how that can allow a movement not only to survive, but also to grow under the pressure of opposition and even persecution. Neo-pagans should take note that Masonry is a perfect example of "centralized decentralization." While bound by specific and unchangeable landmarks or specific Masonic signs, symbols, words, documents, and points, there is considerable variation in how Masonic degrees are worked from rite to rite as well as jurisdiction to jurisdiction. Each lodge is obedient to the Grand Lodge that charters it, but it has a wide range of autonomy within which to work.

This autonomy, coupled with localization (meaning that members of a lodge come from within that lodge's community), has given a great deal of uniqueness to Masonic expression, for both better and worse. Masonry demonstrates a workable model for new and emerging spiritual movements to copy if they seek to be more than Renaissance fairs without admission fees or simple counterculture escapism.

Despite the promises of perpetual progress, material abundance, and a world without suffering, everything has its moment and then passes. Through its landmarks, Masonry teaches and demonstrates that which is permanent and unchanging—the essence of a thing—and how to recognize it. For this very reason, the examples in this book have been taken from a variety of published Masonic rituals and jurisdictions. Normally, such an approach would appear haphazard or unduly eclectic. However, since all of Freemasonry is united by its landmarks and its rituals are localized expressions of them at a particular place and time, it is possible to widen our understanding of Masonry and its lessons—lessons that, as we will see, can be applied equally by those outside the Craft—by examining their various expressions.

If asked to define what characterizes a Mason, there could be no single answer. All of the virtues of faith, hope, and charity are embodied in Masonry, as well as the Golden Rule of "Do unto others as you would have others do unto you." If we take our cue from the degrees of Masonic initiation, we can see that a Mason—one who has undertaken to embody the Masonic ideal and who is more than a dues payer or pin wearer—is first and foremost a gentleman. He is slow to anger, quick to forgive, generous with praise, and courteous in speech. How he treats others is the rule by which he is judged and measured, and as such, so is the Fraternity. He is also a scholar, in that he seeks personal self-improvement and knowledge of himself, humanity, and the world in which he lives. Nothing is truly foreign to him, and the Seven Liberal Arts and Sciences are his keys to self-awakening. A Freemason knows that in improving himself, he is an example for his Brethren and for his community. By improving himself first, he improves the world. Thirdly, he is religiously devoted, or more accurately, mystically inclined. His attention is always drawn toward the ineffable and the sublime, as therein lies the Light of the Oriental Chair, and within himself he constructs the Temple of Wisdom. This is done in silence and without the sound of hammer, mallet, or chisel, for only in the depths of silence can Wisdom speak. He is a mystic last, because this is the most private and personal thing about him, and the least that should be known by others. The fact that he is a good man and generous to all and encourages learning and self-becoming is enough for them to know. He does not hide his Light, but he does not wear it as a badge of honor. If others see it in him, then so be it; if not, that is fine as well. Yet when asked, he freely shares its wisdom with others, and if asked still, he shares how they too may find it within themselves, without being a braggart or proselytizing. In this way, the secret of Freemasonry is an open secret for everyone to see, but, like the Gospel, it is often veiled in the allegory of "Let those who have ears hear, and with eyes see."

Many of my Masonic Brethren who read this book will be taken aback by the clear connection it makes between the Craft and the esoteric doctrines associated with the practical aspects of occultism—mainly ritual magic, alchemy, and astrology. This is unfortunate, because for many Masons in the United States, as well as elsewhere in the world, Freemasonry's symbols are seen as extensions of the Christian experience rather than what they truly are: the precursors to it. To those Masons who object to this connection and fail to see what is before them, I suggest they turn to the King James Bible they were presented with upon becoming a Thirty-Second Degree Mason in the Scottish Rite. Herein, they will find a series of questions and answers, many of which will surprise them if they take the time to read them and research the actual meaning of the words and their context. Unfortunately, this is rarely done, and it is in part for this reason that this book was written.

While the questions and answers given below may be of little meaning to the reader, be he a Mason or not at the moment, they will have a clear and distinct meaning when he has completed the final chapter. Regardless, some Masons will still hold true to their belief that Masonry is simply an extension of the Jewish-Christian experience, and to some degree this will always be true. There is a point where this changes, and within the context of the Judeo-Christian experience, the ancient mystery traditions of Egypt, Chaldea, Greece, Rome, and even Persia and India are brought forth into the Masonic ritual experience, making it distinctly doctrinally non-Christian. Anti-Masons will find further justification for their vilification of the Craft here, but then whether it comes from this book and its clearly listed sources or from another, they would have found it anyhow—even if it meant making it up!

The following is found within the first few pages of the Holy Bible prepared for the Scottish Rite and given upon reception of the Thirty-Second

Degree. It is taken from Charles H. Merz's "Ask Me Brother," which was originally published in 1927.

### Questions and Answers Relating to Characters, Places, Words, and Phrases Used in Symbolic Masonry

Q: Hebrew language: Why is it of the greatest importance in Free Masonry?

A: Because the alphabet and its numerical values is the key to the greater number of words employed in Masonry as well as the mysteries of the Bible.

Q: Hermes Trismegistus: Who was he?

A: The "Thrice Great," a celebrated Egyptian legislator, priest and philosopher, who lived about the year 2670. From the Hermetic Arts we have in Masonry, Hermetic Rites and Hermetic Degrees.

Q: Masons Wind: What is the fundamental idea?

A: Blowing from the East, in the belief of the Middle Ages, that all good things, such as philosophy and religion, come from the East.

Q: Monarch: What monarch, [is] the son of David, and [what] is the literal meaning of his name.

A: Solomon: Kabbalistic composition, its outward form expressed the symbolism as the three principal officers of a Masonic Lodge. Sol, the sun; Om, the meridian sun; On, the setting sun—Worshipful Master, Junior Warden, Senior Warden.[4]

Additional questions and answers make reference to Egypt, Enoch, Rosicrucians sharing symbols with Freemasonry, placing the origin of Freemasonry in the oldest of ancient mysteries and the astrological sign of Leo, and the magical creature, or serpent, known as Shermah, which legend says Solomon used to build the Temple.

Once again, those with eyes to see and ears to listen will understand the importance of the above questions and answers within, as well as outside of, a Masonic context.

---

4 Heirloom Bible Publishers, *Master Mason Bible: King James Version* (Wichita, KS: Heirloom Bible Publishers, n.d.).

## A Note to the Non-Mason

Most of readers of this book will not be members of the Craft. Many will know someone who is a Freemason or have a family member who belongs and will simply want to know more about Freemasonry. Others may be interested in the so-called secrets of the Fraternity and what they may be. And some, while intrigued, may be asking themselves, "What does Masonic Philosophy have to do with me if I am not a Mason? How can it make my life better?" Of all these disparate groups, it is for this reader that this book is written. Masonic Philosophy is universal, and the lessons it can teach us transcend sect or cult. Readers who belong to one or more religious, initiatic, or esoteric organizations will find the exercises beneficial to their particular group. Some may even find themselves "a Brother (or Sister) Without an Apron."

## "Nullius in Verba"

"Nullius in Verba," or "On the words of no one," best describes Freemasonry and any attempts to write a definitive book or encyclopedia on the matter. Masonry, as we will shortly see, is a vast topic, and as a living entity, it has no official doctrines or creeds, only the requirement that one believe in a Supreme Being. While every effort has been made to demonstrate the direct relationship of the material presented here to ancient and modern Freemasonry, it is in no way exclusionary. Each Freemason must come to understand the Craft to the best of his ability. This book is simply my effort at fulfilling that oath and obligation.

To be clear to the reader: despite its philosophical and religious overtones, Freemasonry is not a religion, although it shares the purpose of religion, in that it encourages the uniting of man with God. Masonry does not require any specific set of beliefs other than the belief in a Supreme Being, and even this is a fuzzy idea, being individualistic in meaning. While some say Masonry is a religious organization, it would be more accurate to describe it as speculative and philosophic. Masonry has no creed or sacraments and no means of salvation, and it is a human creation, not a divinely revealed one. In the end, Freemasonry is about self-improvement and helping others—what we do on this earth as an expression of our understanding of our relation to divinity. The rest is simply details.

Mark Stavish
Director of Studies, Institute for Hermetic Studies
Wyoming, Pennsylvania
Saint John's Day, December 26, 2006

# How to Use This Book

While many books explain the rituals and symbols of Freemasonry, none have truly put them in the proper context so that modern men (and women) can understand why they are as important to us today as they were three hundred years ago. *Freemasonry: Rituals, Symbols & History of the Secret Society* shows the reader how to understand the events that gave rise to Freemasonry, why they matter, and how to live a "Masonic" life as a creator, builder, and friend of God and humanity, whether or not you ever wear a Masonic apron.

While this book can be read as an overview of Masonic symbolism and ideas and their relationship to Renaissance and classical thought, it should be used primarily as a workbook for self-improvement, for self-improvement is what Masonry, esotericism, and various modern therapies most readers will be familiar with are all about.

1. Have a notebook handy and some colored pencils or pens. Write down key ideas and go back to study them before reading the next chapter.

2. Read at least one of the books from each chapter's Suggested Reading list.

3. Pay attention to your dreams as you progress through this book. Read slowly and casually and allow the ideas to stimulate your creative

energies. Practice at least one of the assignments given at the end of each chapter.

4. Write down ideas, inspirations, and other things that come to you from "out of the blue" as you progress.

5. Begin each reading session with a prayer to the Divine Architect of the Universe, the God of your understanding, to enlighten you on this very special and unique journey.

6. Take what you have learned and put it to use in the world of action. Join a civic group or volunteer some time regularly to a non-political, nonreligious cause. Make cash donations as well, and see how much you are blessed by helping others and how much you have to give but had not realized it.

7. Give thanks daily for the blessings you have, and spend time in meditation and prayer as often as possible.

# I

# What Is Freemasonry?

OVERVIEW
- *Operative and Speculative Masonry*
- *The First Grand Lodge*
- *Antients and Moderns*

Freemasonry has captivated the public's attention since its inception because of its reputation as a society that contains secrets. However, in addition to secrets, or things known only to its members, Freemasonry is also an organization that possesses many mysteries—foremost among them the very origins of the Craft itself.

As an organization, Freemasonry defines itself as "A peculiar system of morality, veiled in allegory and illustrated by symbols." And, as such, "Freemasonry makes good men better."

While interesting, these definitions are not terribly informative, as we are left asking ourselves the usual questions of "how," "why," and "what for." To answer these questions, we need to examine the history of Freemasonry and how it came to be the meeting ground for men from all walks of life and philosophical persuasions at a time when class structure was rigid and religious wars ravaged Europe.

The symbolism is in part the mystery as well as the secret. Freemasonry (or, more accurately, the Order of Free and Accepted Masons) derives its system of initiation of three degrees from the techniques and methods of the stonemasons' trade, or those Operative Masons who actually worked with stone, as well as biblical accounts of the construction of the Temple of Solomon. From these two relatively simple ideas, a complex structure of ritual, symbolism, philanthropy, and philosophy has arisen. In addition, some things unique to Masonry, such as "the Mason's Word" and the legend of Hiram Abiff, have been the source of a great deal of speculation, suggesting that Freemasons were privy to secret esoteric teachings and occult operations. This, coupled with the length and breadth of the order as it grew, created a perfect climate for Freemasonry to become a vehicle for the promotion of certain spiritual ideas that were outside the mainstream. While such promotions were more often private affairs than centrally directed by a Grand Lodge, Freemasonry became the happy hunting grounds for esoteric groups seeking members as early as thirty years after the formation of the first Grand Lodge. The reasons for this are simple: Masons were educated, socially connected, and able to travel more freely, and perhaps there were some early occult influences in the formation of the first Grand Lodge.

## Operative and Speculative Masonry

The medieval building guilds, or early unions, had their origin in the construction of the great cathedrals and public building projects of the day. Given that many trades were passed down from father to son or master to apprentice, methods and techniques were jealously guarded not only to ensure proper training, but also to limit the number of workers in any given craft. Rites and rituals of progression developed around these organizations, all reflecting to some degree the dominant theme of religion in daily life, as well as providing a means of "linking" their trade in a religious or philosophical sense. Roman Catholicism and Eastern Orthodoxy are filled with patron saints, with each holy person forming a direct link to Christ or divinity, a conduit for divine blessing upon a particular field of work or endeavor.

Members of these guilds had means of recognizing one another during their travels as well as when applying for work on a specific project. This thereby fostered a sense of fraternalism that extended beyond simple daily employment. In addition, the means of transmitting knowledge meant that in some way, even if tenuously thin, members of these guilds could see themselves as connected to great builders of old, going back to the Roman architectural colleges, the temples of Egypt, and even to Solomon himself.

Despite their exact and precise knowledge, most members of trade guilds were illiterate. Those who were literate would have acted as the contractors on projects and communicated with the church or royal sponsors, thereby giving them some interaction with the ruling elites in the various cities, regions, and countries in which they traveled and worked.

Given this intimate connection, and the well-established network of building lodges and related guilds that existed across Europe, it is no surprise that around 1,640 men who were not operative stonemasons were admitted (or *accepted*) into Masonic lodges; as such, they were known as Accepted Masons. The initial reason for admitting non-stonemasons into the lodges appears to have been purely financial. This admission was limited as well, with preference given to relatives of operative stoneworkers. The fees associated with membership were substantial, so along with them must have come benefits to outweigh the costs. What made this unique—even pivotal—is that in opening the doors to non-stonemasons, a host of middle-class professions suddenly found themselves seated together as never before. Within half a century, the majority of masons in most lodges were Accepted Masons and not Operative Masons—that is, not men who actually laid stone for a living. In the 1700s, this trend continued, with many lodges composed exclusively of Accepted Brethren, not a single bricklayer among them.

This would be of little consequence if it were not for a series of events also occurring in Europe during the seventeenth century. Just as operative building guilds were accepting non-stonemasons into their ranks, the Thirty Years War was beginning to come to a close. The Rosicrucian Enlightenment had failed, and numerous groups and networks of educated and wealthy men with an active interest in esotericism, alchemy, Qabala, Hermeticism, and utopian ideals needed a safe place to hide as well as meet. For many, the guild of Freemasonry may have been the perfect place, and not without precedence. As we will later see, there is also the possibility that Knights Templar on the run after the arrest of their brothers in arms in 1307 fled to Scotland, and possibly other areas not under strict papal control, and hid themselves among the stonemasons. This allowed them to continue communicating with each other and to travel without attracting too much attention to themselves.

The same would apply centuries later to Hermeticists on the run or seeking to have a safe means of travel, contact, and lodging when in foreign lands. The speed with which the Operative lodges were taken over by Speculative members is critical to this line of thinking, as is the justification given for the formation of the first Grand Lodge, the Grand Lodge of England. The question we are constantly faced with is, "Why would men actively seek to associate with other men who were clearly of a lower social class? What is it that they had to offer?" The answer, as we will see, may very well have to do with one word: *geometry*.

During the Renaissance and early period of the Enlightenment, mathematics was seen as a means to pure knowledge—access to the celestial realms of pure mind and idea. Math gave certitude, a repeatable and demonstrable method that faith alone could not. It was the gateway to the rule of reason (rather than faith). As a result of this, as well as the association of numbers with the occult, math was against the law in the medieval era, and zero was forbidden as the devil's number.

Despite the climate of fear that surrounded the study of such things, not all societies investigating the hidden realms of nature were secret at the time. Among the most famous and influential was the College for the Promoting of Physico-Mathematical Experimental Learning, renamed the Royal Society of London for Improving Natural Knowledge in 1663. The Royal Society, as it became known, had King Charles II as one of its benefactors and included some of the most well-known Freemasons as its first members. What is also critical here is that at this time, science, philosophy, and esotericism were not completely separate fields of study, but rather had considerable overlap. Men of learning were at least superficially familiar with Jewish mysticism or Qabala, alchemy, and astrology, as well as the theories of natural magic. *Natural magic* was the cornerstone of Renaissance philosophy and occultism; it proposed that the universe was composed of a series of interconnected energies, ideas, and planes of consciousness (complete with elemental, celestial, and demonic inhabitants) and that they could be affected through symbols, sounds, and physical acts such as alchemy and ceremonial operations.

Sir Christopher Wren, the London architect who played a key role in rebuilding London after the Great Fire of 1666;[1] Dr. John Theophilus Desaguliers; Robert Moray, military engineer and associate of Francis Bacon and Descartes; and Elias Ashmole, scholar, were among the first members of the Royal Society. Elias Ashmole's connection is among the most well known, thereby linking the Royal Society, Freemasonry, and Hermeticism in seventeenth-century England.

## Ashmole: Angel Magician and First Freemason

Elias Ashmole (1617–92) is often referred to as "the first Freemason" and is falsely given credit in some histories as having cofounded the order. This high praise, while incorrect, does point to the influence he had in the formation of early Masonic ideals, made possible through his love of learning and obsession with antiquity. On October 16, 1646, Elias Ashmole, assisted by his cousin by marriage, became a Freemason. Ashmole was an avid antiquarian who collected numerous books and manuscripts. Born in the town of Lichfield, Staffordshire, he attended school to become employed as a lawyer.[2] Upon marriage, his wife's estate allowed him to devote his entire time to scholarly research, which included alchemy, Qabala, magic, and astrology. His extensive collection eventually formed the Ashmolean Museum at Oxford University, and among its most famous books were the original notebooks of Dr. John Dee and Edward Kelly's Enochian experiments. These notebooks eventually became part of the holdings of the British Museum and formed the core elements of the Enochian system utilized by the Hermetic Order of the Golden Dawn,

---

1 Forty thousand buildings and eighty-six churches were destroyed; as a result, Operative Masons from across England were needed to rebuild the city.

2 A small plaque adorns his birthplace and reads, "Priests' Hall—The Birthplace of Elias Ashmole, Windsor Herald to Charles II. Founder of the Ashmolean Museum, Oxford. Born 1617, Died 1692. Educated at Lichfield Grammar School."

Aleister Crowley, and later ceremonial magicians. In addition, Ashmole preserved important Hermetic and alchemical texts, including Norton's *Ordinall of Alchemy*, and authored a book on the early origins of the Order of the Garter, which was published in 1672. Titled *The Institutions, Laws, and Ceremonies of the Most Noble Order of the Garter*, this was to be his magnum opus.

Ashmole was close friends with William Lilly, Parliamentary astrologer; both appeared to have assisted each other in staying out of harm's way during the troubled years of the English Civil War and then the Restoration of Charles II. Lilly, by all accounts, is the father of English astrology, having earned an amazing sum during his lifetime because of the accuracy of his predictions. His masterpiece of over eight hundred pages, *Christian Astrology*, was the standard reference book on astrology in the English language until the astrological revival of the late nineteenth century.

Like Lilly, Ashmole was not content to be merely a bookish scholar of the occult arts. He eagerly pursued operative methods of alchemy, astrology, and angelic magic in his search for wisdom and knowledge of God. Coincidentally, the notion of an "angelic language" or primordial tongue, sought by many during this period, would eventually find itself in later Scottish Rite degrees, even referencing works by Athanasius Kircher and his discussion of an angelic alphabet, works well known to Ashmole and other Hermeticists. Ashmole cast a horoscope on October 23, 1667, to discover the most beneficial time for King Charles II to ceremonially place the first stone of the Royal Exchange. Unfortunately, with the publishing in 1659 of Meric Casaubon's *A True and Faithful Revelation of What Passed for Many Years Between Dr. John Dee and Some Spirits*, attacks on the works of Dee, known to be in Ashmole's collection, created a whirlwind of controversy that would later be understood as the beginning of the end of the Hermetic worldview.

While much of the antimystical thought of the period was aimed at ending the proliferation of sects and the religious warfare that had first decimated Central Europe and England, it was also the beginning of a profoundly materialistic, mechanistic, and atheistic worldview that would come to full fruition in the twentieth century, with Communism and laissez-faire capitalism as the primary examples.

Over the next three centuries, the scientific model—the basis for modern society—would become perfected, but it would not be fully understood. As a result, its technical applications became a replacement for genuine introspection, spawning such false philosophies as Modernism, or the belief in eternal progress and a world without limitations, and the so-called scientific materialism of Marxism, atheism, and contemporary "consumerism."[3]

## Robert Moray: Alchemist and Freemason

Moray was among the original 114 founders of the Royal Society and was an avid researcher into alchemy during his twilight years. Alchemy was the science of the age, or more accurately the previous one: it was increasingly coming under attack by more pragmatic and objective methodologies. To fully understand the importance of the Royal Society and the contributions of its founding members, it is important to recognize that, like any new organization, it did not spring fully formed into existence. It took time to organize and grow, and it had its detractors in the press and the church—as well as that section of individuals who are little more than ignorance and hypocrisy wrapped in a veneer of respectability, known as "polite society."

The Royal Society was a friend of Francis Bacon and, in being so, was part of a stream of transmitting ideas and forming groups aimed at transforming society and the world at large. This transformation was outlined by Francis Bacon in *The Great Instauration: The Universal and General Reformation of the Whole Wide World through the Renewal of the Arts and Sciences* and was based on the fundamental learning of the day, which included all aspects of knowledge in terms of divine, human, and natural. To promote the studies of these things, particularly since divine and natural knowledge often involved the study of Qabala, magic, alchemy, and astrology, Bacon created two schools, or groups. One school, the School of the Day, was open; the other, the School of the Night, was private. The secret School of the Night would give rise to the so-called Invisible College,

---

3 This is most clearly seen in science fiction, particularly the *Star Trek* television series and movie franchise, in which there is not a problem encountered that cannot be solved technologically.

some of whose members would later form the Royal Society and thereby influence the development of Freemasonry.

## The First Grand Lodge

In 1717, four lodges located in London came together and created the first Grand Lodge, the oldest Masonic Grand Lodge. It is important to remember that this is the date given for the *formation of the Grand Lodge of England*, not the beginning of Freemasonry. For the Grand Lodge to have been created, lodges would have to already have been in existence. However, given the nature of Masonic history, many histories simply work from 1717 forward, as here the greatest number of documents, records, and other forms of suitable evidence exist. As pointed out, prior to 1717 little is known about the origins of the Craft, and speculations abound by both Masons and non-Masons alike.

Masons met in taverns and coffeehouses, naming their lodges after the places they met. In February 1717, the Apple Tree, the Crown, the Goose and Gridiron, and the Rummer and Grapes lodges met in the Apple Tree Tavern on Charles Street in the Covent Garden district of London. Of the four lodges present, three of them were composed primarily of Operative Masons, with some Accepted Masons in the ranks. Rummer and Grapes was a different story, composed exclusively of Accepted Masons, all gentlemen, and a few nobles as well. Their discussion centered around the future of Freemasonry in England.

What most concerned the members present was how to distinguish Freemasonry from other clubs and social groups in London at the time. Given that many of these clubs existed solely for the purpose of drinking, eating, gambling, and frequenting brothels, they wanted rules that would establish who could be a member, as well as a code of conduct for members.

The men who met at the Apple Tree Tavern wanted to see Freemasonry grow. They were living in the largest and fastest-growing city in Europe. Social mobility was increasing as the workers moved in from the countryside and a merchant middle class exploded to meet their needs. Now, suddenly, skilled laborers, merchants, bankers, and nobles were all sitting together in one place: a Masonic lodge. To govern this body of men of mixed social rank—something unheard of before then—they formed a Grand Lodge, and on June 24, 1717, also known as Saint John the Baptist's Day, they elected Anthony Sayer the first Grand Master for the Grand Lodge of England. Sayer was a gentleman and Accepted Mason, and with his election, Freemasonry split further from its Operative roots and moved into the future of Speculative and, as we will later see, occult and philosophical Freemasonry.

## Anderson's *Constitutions*

During the early years of the Grand Lodge of England, James Anderson, a Presbyterian minister, was asked to write a history of Masonry and in doing so outline its rules and principles. The result was his *Book of Constitutions*, which was published in 1723. In addition to always referring to "constitutions" in the plural, thereby demonstrating that this was not the idea of a lone individual or lodge but instead a synthesis, Anderson's *Constitutions* contained an important element, an updated rendition of the Ancient Charges. It is important to note that the Charges have been adopted almost universally by the various Masonic jurisdictions, and their annual reading to the membership is a common practice. The Charges state how a member of the Craft is to behave in relation to his Brethren and society at large, and they extol the importance of religious observance, generosity, moral and ethical propriety, and service to God and community, as well as dictating that the member do nothing in public or private with a Brother or the profane (non-Masons) that would injure the good name and reputation of Freemasonry. In the writing, accepting, and application of these guidelines, Anderson's *Constitutions* became one of the earliest recorded landmarks of Freemasonry in the post-1717 era.

Among the most important of the rules presented was that in order to maintain peace, harmony, and the good order thereof within lodges and in activities outside them, Freemasons were forbidden to discuss politics and religion. The *Constitutions* requires that Masons believe in a Supreme Being, but the text does not state what that must be; it simply refers to the "Grand Architect of the Universe." This created almost immediate love or hate for Masonry in an era when sectarian strife was always just below the threshold of all social, political, and economic activities. For the first time, men of all known sects and social status in England were sitting together in brotherly love and friendship in the same room. In the minds of many, this clearly could lead to no good. As a result, the Roman Catholic Church issued an edict banning its members from being Freemasons (as have various other religions across the years, including Islam), and membership became a criminal offense in some countries. The Grand Architect of the Universe was seen as something other than the one God of the "one true faith," and Freemasonry's rituals were condemned as being the last vestiges of occult practices and, as such, contrary to the teachings of the Church.

Among the most damning of protests came in 1738 from the Roman Catholic Church, forbidding its members to become Freemasons; later, other Christian sects issued prohibitions stating that Freemasonry was inherently a deist movement and that leaving individuals to discover God for themselves could only lead back to the sectarian fighting that had plagued Europe for generations. The Roman Catholic Church would continue to repeat this ban, as well as reasons for its justification, in increasingly hostile language. The most famous was Pope Leo XII's encyclical "Human Genus," published in 1882. The twenty-five-page document stated unequivocally that from the viewpoint of the Roman Catholic Church, Freemasonry was evil, as it was based on reason and not faith. Pope Pius XII picked up the anti-Masonic banner again when in the 1950s he publicly denounced Freemasonry along with other civic organizations for being too liberal in their associations and religious views.

Only in the early 1980s would the Roman Catholic Church take a position that was less damning of Masonry in general, though it still prohibited its members from joining; should they do so, they would not be able to receive the sacraments and would be in "a state of grave sin." Pope Benedict XVI restated this position in 1983, when as Cardinal Joseph Ratzinger he led the Office of the Sacred Congregation for the Doctrine of the Faith, the successor organization to the Office of the Inquisition.

Forbidding members from discussing politics and religion and sitting in the same room with men of all classes became a sore spot for those who saw in Freemasonry the seeds of egalitarianism. Here, it was feared, plots against governments would be hatched (and some were), and the right to have a say in representation (republican government) or the right to vote (democratic reforms) would undermine the inherited rule of royalty. In many countries, Freemasonry was forced underground to survive, as some saw it as a threat to the natural order of things. The principle that all Masons must be good citizens of the country in which they live was simply ignored by the Craft's detractors.

## Masonic Landmarks and the Making of a Movement

Among the more interesting aspects of Freemasonry are its landmarks. *Landmarks* are often defined as ancient customs, usages, practices, or peculiarities used by Masons in the performance of their rites. Often one hears Hebrew or Latin mispronounced—but mispronounced uniformly across a particular jurisdiction. This pronunciation is unique to Masonry, and therefore the accepted usage of the term or word. Landmarks are a strange thing, in that no one agrees on how many there are, with some lists as short as three and others containing as many as fifty-four identified landmarks. There is no agreement on exactly what they are, either, but the majority of them are agreed upon by the various Grand Lodges and easily recognized by a visiting Brother. As such, the performance of an initiation may be very different in some elements of form, but the key parts and elements will easily be recognized by a visitor who himself has experienced the same initiation elsewhere. For example, the structure of the lodge room, the placement of the officers, their duties and methods of performing them, and the general dress and decorum are nearly identical across the Masonic landscape. Landmarks provide for a string or core of connection and continuity in a worldwide system that is quite diverse and independent in many regards.

Some of the landmarks listed by various authorities such as Albert Mackey are also administrative in nature, such as personal recommendation for membership, the requirement to keep meeting, and petitioners being able to pay for their membership from their own funds and come of their own free will. This last part is most critical, as no Mason should ever become a Mason unwillingly—because of undue pressure from friends or

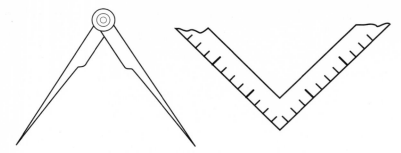

**The Square and Compass: Two of the Greater Lights**

relatives, or for mercenary or other reasons—as this would make the ideals of Masonry null and the oaths a lie.

Landmarks are subject to change or innovation, such as the use of the Bible on the altar. Prior to its use, a small equilateral triangle was used to represent the Grand Architect of the Universe. With the Bible came the adoption of the following Scripture passages for use in each of the degrees: Entered Apprentice, Psalm 133; Fellowcraft, Amos 7:7–8; and Master, Ecclesiastes 12:1–7. However, these are only the most commonly used passages, and their use is by no means uniform across jurisdictions and rites. Some rites and rituals continue to use the triangle in conjunction with the Bible or whatever version of the Volume of the Sacred Law is present. *The Volume of the Sacred Law*, also known as *VSL* or simply the Book of the Law, distinguishes Freemasonry from a strictly religious or sectarian organization in that it varies from lodge to lodge and can even be changed at the time of initiation at the candidate's request.

In addition to the VSL, two other landmarks form the most rudimentary and basic tools, or *furniture*, as they are called, for a Masonic lodge to be opened: these are the *square* and *compass*. Together with the VSL, the three of them are known as *the Greater Lights*. Despite whatever differences there are between rites, rituals, and jurisdictions, these three Lights are required and must be present for a lodge of Masons to be in session. *The Lesser Lights* are the sun, the moon, and the Master of the Lodge, for as the sun rules the day and the moon rules the night, the Master rules the lodge with justice and equity for all members. He is a living example of Masonic idealism.

## Philosophy, Fraternity, and Charity and the Making of a Man

Freemasonry is fundamentally a spiritual organization, encouraging individual spiritual research and expression without binding members to a specific creed or doctrine of belief or practice. As a result of this, individual Masons must adhere to a moral code to improve their individual characters and, as such, the community—one person at a time—rather than attempting improvement through mass movements or legislation.

Action in terms of education comes via rituals that portray specific moral and ethical virtues as illustrated in sacred literature and historic and mythic events. These are *initiations*, and they instill a particular set of symbols and ideas into the psyche of those who participate in them. Charity is the highest of virtues, as it embodies all other virtues in itself. This then manifests primarily in personal conduct, community service, and defending liberties.

All members of the Fraternity are equal and may avail themselves of the rights and privileges of membership without prejudice. One is often reminded of instances in which men of great rank, power, and privilege sat in lodges while one of their servants presided as Master of the Lodge, and they were subordinate to them in that responsibility. It is important to think of the role of Master of the Lodge as a responsibility, for it is a great one, not simply a role one plays and then goes home. A great deal of time and attention is required while serving in that capacity. For this reason, Past Masters, or those who have served and completed their terms, are given a special respect among members.

## Antients and Moderns: The Craft's First Crisis

The ideals of Freemasonry were quickly put to the test, and not only with the assertion of the Grand Lodge of England over other lodges, particularly Ireland (1725) and Scotland (1736). Grand Lodges opened in France as well; although the dates are obscured, they appear to have been in existence prior to the mid 1730s. Germany (1737), Denmark (1745), and the Netherlands (1756) all established Grand Lodges also. The first Grand Lodges in the Colonies were chartered by the Grand Lodge of England and located in Philadelphia (1731) and Boston (1733), with other Grand

Lodges quickly following. Competing Grand Lodges soon came into the picture, forming in various countries to oppose what they perceived as an imposition on their independence by the dictates of the Grand Lodge of England. Many of these Grand Lodges existed for several generations but were eventually absorbed into the United Grand Lodge of England; others, such as those in the Colonies and on the Continent, maintained their independent status. However, the most significant of these counter–Grand Lodges created many of the more interesting aspects of modern Masonry, including the formation of York and Scottish Rites and the battle between the Antients and the Moderns.

In 1751, within a generation of the publishing of Anderson's *Constitutions*, which outlined the rules and regulations for Freemasons, a group of Irish Masons living in London formed the Antient Grand Lodge.[4] This new Grand Lodge was formed in response to what its members saw as changes to the ritual structure and constitutions. This crisis erupted between two camps: one advocating for the older, simpler, and traditional methods, known as the *Antients* or *Ancients*, and one advocating newer, more symbolically elaborate and philosophical rituals, known as the *Moderns*. The primary concerns of the Antients were the omission of prayers, no longer celebrating the holy days of the saints John the Baptist and John the Evangelist, and the perception that the rituals of the Craft were being de-Christianized and replaced with deism.

Eventually, the two camps would come together in an elaborate ceremony of harmony and union—true Masonic splendor—and form the United Grand Lodge of England. While this may appear to be a minor point to some, it is critical to see that Masons of the period were men of convictions and honor and that even when in deep disagreement with each other on issues they considered fundamental to the Craft, they were eventually able to come to a reasonable and workable resolution in true Masonic form and fashion. Their ideals were not simply ideals of convenience, but ones that they stood by—even if imperfectly—when tested.

---

4 *Antient* is the Old English spelling of *ancient*.

The crisis of the Antients and the Moderns was another critical turning point for Freemasonry. Just as the acceptance of "gentlemen" into the lodges less than a century earlier had begun their transformation away from purely operative guilds into wider social organizations, and just as the formation of the first Grand Lodge had begun the formation of a larger cultural and civic movement, the struggle between the ideals of the Antients and the Moderns would create a third transformation in Masonry in less than a century: the rise of appendant bodies.

## Proliferation of the Craft

Since the days of the medieval guilds, Freemasonry had changed organizationally in its outward as well as its inward appearance. The metaphors, rituals, and morality plays of stoneworking were easily transformed into the metaphor of human development on both the individual and social level. A better person was "built" and "raised," as was a better society. Just as a building was planned and designed for beauty, inspiration, reverence, worship, and function, the same process of reasoning could allow us to lead better lives. Reason, intellect, and study of the Seven Liberal Arts and Sciences would supplement—and in many instances replace—the blind faith and devotion that the medieval Church had required, which was weakened during the Renaissance. Now, as Western Europe stood on the edge of the Age of Enlightenment, God existed, but to know and understand the Grand Architect of the Universe, one had first to know and understand one's very self. Self-reflection, moral and ethical conduct, and self-improvement via the path of knowledge and wisdom—and its most precise instrument, that of the scientific method—were the tools Masonry would encourage its members to use on their journey of self-discovery.

Embedded within the symbols of Masonry, just as they were embedded within the Gothic cathedrals centuries earlier, were the keys to that improvement—an improvement deeply personal, deeply spiritual, and, as some of the key members of the Royal Society demonstrated, deeply esoteric. In the degrees of York and Scottish Rite, as well as numerous other rites long since dormant, mythology, history, and Hermetic symbolism would be preserved and demonstrated to the members. In keeping with true Masonic form, the symbols and ideals would be "shown" visibly and be presented in rituals and initiations, but they would not be explained. This final note is critical, as each Mason must come to understand what is presented to him in his own manner. The keys of Hermeticism and related topics are ever present and ever hidden (in plain sight) in Masonic rituals, most of which were created during the prolific period of Masonic expansion during the eighteenth century.

## Key Points

1. Freemasonry defines itself as "A peculiar system of morality, veiled in allegory and illustrated by symbols."

2. The aim of Freemasonry is to "Make good men better" through philosophy, charity, and fraternity.

3. The rituals of Freemasonry are composed mainly of scriptural references to the building of the Temple of Solomon, specific Masonic mythology, and earlier trade-guild practices dating from at least the Middle Ages.

4. *Operative Masonry* is a term that refers to stonemasons engaged in the building arts.

5. *Speculative Masonry* is a term that refers to members of Masonic guilds who were not Operative Masons and saw in Masonry symbols and practices that they interpreted as having an esoteric, philosophical, or moral meaning.

6. Among those involved in Freemasonry prior to 1717 were Elias Ashmole and Robert Moray.

7. Elias Ashmole is often referred to as "the first Freemason" and falsely given credit for cofounding the order; however, this points to the significant influence he may have had on the Craft in the late seventeenth century. Ashmole was an associate of William Lilly, author of Christian astrology, who was himself an avid collector of esoteric and occult manuscripts. Ashmole's collection of John Dee's materials resides in the British Museum.

8. Robert Moray was one of the original founders of the Royal Society and an avid researcher into alchemy.

9. Masonry existed prior to 1717, a date that refers to the formation of the first Grand Lodge, or the Grand Lodge of England.

10. Under the direction of the Grand Lodge of England, James Anderson, a Presbyterian minister, wrote a history of Freemasonry and outlined its rules and practices. This is known as the *Book of Constitutions*, which was published in 1723.

11. There exist within Freemasonry ancient customs, usages, practices, and peculiarities unique to Freemasonry in the performance of its rites. These are known as landmarks, of which there is no set number. Lists of identified landmarks are as short as three and as long as fifty-four; they are often easily identified by visiting Freemasons regardless of where the members may be from.

12. The first major crisis in Freemasonry came in 1751, when a group of Irish Masons living in London formed the Antient Grand Lodge, splitting English Masonry into two camps. The dispute was over what the Antients, as they were known, claimed was adherence to older traditions. The Moderns, as the other group was known, were said to be favoring a more elaborate and philosophical presentation of the rituals. This split was eventually reconciled and gave rise to the current United Grand Lodge of England.

## Assignments for Chapter 1

1. Read one or more of the books from the Suggested Reading list that follows and, to the best of your ability, imagine the social environment of the seventeenth and early eighteenth centuries. Using this image, think about what you would do if you were in the same or a similar environment. How would you attempt to bring people together? What kind of network would you need? What would the rules be? How would you select, admit, and recognize members? What would be the most important unifying ideals? How would you begin to put those into action?

2. Reflect upon your current involvement with society. What organizations do you belong to? Are they primarily for business advancement, entertainment, or personal development purposes? Based on your self-assessment, identify the various service organizations in your community, for example the Lions, Rotary, or Kiwanis, and resolve to join one as a means of putting your highest ideals into action in a nonsectarian, nonpolitical, and anonymous fashion.

## Suggested Reading

*The Freemasons: A History of the World's Most Powerful Secret Society*, by Jasper Ridley (Arcade Publishing)

*The Golden Builders: Alchemists, Rosicrucians, and the First Freemasons*, by Tobias Churton (Inner Traditions)

*Freemasonry and the Birth of Modern Science*, by Robert Lomas (Fair Winds Press)

*Gnostic Philosophy: From Ancient Persia to Modern Times*, by Tobias Churton (Inner Traditions)

*The Great Instauration: The Universal and General Reformation of the Whole Wide World Through the Arts and Sciences; A Commentary*, by Peter Dawkins (Francis Bacon Research Trust)

*The Occult Philosophy in the Elizabethan Age*, by Frances A. Yates (Routledge)

*The Origins of Freemasonry: Facts and Fictions*, by Margaret C. Jacobs (University of Pennsylvania Press)

*The Rosicrucian Enlightenment*, by Frances A. Yates (Routledge)

*The Thirty Years' War*, edited by Geoffrey Parker (Routledge)

*The Genesis of Freemasonry*, by Douglas Knoop, MA, Hon. ARIBA, and G. P. Jones, MA, Litt.D. (Manchester University Press)

*The Radical Enlightenment: Pantheists, Freemasons and Republicans*, by Margaret C. Jacob (The Temple Publishers)

*Living the Enlightenment: Freemasonry and Politics in Eighteenth-Century Europe,* by Margaret C. Jacob (Oxford University Press)

*The Origins of Freemasonry: Scotland's Century, 1590–1710,* by David Stevenson (Cambridge University Press)

*The Rise and Development of Organized Freemasonry,* by Roy A. Wells (Lewis Masonic/The Masonic Book Club, vol. 17)

## 2

# The Temple of Solomon
# and the Legend of Hiram Abiff

OVERVIEW
- *The Temple as Symbol of the World*
- *Solomon as Magician*
- *Hiram Abiff and the Unique Mythology of Masonry*

What is passed off as architecture in the modern world is often little more than a cross between crass utilitarianism, such as the poured-concrete housing blocks of the Soviet era, and expressions of psychic neuroses come to three-dimensional life, in such acts of hubris as the Sears Tower, entire cities like Las Vegas, and the Arab resort for the ultra-rich in Dubai where you can ski indoors despite a temperature outside well above 100 degrees Fahrenheit. From these creations, we clearly, albeit unconsciously, see the truth that each building is a temple of sorts, and each culture pays tribute to its gods by building them the largest and most centrally located temple they can conceive of. During the medieval and Renaissance periods, churches and cathedrals were cities' largest buildings and occupied the central square. As civic life increased, this space was shared with government buildings, and by the nineteenth century, we see the early beginnings of both religion and government beginning to literally stand in the shadows of commerce and banking. By the middle of the twentieth century, the skyscraper became the new tower of light to guide human footsteps, and by the end of the twentieth century, many of the largest and most centrally located buildings were for governmental social service programs.

Each one represents the true and most deeply held unconscious beliefs of its generation, and with each one we see a passing from art to function, from ideal to utility, from inspiration to death in a cubicle. The building is the inner world made manifest, the vision of the cosmos—and nowhere was this more visible than in the classical through medieval periods. The temple is the collective microcosm for everyone to see and participate in; it is the mythic history made flesh.

In the ancient world, the dominant assumption was the imminent presence of the divine. In the modern world, either in the false utopia of Communism (as well as its contemporary insidious spawn of political correctness) or in the vacuous consumerism and excessive quest for material wealth that capitalism has morphed into, the dominant theme is eternal progress under the direction of scientific materialism. It is no surprise that for decades, and with no end in sight, simplistic and radical forms of religious fundamentalism have attracted followers from not only the lowest classes of society, but increasingly from the middle and upper classes as well.[1]

## The Temple of Solomon

The construction of the Temple of Solomon is the most important historical event in Masonic lore and is the basis for all degree work, including the explanatory work beyond the degree of becoming a Master Mason that forms the basis of Scottish and York Rites. It is, in no uncertain terms, the most important building in Western esoteric symbolism. While the Great Pyramid complex, the temple of Luxor, and even the purely symbolic vault of Christian Rosenkreutz play important roles, only the Temple of Solomon has continued to be both a historical and spiritual focal point since its construction, for both exoteric and esoteric beliefs and practices.

---

1 It is only fitting that in this light we remember the Shiva Purana, which states, "The end of the Kali Yuga is a particularly favorable period to pursue true knowledge. Some will attain wisdom in a short time, for the merits acquired in one year during the Treta Age [the second cycle, the Age of Ritual] can be obtained in one day in the Kali Yuga."

In *The Temple at Jerusalem: A Revelation*, John Michell, one of the world's leading exponents of sacred geometry, makes the following observation about the Temple:

> The plan of the Temple as revealed to King David was, like the plan of the Tabernacle that proceeded it, a composition of proportions and harmonics that represented the structure of the universe. It was measured by certain "sacred units," all related to the foot used today, and also related to the dimensions of the earth. Describing his vision of the Temple, the prophet Ezekiel mentioned three units in its dimensions: the cubit, the cubit-and-a-handsbreadth or greater cubit and the reed of six greater cubits.[2]

Michell further explains that the cubit is 1.728 feet, the duodecimal aspect of $12 \times 12 \times 12$ when represented in feet, and can be directly traced back to the units of measure used in the construction of Egyptian monuments, the Great Pyramid in particular. He further points out that the various units of ancient measurement are called by the civilizations in which they are found—Greek, Roman, Egyptian, or Hebrew—but in fact relate to each other by simple ratios. Their essential unity and use worldwide suggests that they belong to an older civilization, as of yet undiscovered, that once occupied planet Earth.[3]

In this same context, Michell suggests that while the Temple of Jerusalem is generally seen only in the context of the Abrahamic religions, it is also important to an older faith that precedes them and issues from the same cosmological font:

> Whether by chance or divine intent, Jerusalem has become the temple of four types of religion, issuing like the four rivers of paradise that rose from beneath the Temple towards the four directions, Jews to the east, Muslims to the south, Christians to the West and, in the direction of the north pole, followers of that ancient religious system that preceded the others.[4]

---

2 John Michell, *The Temple at Jerusalem: A Revelation* (York Beach, ME: Weiser, 2000), 46.

3 For a detailed discussion of this topic, see also Christopher Knight and Robert Lomas, *Uriel's Machine: Uncovering the Secrets of Stonehenge, Noah's Flood and the Dawn of Civilization* (Beverly, MA: Fair Winds Press, 2001).

4 Michell, *Temple at Jerusalem*, 60.

Constructed in the city of Jerusalem (meaning "new peace") around the middle of the tenth century BCE and made of stone, cedar timbers, and gold, the original Temple of Solomon was a smallish structure designed to house the Ark of the Covenant. Details of the Temple's design and furnishings are given in 1 Kings 5:15–7:51 and 2 Chronicles 1:18–5:1 and give the following dimensions: 60 cubits long, 20 cubits wide, and 30 cubits high. A *cubit*,[5] later standardized in the Middle Ages, is approximately the length from the elbow to the tip of the middle finger, about 18 to 22 inches. From this we can see that the Temple was slightly over 100 feet long, 30 feet wide, and 50 feet high. The central portion of the Temple was 40 cubits long and constituted the Holy of Holies, or inner sanctuary. Here, behind a thick curtain, with only the high priest allowed to enter, and then only once a year, the Ark of the Covenant was kept.

The Ark of the Covenant was critical to early Jewish identity, as it contained the broken tablets of the Ten Commandments as received by Moses on Mount Hebron and shattered by him when he saw the Jews worshipping before a golden calf. A great deal of legend and lore, both ancient and contemporary, has grown up around the Ark of the Covenant and it possibly having occult powers.[6]

It is interesting from a Masonic perspective that the ratio of length to width to height is 3:1:2, similar to the battery of knocks or raps made by the Master with his gavel to undertake business in the lodge. This ratio, as well as the raw numbers of 60, 20, and 30, has also been the subject of endless speculation from the perspective of sacred geometry and its numerology.

A Masonic lodge room is laid out according to traditional geographic symbolism, with the entrance in the west, seating along the north and south sides, and the Master's station in the east. The Senior and Junior Wardens have their positions in the west and south, respectively. No officer

---

5  From the Latin *cubitus*, or "elbow."

6  *Raiders of the Lost Ark* is the most famous of this genre, but recent publishers have turned the Ark and anything related to the Holy Grail, the Temple of Solomon, the Knights Templar, and Masonry into a publishing industry. Much of the material is pure speculation, hung on the skeletal framework of a historical timeline and purporting to fill in the missing pieces.

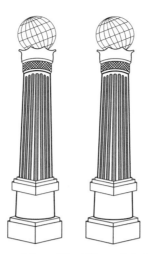

**Jachin and Boaz: The Pillars of the Porch**

sits in the north. Additional officers are placed around the lodge, as well as outside of it, and carry out both administrative and ritualistic functions.

Two large pillars, Jachin and Boaz, flanked the entranceway to the Temple of Jerusalem; they are called the Pillars of the Porch, as regardless of where they appear in the lodge room, in the historical Temple they are on the exterior at the entrance. This hints at something few may notice about Masonic ritual: all three degrees take place on or around the entrance to the Temple of Solomon and never inside the Temple proper or the Holy of Holies in particular.

In modern Masonic lodges, the general theme of the Temple is kept, with an area between the Master's station in the east and the altar in the center of the lodge room being designated as the Holy of Holies. Depending on Masonic jurisdiction, some lodges will have two large pillars representing Jachin and Boaz directly inside the entrance of the lodge room. In other rites, they are represented by the columns carried by two of the most important officers of the lodge—the Junior and Senior Wardens. (Other aspects of the lodge draw more upon Masonic allegory and mythology than historical facts. These include the *ornaments* of a lodge, whose major symbols are a checkerboard floor, tessel border, and pentagram. These ornaments are by no means universal and, like so many things, will be present in one jurisdiction but absent in another.)

We find in 2 Chronicles 3:15–17 the following information:

> Also he made before the house two pillars of thirty and five cubits high, and the chapiter that was on the top of each of them was five cubits.
>
> And he made chains, as in the oracle, and put them on the heads of the pillars; and made a hundred pomegranates, and put them on the chains.
>
> And he reared up the pillars before the temple, one on the right hand, and the other on the left; and he called the name of that on the right hand Jachin, and the name of that on the left Boaz.

Jachin and Boaz are probably the most well known and recognized symbols of Masonry that give it a powerful link to earlier esoteric traditions, particularly Jewish mysticism or Qabala. In the *Sepher Yetzirah,* among the earliest of Qabalistic manuscripts, these pillars are mentioned in relation to the Tree of Life and the Ten Spheres of Creation, or Sephiroth. These spheres are utilized extensively in Qabalistic practices, and together they are said to represent a ladder to the heavens. Here again, the ladder, as well as the staircase, is used within Masonic symbolism to represent man's rise from ignorance to Illumination, from crudeness to refinement.

In chapter 1, section 5, of the *Sepher Yetzirah,* we read:

> The appearance of the ten spheres out of nothing is like a flash of lightning, being without an end, His word is in them, when they go and return; they run by his order like a whirlwind and humble themselves before His throne.[7]

And then in chapter 1, section 9:

> These are the ten spheres of existence, out of nothing. From the spirit of the Living God emanated air, from the air, water, from the water, fire or ether, from the ether, the height and depth, the East and West, the North and South.[8]

---

7   Isidor Kalisch, ed. and trans., *Sepher Yetzirah: A Book on Creation; or, The Jewish Metaphysics of Remote Antiquity* (1877; Everything2, 2001), http://everything2.com/index.pl?node=Sepher%20Yezirah%2C%20A%20Book%20on%20Creation.

8   Ibid.

And in chapter 2, section 6, of the *Sepher Yetzirah*:

> He created a reality out of nothing, called the nonentity into existence and
> hewed, as it were, colossal pillars from intangible air.[9]

The First Temple of Solomon stood for approximately five hundred years, or until 586 BCE, when it was destroyed by the Assyrians after a failed revolt by the Jews. For seventy years, it was in ruins, after which much of the population of Israel was deported to Babylon, beginning the period known as the "Babylonian Captivity." It was during this period that the "Babylonian Talmud" was created, and Jewish angelology and demonology were influenced by prevailing Babylonian traditions and magical practices. When the Babylonians were in turn conquered by the Persians, King Cyrus allowed Ezra and seventy followers to return to see what had become of their former homeland and its remaining inhabitants. What Ezra found was little more than people living in hovels and ruins, Jews in little more than name only, with no knowledge of their religious beliefs or practices. When the remaining Jews were allowed to leave Babylon and join with Ezra, the Temple was reconstructed, approximating the original design of the First Temple. This Second Temple was later renovated by King Herod, with construction beginning around 20 BCE, and razed by the Romans in 70 CE after another failed Jewish uprising.

The Temple was a source of much myth and mystery throughout the Middle Ages, when during the Crusades the Knights Templar established their first headquarters in the old stables of the ruined Temple. This in turn would give rise to endless speculations about their activities, with recent archeological evidence showing that extensive tunneling was undertaken during the Templars period.

## Solomon as Magician

Solomon ascended to the throne upon the death of his father, King David, at the end of the tenth century BCE. Reigning for forty years (c. 986–c. 933 BCE) as Israel's third king, Solomon's reign was the high-water mark

---

9 Ibid.

of the Israeli kingdom. This was due in no small measure to David's accomplishments, Solomon's own managerial skills, and the temporarily weakened neighboring empires of Egypt and Babylon.

Solomon's reputed wisdom is well known, recorded in biblical narratives, popular myth, and even modern media. Like the Egyptian god Thoth, Solomon's learning and wisdom also encompassed the fields of magic and related occult arts, soon placing him as a magus supreme. Books on invocation and magic are attributed to his authorship as early as the first century CE. Gnostic references also exist, including one of the Nag Hammadi texts.

*The Testament of Solomon*, one of these first-century books attributed to Solomon, tells how he built the First Temple through magical means that constrained the power of fifty thousand *jinn*, or magical beings (possibly demons), to do his work.

In *Antiquities of the Jews*, Jewish historian Flavius Josephus wrote:

> He [Solomon] is in no way inferior to the Egyptians, who are said to have been beyond all men in understanding. . . . God also enabled him to learn that skill which expels demons, which is a science useful and sanative to men.[10]

This image of Solomon as magus continues to expand and grow, even paralleling that of Thoth or Hermes Trismegistus so that during the Middle Ages and early Renaissance these two figures—one Egyptian or "pagan," the other Jewish—are seen as the archetypal magicians. In an age when magic was seen as the work of the devil, the pentagram known as the "goat's foot," and witch hunting (and pogroms against the Jews) in one form or another just a memory away, there was considerable effort made to sanitize and mainstream esoteric ideas.

To make them acceptable, Hermes was said to be a contemporary of Moses, and, of course, Solomon the Wise a magician who used his knowledge only for good.

---

10   Flavius Josephus, *The Antiquities of the Jews*, trans. William Whiston (1737; Internet Sacred Text Archive, n.d.), bk. 8, http://www.sacred-texts.com/jud/josephus/index.htm#aoj..

However, this whitewashing was less than universally accepted. A collection of writings known as the Solomonic literature formed a branch of magic known as "Solomonic magic." These books include the well-known *Lesser Key of Solomon* and *Greater Key of Solomon*, the *Testament of Solomon*, *Book of Solomon on Gems and Spirits*, the *Shem ha-Mephoresh of Solomon the King*, and a variety of books on the notary arts. The *notary arts* is an area of magic that would have been of particular interest to Renaissance scholars, in that it is purported to allow one to learn any subject quickly and without difficulty. Solomon is reputed to have received his knowledge directly from God, and yet despite this (or possibly because of it being too Gnostic in tone), the Roman Catholic Church took exceptional rebuke to the notary arts, condemning them repeatedly and destroying copies of related books whenever they were found.

Much of what we know regarding impressions of Solomon in Middle Eastern and neighboring Asian folklore has come to us from *A Thousand and One Arabian Nights*. Translated by Sir Richard Francis Burton, the unexpurgated stories are contained in sixteen volumes and were published between 1885 and 1888. It says herein that Solomon is named Sulemain and that the demons, or jinn, are sealed in a brass vessel and controlled by a magic ring bearing "Solomon's Seal."

Burton is among the world's most renowned travelers, linguists, and lovers, and his adventures document the height of the Victorian era. He was a Freemason, initiated into Hope Lodge, Kurrachee, Scinde, India. His fascination with the *Nights* began early in his career, and he made a point of collecting as much information about and variations of the stories as he could in his extensive travels across North Africa, the Middle East, and Asia. The Arabic title is properly *Alf laylah wa laylah*, translated by Burton into *The Book of a Thousand Nights and a Night*. Burton's translation is still considered unsurpassed, not only because of its rendering of the poetry, but also, and maybe even more importantly, because of his notations, which were drawn directly from his experience with Arab and Muslim culture, lore, folk magic, Sufi mysticism, and sexuality.

The *Nights* is essentially a series of stories within the framework of a larger story, with magic, mysticism, and various mythical beings playing key roles. The longest of the stories, told for fifty-three nights, is "The Queen of the Serpents," which is directly connected to the mystical experiences revered in many Eastern cultures. Alchemical and magical symbols form the imagery, among them the famous Ring of Solomon, the mystic symbol of divine union. Of interest to Masons and Rosicrucians, however, is that the main focus of "Queen of the Serpents" is the quest to find the tomb of Solomon, said to be hidden in the sacred mountain of Qaf. Qaf, according to Burton, was a rendition of the Persian Alborz. It is in Alborz that the Zoroastrian redeemer waits for the Second Coming and the end of the world. According to legend, it is here in this sacred mountain that the coffin of Solomon rests after having been transported across the Seven Mystical Seas.

Burton further notes that the symbolism used in the *Nights* is definitively Sufi in many respects, and the symbol of the bird, the Middle Eastern ideogram of the soul, is a common motif. The flight of the bird denotes the human search for divine realities, its pilgrimage across life. For Burton, this wandering is translated as "traveling," and those who undertake it "travelers," a common term for a Freemason.[11] These themes are also mentioned in the Renaissance magical text the *Picatrix*.

## The *Picatrix*

The *Picatrix*[12] is a comprehensive text on sympathetic and astral magic that carried substantial weight in Renaissance circles. It is primarily concerned with the construction of talismans (or *physical* magical images) based on zodiacal position of the planets and the creation of prayers, or invocations, to the spiritual power personified by the planets. Over fifty images,[13] along with the appropriate times, places, attitudes, and ritual gestures, are described, so that operators might successfully invoke the

---

11  Edward Rice, *Captain Sir Richard Francis Burton: The Secret Agent Who Made the Pilgrimage to Mecca, Discovered the Kama Sutra, and Brought the Arabian Nights to the West* (New York: Charles Scribner's Sons, 1990), 462–63.

12  Possibly a corruption of *Hippocrates*. See Jean Seznec, *The Survival of the Pagan Gods* (Princeton, NJ: Princeton University Press, 1981), 53.

13  Possibly of Babylonian origin. Ibid., 160.

power of their chosen planet. The title of the work is the name in Latin given to the 1256 translation of an Arab text on magic.[14] The work was originally translated into Spanish under the sponsorship of Alphonso the Wise, king of Castille. The Latin text, widely used during the Renaissance, differs slightly from the Arabic original and is shorter.[15] Unfortunately, the Spanish manuscript has not survived. While never printed, it enjoyed a wide circulation in manuscript form throughout the fifteenth and sixteenth centuries.[16]

Precious stones and gems are the preferred substance upon which to make a talismanic image. In fact, gems bearing the images of deities were in use into the medieval period, and many monasteries had their own cameos, as well as relics, crosses, books, altars, and reliquaries mounted with carved gems of one sort or another.

While the knowledge of how to actually carve these images into the gems was lost somewhere between the second and third centuries CE, the practice, as well as the actual passage in the *Picatrix* regarding making such images on gems, was replaced with simply having the corresponding gem itself.

## The *Clavicula Salomonis*

The *Clavicula Salomonis*, or *The Key of Solomon*, is among the most famous magical texts written, and it continues to exert an influence in magical circles to this day. Purported to have been written by King Solomon, the text gives thirty-six different talismanic images, as well as detailed instructions for their construction, use, and purpose. The talismans are described according to their relationships to the seven ancient planets of the solar system.

---

14  *End of the Sages by Means of Magic* (*Ghayat al-Hakim fi'l-sihr*), attributed to al-Madjriti (died c. 1004–7).

15  It was also translated into Hebrew, with the title *Takhilt he-Hakham*. See Gershom Scholem, *Kabbalah* (New York: Meridian Books, 1978), 187.

16  Frances A. Yates, *Giordano Bruno and the Hermetic Tradition* (Chicago: University of Chicago Press, 1964), 50.

Solomon, like Moses, Hermes, and others, often has magical texts attributed to him because of the extensive mythology that surrounds his kingship. He is said to have possessed a magic ring and used it to control fifty thousand demons for the construction of his famous Temple. Despite being pseudepigraphical—that is, written or compiled by someone other than their attributed author—many of these books are still of value.

The *Clavicula Solomonis* was in fact not Jewish but was translated into Hebrew for the first time in the seventeenth century; it is composed of Christian, Jewish, and Arab magical elements. The famous work *The Book of the Sacred Magic of Abra-Melin*, purported to have been written by "Abraham the Jew of Worms" in the fifteenth century, was first written in German.[17]

The majority of the talismans described in *The Key of Solomon* in some fashion use either a five-pointed star (pentagram) or a six-pointed star, often called the Shield of David (*Magen David* in Hebrew) or the Seal of Solomon. This symbol, now universally identified with Judaism, was used as early as the Bronze Age and appears in cultures as widely dispersed as Britain and Mesopotamia, with Iron Age examples coming from India and Iberia.[18]

While the symbol appears as early as the seventh century BCE and is used by Jews and their neighbors alongside the pentagram in the Second Temple Period and along with the swastika in the second or third centuries, it may have had only decorative purposes. The hexagram does not appear in any of the magical papyruses or Jewish magical sources and is not associated with such practices until the early medieval period.

In Arab texts, the hexagram was used along with other geometrical symbols and was known as the *Seal of Solomon*, a term later adopted by many Jews. By the sixth century CE, the name *Seal of Solomon* was in use by Byzantine Christians. From the thirteenth century onward, the symbol appears in Hebrew Bibles from both Germany and Spain.[19]

---

17  Gershom Scholem, *Kabbalah* (New York: Meridian Books, 1978), 186.

18  Ibid., 362.

19  Ibid.

Arab magicians used the symbol widely, even to some degree interchangeably with the pentagram. In Jewish circles, its use was much more limited. However, the idea of it having some kind of magical power may have come from Islamic sources. It is in the Koran that David is first seen making use of the hidden, inner magical teachings of Judaism.[20]

From the thirteenth through seventeenth centuries, the magical meaning and use of the Shield of David increased in popularity, complexity, and meaning. In the fourteenth century, Charles IV allowed Jews in Prague to create a flag for their community. It is here that the Star of David appears to be used for the first time to symbolize a distinctly Jewish community. By the nineteenth century, in the Jews' desire to imitate Christians and have a symbol that represented Judaism in the same fashion that the cross does for Christianity, the Shield of David took on widespread use. It began appearing on books, religious literature, synagogues, and letterheads of organizations. Less than a century earlier, its use had been restricted to ecclesiastical paraphernalia.[21]

## Shekinah: Goddesses of the Temple

The Temple of Solomon was unique in that within it, the presence of God was said to dwell and be directly experienced by those present. While only the high priest, like his Egyptian counterpart in the Temple of Karnak, could enter the Holy of Holies on one day a year, the area around the inner sanctuary containing the Ark of the Covenant was occupied by other members of the priestly class at various times.

This "divine presence," known as *shekinah*, is described as being a great billowing cloud and as physically palatable and tangible. Shekinah has distinctly feminine attributes, and her presence is described in sexual imagery. While it is suggested that this may be a reflection of the survival of earlier polytheistic traits within primitive Judaism, it is important to note that it is also suggested that Solomon may have secretly been involved in a cult of Astarte and that during the Roman period a temple to Venus was established on the Temple Mount.

---

20 Ibid., 365.
21 Ibid., 367–68.

The Temple of Solomon, and even Solomon himself, is linked to the worship, expression, and concrete union with the creative power of the cosmos in distinctly feminine and sexual terms. While this is lost to most Jews and Christians, it may find its partial survival in the description of the "Genius of Freemasonry," which is clearly feminine.

As we will see later on, this notion of a feminine presence of deity in and throughout the immediate material world was of great importance to the Renaissance adepts. The *anima mundi*, or "soul of the world," is described as being female, and alchemy and geometry are both personified as being female. We even see the great revelations of the period, such as the "Chemical Wedding" of Christian Rosenkreutz, being preceded by the visitation of a feminine angel. Additional important concepts, such as Wisdom, the Word, and Holy Spirit, are also feminine in nature and are cornerstones of Masonic symbolism.

## Solomon and the Divine Feminine

It is clear that Solomon worshipped more than just at the altar of Yahweh, God of the Jews, in part as a result of his introduction of neighboring workmen into Jerusalem to assist in the construction of the Temple. The design and construction of the Temple adhered closely to the standards of their own Canaanite and Syrian temples, in particular Tell Tayinat, a ninth-century BCE Syrian temple. The uncovered remains of Tell Tayinat show a temple divided into three sections—entrance, nave, and vestibule—along with two pillars at the entrance. Brasswork executed by Hiram of Tyre was also similar to other Eastern Mediterranean cults. The reason for this was simple: during this period, the fundamental ritualistic differences between the cult of Yahweh and neighboring cults was nominal, the main difference being in their moral and cosmological teachings.

Yet despite Solomon having compromised his devotion of Yahweh, biblical condemnations of him are tame by comparison to others who deviated from the one true faith. It is clearly stated that his introduction of additional cults into Jerusalem was a result of his marriage to foreign princesses; however, the apologists are only partially correct. These introductions did not occur when he was old, but rather were essential to the very building of the Temple to begin with. Political marriages were crucial to Solomon's maintaining peace on his borders; in this way, instead of maintaining a large army, he could free up manpower for his massive civil and religious construction projects.

Solomon is said to have worshipped at the altar of Astarte; however, this is possibly a confusion with the goddess Asherah, who was well known to the Jews and would have been introduced into Jerusalem as a result of Solomon's marriage to a Sidonian princess. Asherah was an agricultural and fertility goddess, and like many deities in polytheistic culture, she is often amalgamated, and at times confused, with other deities. Asherah would have been well known to the Sidonian and Tyrian workmen Solomon was importing to construct his Temple to Yahweh.

## Hiram Abiff and the Unique Mythology of Freemasonry

While Masonic initiation and allegory quote liberally from the Jewish scriptures, there is in fact little about Masonry that can be historically linked to the Bible. The majority of Masonic ritual is a composite myth or morality tale, created to make a philosophical or moral point rather than an intellectual one. However, since few of the rank-and-file members of the Fraternity are well versed in either religious scriptures or history, this point is often missed, and they will routinely state that Masonry is found in the Bible. It is more accurate to state that the Jewish and later Christian scriptures can be found in Freemasonry. A perfect example of this kind of myth making comes in one of the core figures of Freemasonry: Hiram Abiff, the slain Grand Master to whom the entire Third Degree is devoted. As Arthur Edward Waite writes in *A New Encyclopedia of Freemasonry*,

> The Legend of the Master-Builder is the great allegory of Masonry. It happens that his figurative story is grounded in the fact of a personality mentioned in the Holy Scriptures, but this historical background is of accidents and not the essence; the significance is in the allegory and not in any point of history which may lie behind it.[22]

---

22 A. E. Waite, *A New Encyclopedia of Freemasonry* (New York: Weathervane Books, 1970), 366–67.

To confound matters, the name Hiram is used twice: Hiram, King of Tyre, and Hiram the Builder. Together with King Solomon, they constitute the three traditional Grand Masters of primitive Freemasonry.

### Hiram, King of Tyre

Hiram, King of Tyre, was a friend of King Solomon who, according to the Scriptures, assisted him in building the First Temple, the temple around which all Masonic initiation is predicated. Upon Solomon's coronation, Hiram sent ambassadors and gifts. Solomon requested King Hiram's assistance in constructing the temple at Jerusalem, and Hiram in turn sent money, men, and supplies.

In 1 Kings 5:8–9, it is said that he replied,

> "I will do all thy desire concerning timber of cedar and timber of fir. My servants shall bring them down from Lebanon unto the sea; and I will convey them by sea in floats, unto the place that thou shall appoint me, and will cause them to be discharged there, and thou shalt receive them; and thou shalt accomplish my desire in giving food for my household."

Necessary timber was cut and sent to the seaport of Jaffa, and from there, moved overland to Jerusalem.

In return, Solomon gave extensive wheat and oil to support the labor Hiram had sent, to King Hiram as well as twenty cities in the region of Galilee. Apparently, Hiram was not pleased with this gift and personally visited Solomon to inform him of his displeasure.

### Hiram the Builder

While King Hiram of Tyre and King Solomon of Israel play important roles in Masonic mythology, they are behind-the-scenes players compared to Hiram Abiff. This Hiram was among the builders sent by the king of Tyre to assist in the construction of the Temple. He is described in Masonic ritual and Jewish Scripture as "a cunning man, endued with understanding" (2 Chronicles 2:13) and "a widow's son of the tribe of Naphtali, and his father was a man of Tyre, a worker in brass; and he was filled with wisdom and understanding, and cunning to work all works of brass" (1 Kings 7:14).

Hiram was responsible for all ornamentation of the Temple. He is referred to as Hiram Abiff, in reference to his high standing in the courts of both the king of Tyre and Solomon. He was, in fact, an advisor and friend to both kings. *Abiff* is derived from the Hebrew word for "father," or *ab*, and is a designation of high standing and respect. *Huram abif* means "Hiram, his father" in Hebrew and is used to make a clear distinction between Hiram, King of Tyre, and his loyal friend Hiram the Builder, or architect.

This unique use of the name Hiram within Masonry gave rise to the now-archaic term *Hiramites*, used in reference to Freemasons in general and to those in particular who claimed the Fraternity descended from the architect of the Temple.

The esoteric significance of this is that the Builder constructs two pillars, and it is the Builder himself, in addition to Solomon, who is filled with Wisdom (Hokmah) and Understanding (Binah), the two spheres of the Tree of Life that cap the pillars of Jachin and Boaz. On a spiritual level, Hiram the Builder and Solomon are equal—possibly even unequal, with the Builder being the superior of the two, since it is he who will be slain and it is around him that the legends of the Craft and its secret wisdom will be woven.

> He set up the columns at the portico of the Great Hall; he set up one column on the right and named it Jachin, and he set up the other column on the left and named it Boaz. Upon the top of each column there was a lily design. Thus the work of the columns was completed.[23]

The columns were decorated with pomegranate designs, signifying fertility and abundance—the original apple of the Tree of Knowledge of Good and Evil from the Garden of Eden. If the Tree of Knowledge could corrupt man and cause his "fall from grace," then the Tree of Life could provide the means of restoring man to his original glory.

From this we have a peculiar insight into Masonic allegory and its subtle teachings of equality and authority. While the three traditional Grand Masters are all equal in the work, as it takes Solomon's wisdom to envision the

---

23  1 Kings 7:21–22.

Temple and the King of Tyre's wealth or strength to construct it, it is the skill of Hiram the Builder that adds beauty to the finished design. Herein lie the three pillars of Freemasonry: Wisdom, Strength, and Beauty, symbolized by the three principal officers of a Masonic lodge—the Master, Senior Warden, and Junior Warden. These officers each in turn rule a lodge, direct its work, and initiate new members. If they are absent, no lodge can be opened.

## Key Points

1. Modern architecture is utilitarian and devoid of any spiritual value. That is, it fails to inspire us to greatness or encourage selfless acts or visions beyond materialism.

2. Civilizations are known by their architecture, as a building is the inner world made manifest in three dimensions in the material world. It is a collective microcosm for everyone to see and participate in: the myth made flesh.

3. The construction of the Temple of Solomon in Jerusalem is the single most important event in Masonic lore, and in some fashion it is the basis for all of Masonry's rituals and degrees.

4. The Temple is a composition of proportions and harmonics that represent the structure of the universe.

5. Two sacred pillars were built on the porch to the Temple: Jachin and Boaz, meaning "I will establish" and "In strength." These pillars are similar to pillars found in other Near Eastern civilizations.

6. The pillars are often said to have been made out of various materials, including brass and stone, and it is claimed they were hollow in order to contain the secrets of Masonry and preserve them against future cataclysms.

7. A description of the pillars is found in the *Sepher Yetzirah*, an early Jewish mystical text, and thereby associates this aspect of Masonic symbolism with both biblical and esoteric interpretations linking it to the Tree of Life.

8. Masonry is constructed upon the three pillars of Wisdom, Strength, and Beauty. These represent ideals that are made present in the lodge through the three key officers: Master, Senior Warden, and Junior Warden.

9. Masonic lodges have ornaments that distinguish them from other buildings. Among these are the checkerboard floor, tessel borders, and the pentagram. These ornaments are not universal to all jurisdictions.

10. Solomon is known across the Middle and Far East, particularly within Jewish and Arab folklore, as a magician who used occult means to construct the Temple. Many of these stories are found in Sir Richard Francis Burton's sixteen-volume translation of *A Thousand and One Arabian Nights*.

11. Medieval and Renaissance images of Solomon adhere to the image of him as a magician, which resulted in numerous manuscripts being attributed to him. Together, this is known as the Solomonic magic. *The Greater Key of Solomon* and *The Lesser Key of Solomon*, better known as *Goetia*, are the most popular works in Solomonic literature.

12. During the Temple rites, the divine presence known as shekinah, having distinctly feminine attributes, was said to manifest. This has led many to believe that Solomon was also secretly worshipping the goddess Astarte. During the Roman period, a temple to Venus was established on the ruins of the Temple. Masonry refers to the "Genius of Freemasonry" in distinctly feminine terms.

## Assignments for Chapter 2

1. Read one book from the Suggested Reading list or, using a reference work such as *The Encyclopedia of Religion*, edited by Mircea Eliade, or John Michael Greer's *The New Encyclopedia of the Occult*, look up the terms *Solomon, Masonry, magic, shekinah, Sepher Yetzirah*, and *Qabala*.

2. Examine the buildings in your immediate environment and write down clearly the feelings they evoke within you.

3. Using these feelings, write down ways you can improve the spiritual qualities of your architectural environment.

4. Explore ways you can expand this to your neighborhood and community.

5. Research the concept of the Divine Feminine in your particular spiritual tradition and its importance in physical and psychological well-being.

## Suggested Reading

*The Key to Solomon's Key: Secrets of Magic and Masonry*, by Lon Milo DuQuette (CCC Publishing)

*The Hebrew Goddess*, by Raphael Patai (Wayne State University Press)

*The Temple at Jerusalem: A Revelation*, by John Michell (Weiser)

*From the Ashes of Angels: The Forbidden Legacy of a Fallen Race*, by Andrew Collins (Bear & Company)

*The Mysteries of Freemasonry; or, An Exposition of the Religious Dogmas and Customs of the Ancient Egyptians*, by John Fellows, AM (Reeves and Turner)

## 3

# Masonic Initiation
# and Blue Lodge

OVERVIEW
- *Initiation: The Making of a Mason*
- *Isolation, Individuality, and the Beginning of Masonic Awakening*
- *Symbolic Masonry: Blue Lodge and the Starry Vault of Heaven*

Initiation essentially aims to go beyond the possibilities of
the individual human state, to make possible the transition
to higher states and finally to lead the individual beyond any
limitations whatsoever.

—RENÉ GUÉNON, *Glimpses of Initiation*

Masonry is a fraternal organization whose activities are centered around
the lodge ritual and for whom membership consists of applying and being accepted as a candidate for Masonic initiation. This is critical, in that
one can ask to become a Mason but cannot demand it. It is possible to
apply for lodge membership and undergo investigation by the membership committee only to find that one's application has been rejected, or
"blackballed," referring to the use of black and white balls when vot-
ing on an application. The vote must be unanimous. A single black ball
means automatic denial. However, in theory, one can only be rejected
from a lodge for Masonic reasons; that is, the applicant has committed a
serious legal or moral offense and is not considered a good representative
of the ideals of Masonry. While this has been abused and often falls short

of the mark, the process has managed to maintain a basic level of trust and respect among the membership of lodges as well as across rites and jurisdictions.

Membership in Freemasonry is a privilege, not a right, an idea that is foreign to modern society's obsession with forced inclusiveness and individual rights that are devoid of personal responsibilities. This sets Masonry apart from many organizations and is in part why it is considered more than just a "fraternity" but rather a gateway to genuine initiation—not only ceremonial, but also spiritual. Masonry has always been viewed as being composed of a select group of men who choose of their "own free will and accord" to undertake membership in an organization that states as its objectives the improvement of all members, their community, the Fraternity, and service to a higher ideal of "brotherly love and affection" in the name of God. Such ideals can only take place under harmonious circumstances, or circumstances in which harmony can be restored through the accepted authority of the rules and regulations—the landmarks—of the Fraternity.

## Initiation: The Making of a Freemason

Initiation is defined as a beginning, but a beginning of what? In modern life, where we have virtually destroyed all contact with our traditional values and social conventions, the nature of ritual initiation is mysterious, foreign, and terrifying. Mysterious because it is something rarely heard of, let alone experienced. Foreign because it rarely occurs in our lives except in the most crude and sophomoric fashions, such as college fraternities and sororities or membership in a special club or clique. Terrifying because to undertake it requires, now more than ever, a willing surrender of our personal liberty—to trust another group of human beings whom we do not really know with our well-being and security. This security is rarely physical, but rather completely psychological and ego-centered. For this reason, many Masonic lodges have actually destroyed the effectiveness of their own ritual initiations by desacralizing them, joking openly about the "goat" or other such nonsense when a profound and deep sense of solemnity and silence should be manifest.

Initiation is distinct from religious worship in that while there is often an element of the divine in initiation rites, particularly those of a mystical and occult nature, initiation is not a form of worship but transformation. The candidate takes part in a play performed for his benefit, so that he may have specific and distinct experiences that will have the potential to transform him on one or more levels. The candidate is both spectator and participant in the events that unfold around him.

Symbols are placed before the candidate, words stated, and stories told that hold within them a veiled truth, a connection to an ancient and mythological period that participates in yet also transcends human history and knowledge.

Initiation takes candidates beyond time and space and impacts them deeply on a subconscious level. Even if they never reflect again upon the symbols put before them, Masons will find their mind drifting back to one or more of the key experiences in their initiation and knowing that "something" intangible happened to them at that moment. Be it by an inch or a yard, they were transformed and connected to something bigger than themselves. For some, this bigger something is the lodge and their community; for others, it is the Masonic fraternity as an entity of importance; for a small number, it is the mystical stream of which Freemasonry is a distinct and unique expression; and for but the most elect, in the experiences of initiation can be found a direct epiphany of the cosmos—their connection to God.

Masonic initiation is designed to change on a deeper level those who experience it. It does not make members perfect, nor does it promise salvation; it simply provides to those who seek it out and are accepted the tools and opportunity to make themselves better human beings, each in his own way. Through initiation and lodge work, the nature of the sacred is revealed as being an everyday occurrence. This is why when Masons meet, formally or informally, they recognize the presence of the divine through invocation and prayer, bringing forth the full potential of a spiritual life.

## Isolation, Individuality, and the Beginning of Masonic Awakening

The Chamber of Reflection is a unique aspect of Freemasonry that is not present in every rite or jurisdiction. The importance of it, however, is such that no Mason should be unaware of it, and in fact, each should replicate it in his own dwelling space as a means of understanding the deeper aspects of the Craft.

The Chamber of Reflection sits outside of the Temple, or "Tempus," and as such symbolically sits outside of time and space. This is nothing more or less than our very consciousness—our awareness—and challenges us to understand why we do what we do and consider the consequences of our actions. Each man who desires admittance into the brotherhood does so of his own free will and accord. No one can be forced to join. In the Chamber of Reflection, the candidate is asked to reflect upon his reasons for desiring admission and the consequences it may bring. The Chamber of Reflection came into use at a time when Masonic membership was persecuted and declared heretical to dominant church doctrines, as well as seen as politically subversive. Membership could mean one's imprisonment, torture, or death in some instances.

The Chamber of Reflection, even in its most basic form, is clearly linked to the Renaissance practice of the studio. These *studiolos*, also known as *kunstkammer*, or "Chambers of Art," were special rooms highly prized among the wealthy and ruling classes. Here, in their small rooms, (and in some instances not so small), shut off from the daily concerns of the world, they would surround themselves with painting, sculpture, wood relief, and objects to inspire and impress the imagination.

The purpose of these chambers, however, was not that of a study as we understand it in the modern sense of the word. It was not a place of work, in particular intellectual pursuits, but rather a place that allowed one to connect more deeply with both the material and spiritual worlds in a single moment through the suggestive power of art and science.

In *The Pagan Dream of the Renaissance*, Joscelyn Godwin writes:

> One of the most attractive inventions of the early Renaissance is the studiolo, a small, private, decorated study . . . a place of retreat from the public

world into a private universe. As we understand it here, it is not a study for writing, nor a library, a treasury, or a monastic cell, though all of these contribute to its ancestry.

What distinguishes the studiolo from the cell of a monk or a nun is its decoration. . . . It is not so much to take the owner out of this world, as to situate him within it. The decorations served as mirrors to qualities, aspirations, and knowledge already latent in the individual, but place them in a historical, moral, Hermetic, or cosmic context. The room was a model of its owner's mind and an exteriorization of his—or more rarely, her—imagination.[1]

This idea of a special chamber of isolation designed to stimulate the imagination along specific courses of thought, but with the intent of helping the occupant to better engage in his daily activities, is echoed in Albert Mackey's *Encyclopedia of Freemasonry*:

In the French and Scottish Rites, a small room adjoining the Lodge, in which, preparatory to initiation, the candidate is enclosed for the purpose of indulging in those serious meditations which its somber appearance and gloomy emblems with which it is furnished are calculated to produce. It is also used in some high degrees for a similar purpose. Its employment is very appropriate, for, as Gaedicke well observes, "It is only in solitude that we can deeply reflect upon our present or future undertakings, and blackness, darkness, or solitariness, is ever a symbol of death. A man who has undertaken a thing after mature reflection seldom turns back.[2]

The objects that occupy the Chamber of Reflection can be as simple as a chair, writing desk, single candle, human skull, mirror, and writing paper and pen. The symbolism is obvious. In more sophisticated chambers, additional symbols taken directly from the Scriptures, alchemy, and Qabalistic Hermeticism are utilized. These include a small vial of sulphur and its alchemical symbol, salt, water, the image of the rooster, and the alchemical motto VITRIOL.

---

1 Joscelyn Godwin, *The Pagan Dream of the Renaissance* (Grand Rapids, MI: Phanes Press, 2002), 85.

2 Albert G. Mackey and Charles McClenachan, *Encyclopedia of Freemasonry*, revised edition by Edward Hawkins and William Hughan (New York: Masonic History Company, 1924), 141.

While it is easy to confuse the Chamber of Reflection with the more religiously minded monastic cells or a hermit's cave, which are clearly its antecedents, the *function* of the chamber is most easily identified by its contents, which connects it to the Renaissance studiolo. The contents identify the function of the chamber, and while death plays an important part, its presence is designed to anchor the candidate in the present world—in the reality that the field of work is here on earth—and remind him not to escape from it. He is a physical being, but with divine essence, and in working on his rough nature, his character through actions, he creates the smooth ashlar of Masonic fame. This chamber isolates him from the world so that he may better go out and work in it as a laborer for the common good and the divine ideal.

Masons live in the world, but endeavor not to be a part of it. They recognize their physical mortality and seek to build the immortal within themselves, while still carrying out their daily duties to family, community, and self. Since all initiations are in some way connected with death, or leaving the old to embrace the new, it is appropriate that death be the major theme in the Chamber of Reflection. Yet death is just another form of birth, and, as Masons soon discover as they pass through the Gate of Initiation, we must learn to trust in something other than ourselves if we are to find the Light.

## The Trestle Board: Masonic Instruction through Symbols

The *trestle board* (also spelled *tresle* or *tressle*) is one of the most unique aspects of Masonic instruction. While it is composed of symbols, it is also in fact a symbol itself. Also known as a tracing board, the trestle board is derived from the French *tresteau*, a board placed on a tripod for display and instruction. In both Operative and Speculative Masonry, it is where the Master draws his plans and directs the workmen in their labor. In Freemasonry, it takes on the added dimensions of being a form of the Book of Nature, or a means whereby the Grand Architect of the Universe reveals the supreme design for creation.

Traditionally, tracing boards were drawn on the floor of the lodge room by the Tyler in chalk or coal and erased with a mop and bucket after their

**The Trestle Board Display**

use. The *Tyler* is the outer guardian who sits outside the lodge room to see that no one who is not a Mason is allowed to enter while lodge is in session. This duty traditionally falls to the immediate Past Master of the lodge once his term of duty is completed, but this is not always the case. The tracing board, or rather the act of its creation, is so integral to Masonry that it became known as the "lodge" or "drawing the lodge," for without it, the degrees could not be conferred. Metal or tin templates were often used to speed up the process, as well as to give greater clarity to the images being created.

The use of chalk fell out of favor by the end of the eighteenth century, although it continued in some lodges even into the nineteenth century as painted floor cloths began to come into fashion. In turn, floor cloths for the most part fell into disuse, and small, more portable painted boards or framed canvases came into favor for displaying images. This innovation did alter the ritual somewhat, in that the Master no longer walked across the chalk drawing and pointed to its symbols during initiation. Instead, the candidate was introduced to and instructed in the meaning of the symbols afterward.

At some point, the significance of the *floor cloth* as being the lodge was changed into the *room wherein the meeting took place* as being the lodge. When this occurred, the ornate cloth with all of its instructional designs was replaced with a simple carpet. These carpets on occasion were of a black-and-white checkerboard design, with or without the Blazing Star, surrounded by a tassel, reminiscent of the earlier chalk designs. The checkerboard pattern is well known and intimately associated with Masonry as much as the square and compass, and it represents the duality of life—the fundamental search for balance in a world of constant change. The Blazing Star is the guiding star of Providence that leads each Mason along his path and bestows light, life, and divine blessing to humanity. Floor cloths in some instances were hung on walls, but in most cases they were simply replaced by smaller designs painted on wood or stiffened canvas for ease of transport and display.

## Symbolic Masonry:
## Blue Lodge and the Starry Vault of Heaven

The three Masonic degrees of Entered Apprentice, Fellowcraft, and Master Mason are in what is known as Blue Lodge and are referred to in some rites as symbolic degrees. The degrees belonging to High Grade Masonry are all based on and further elaborate on what is presented in Blue Lodge and are referred to as *Philosophic Masonry*.

The term *Blue Lodge* refers to the color blue, which dominates the ceremonial paraphernalia and decorum of the lodge, as well as the tradition of painting a blue sky, or astrological designs of the heavens, upon the ceiling in representation of the breadth and encompassing nature of the Fraternity's insistence on universal friendship and mercy—that is, that Masons are to be as broad and tolerant as the heavens themselves. Given the Hermetic milieu in which Freemasonry developed, it is consistent to examine its symbols within a late Renaissance Hermetic framework. A clear connection to Egyptian symbolism can be made here, as the Egyptian gods were often depicted as blue skinned (similar to the Indian and Tibetan practice) to show their heavenly, nonphysical origin and nature. In Qabala, the color blue is given the sphere of Chesed, or Mercy, on the Tree of Life and fits well with the idea of benevolence, as well as being reminded of the universal nature of the Grand Architect's plan. In alchemy, Chesed is related to the Prima Materia, or "First Matter," the secret underlying essence of all things. It is the working matter as well as the plan behind creation as we know it. Astrology, well known in the early days of the Craft and even into the early nineteenth century, associates the color blue with Jupiter and elemental air, signifying breadth, expansion, life, vitality, and clear vision, or a plan for the future. All of these ideas are present in the symbolic teachings of Blue Lodge and are found within the rituals and specific symbols of the tracing board for each degree.

## The Entered Apprentice: The Gate of Initiation

The Entered Apprentice is the first degree in Freemasonry, and its initiation gives the candidate an overview of Masonic ritual form and structure while instructing members to seek the as-yet-undefined light. The Apprentice who has entered a Masonic temple for the first time is prepared for this life-changing moment in the Preparing Room. As part of his due preparation in this room, which adjoins the temple, the candidate for initiation is stripped of all material possessions and dressed in a strange and peculiar garb some say resembles the dress of heretics on their way to be burned at the stake—presumably in reference to the death of Jacques de Molay. This includes a blindfold and a length of rope called a *cable tow*.

The uniform dress reduces all members to the same level and thereby provides the same experience for each Mason, creating a psychological climate in which each Mason remembers forever the moment he was brought before the altar and made a member of the Craft. It is also explained in the lecture of the degree that this uniformity of appearance suggests that Masons learn humility—to turn their attention inward rather than toward material wealth. The notions of charity, personal conduct that is respectable, and loyalty to the Fraternity are moral lessons each Entered Apprentice is to learn and demonstrate during the time of passing from this degree into the next, that of a Fellowcraft. Entered Apprentices are allowed to sit on lodges opened in this degree and this degree only, and they may only observe; they cannot speak or vote on any proceedings of the lodge. Symbolically, they are like a candidate in the ancient mysteries who was allowed to stand on the porch of the temple but not enter the inner sanctum.

The blindfold used represents secrecy, darkness, and ignorance as well as trust. The candidate is led into the lodge room for initiation but is not able to see what is happening. He is bound about the waist and arm with

**The Entered Apprentice Degree**

the cable tow. This appears as a symbol of unity, for a properly drawn trestle board will be enclosed in a cable tow with a tassel at each corner.

The most profound moment in each member's Masonic life is when
he is first exposed to "the Light" at the altar of Freemasonry. The sheer
impact of its presentation is forever memorable and a point of awe. Regardless of what comes and passes during his life or within the Fraternity,
this moment, symbolic of the quest, the essence of human life itself, is the
moment at which each candidate becomes a Freemason.

Part of this Light is represented by the square and compass, the universal symbol of Freemasonry and among the most recognized symbols
across the globe. While presented here for the first time, their meaning
will be revealed in a later degree. In addition, each degree has a special
manner in which it is laid out in the Volume of the Sacred Law. If the
Jewish or Christian Scriptures are used as the Book of the Law, it is to be
opened to Psalm 133, where the opening passage reads, "Behold how good
and how pleasant it is for brethren to dwell together in unity!" With this
prayer, the Entered Apprentice is reminded of the fundamental purpose
of Masonry—to bring men together, dispel personal animosities for the
greater good, and extend the hand of mercy to family, friend, and stranger
in distress. Unity of mind, purpose, and action is the strength of any group
seeking to accomplish something of value. This unity can only come about
when an attitude of forgiveness and mercy predominates and all work is
for the common good. Forgiveness along with renewal are encouraged and
promoted both in daily life and in the life of the lodge.

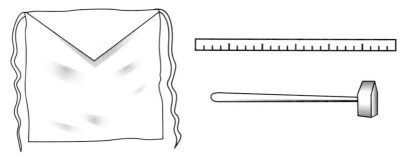

**The Symbolic Lambskin Apron, the Twenty-Four-Inch Gauge,
and the Common Gavel**

Yet oddly, in contrast to these notions of forgiveness and mercy, it is here in the Entered Apprentice Degree that the candidate is told that should he break his oath to the Fraternity by revealing its secrets, terrible and violent retribution will follow. It is unclear if this was meant only to frighten newly made Masons or if the penalties may have actually been carried out at some time. However, to make sense of these threats, it is important to remember that until very recently membership in Freemasonry was often illegal in many countries at various times. To compromise one's self was one thing, but to endanger the livelihoods or even lives of others—particularly in an organization that can only be joined of one's own free will and upon asking—was considered a serious act of treachery. In many modern jurisdictions, it is stated in the ritual that these penalties are traditional and symbolic in nature only, representing the candidate's conscience rather than actual harm.

As a Mason, the Apprentice is invested with an apron symbolic of his work. Traditionally made of lambskin or white leather, both symbols of purity and spiritual strength, it is stated that the apron of Freemasonry "is more ancient than the Golden Fleece or Roman Eagle, and more honorable than the Star and Garter." Three working tools of the Entered Apprentice are then presented: the twenty-four-inch gauge, a common gavel, and a copy of the Book of the Law. The gauge is representative of the hours in a day, the passing of time, and how we use it. The gavel is representative of power and its rightful and constructive use in life. The Book of the Law

**Trestle Board for the Entered Apprentice Degree**

The trestle board for the First Degree features such recognizable symbols as the checker-board floor, the Blazing Star, tessel border, various tools, and the three pillars of Wisdom, Strength, and Beauty.

represents the Apprentice's desire to build his life upon spiritual values. It is up to each Apprentice, under the direction of his mentor, to learn how to use these tools properly and thereby demonstrate his worthiness for the Fellowcraft Degree.

## The Fellowcraft: The Middle Chamber

The Fellowcraft, also known as *Campagnon* in the traditional building lodges, is the Second Degree of Freemasonry. Whereas the Entered Apprentice was but a youth who served "three years" before being allowed to pass on to the Second Degree, the Fellowcraft builds upon the simple moral teachings given—teachings of the heart—and enlarges them through development of the intellect. Symbolically, the Apprentice passes from the porch of the temple into the temple proper, but not its innermost recesses. During his initiation, a peculiar story is told to the candidate: the biblical account of when the Ephraimites wanted to cross the River Jordan. The Gileadites told them to pronounce the word *Shibboleth* in order that the Gileadites might easily identify their friends from foes based on the Ephraimites' pronunciation of the word. At first, this may appear out of place, but for Masons this simple act symbolizes that while the heart must be made charitable and generous, it must also be made wise. Wisdom can be born only from the ability to understand one's experiences. To assist in developing this understanding, the Seven Liberal Arts and Sciences are provided.

The Seven Liberal Arts and Sciences of traditional learning are what create a well-rounded person and creative thinker, someone who is capable of solving problems and understanding the relationships between various disciplines as well as areas of life. These seven disciplines are divided into two groups: the *trivium*, consisting of grammar, rhetoric, and logic; and the *quadrivium*, consisting of arithmetic, music, geometry, and astronomy.

Grammar allows people to express themselves with the correct use of words. Rhetoric adds beauty to this expression so that it may inspire, uplift, and convey a deeper meaning beyond the words chosen. Logic provides clarity and reason and demonstrates the importance of a life of the mind. Arithmetic is the ability to add, subtract, multiply, and divide. This

**The Fellowcraft Degree**

is essential for daily life, and even more so for the Operative Mason. Music demonstrates the mathematical relationship or harmonies that exist and directs the mind to the ultimate harmony of the ancients, the music of the spheres. Geometry, or "the Queen of Science," as it was known, is the practical application of mathematics to the material world, as it allows for the precise measurement of objects both far and near. Astronomy—most likely astrology in the classical, medieval, and Renaissance periods—extends this ability to measure to realms beyond Earth, enlarging our view of creation.

These, along with the teachings of the previous degree, form part of a staircase that will slowly and progressively lead the candidate toward the inner light of the Sanctum Sanctorum—the Holy of Holies.

The image of the Winding Staircase is found in 1 Kings 6:5–8, where it leads to an antechamber for the Holy of Holies. In Masonry, this is called the Middle Chamber. This Middle Chamber is the time of learning, of experiencing the material world and shaping it according to what we have learned. This is a period of the senses, making the symbolic length of time spent as a Fellow of the Craft in the Middle Chamber "five years."

Just as the tools of the Entered Apprentice are for shaping material stone, the tools of the Fellowcraft are for shaping the inner life, improving the life of the mind in preparation for the life of the soul. These tools are an Instructive Tongue, Attentive Ear, and Faithful Breast, or heart. These represent the need of the Fellowcraft to be constructive in his words to others, particularly Apprentices in his care, and his ability to speak in lodge;

**Trestle Board for the Fellowcraft Degree**

The trestle board for the Second Degree shows the pillars of Jachin and Boaz and the Winding Staircase, which leads to the Middle Chamber. The first three steps represent the working tools of the Fellowcraft, the following five the five orders of architecture and the five senses, and the last seven the Seven Liberal Arts and Sciences.

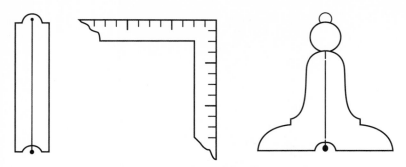

**The Plumb, Square, and Level: Working Tools of a Fellowcraft**

attentive in his listening to instructions from the Master; and faithful in his adherence to what he has received. For this reason, they are known as the Instructive Tongue, Attentive Ear, and Faithful Breast, further demonstrating the oral nature of Masonic ritual and instruction.

The biblical section used in the Second Degree is Amos 7, where the symbol of the plumb line is given to represent the divine standards to which each Mason aspires to adhere so that he may enter the Holy of Holies. The plumb is one of the working tools of a Fellowcraft, along with the square and level.

## The Degree of Master Mason: The Holy of Holies

The degree of Master Mason is the third and final degree in Masonry. At the risk of being repetitive, it is important to recognize that any additional degrees are considered instructive in nature, further elaborating on the basic Masonic framework given up to and including the Third Degree. All Master Masons are equal and may sit in any degree, speak on issues relevant to the lodge, and vote. In this initiation, the greatest of Masonic truths are symbolically revealed, and the sublime nature of the soul and its immortality is inculcated. It is here that the mysteries of life and death are revealed.

This revelation is in part done through the Mystic Chain, or the linking of Brethren arm in arm, as the newly made Master Mason is raised from the stinking stench of death to the bonds of fellowship. The veil

**The Master Mason Degree**

has been pierced, and after the symbolic age of seven years' labor, the Master Mason is a master of life—able to shape himself inwardly and outwardly, to serve his fellows, and to hear the voice of God within.

The Scripture passage used in the Master Mason Degree is Ecclesiastes 12:6, "Or ever the silver cord be loosed, or the golden bowl be broken . . ." This passage is famous for its allusion to the so-called astral cord experienced by many who have had out-of-body experiences. In this degree, the veil of the sanctum is pulled back. The spiritual world is before each Master Mason upon his raising. It is up to each to take the step that will allow him to cross over.

Life for the Master Mason is built upon the three pillars of Strength, Wisdom, and Beauty. Just as the lodge is sustained by these qualities as expressed through the actions of the Three Immovable Jewels—the Master, Senior Warden, and Junior Warden—so does each Mason build his individual life upon these ideals, knowing that, as it is stated in Ecclesiastes 12:14, "For God shall bring every work into judgment, with every secret thing, whether it be good, or whether it be evil." All that we do is known to us and to our Creator. Nothing can escape the rule of conscience of universal justice. This is the ultimate culmination of the first question each Entered Apprentice is asked: "In whom do you put your trust?" The answer is, "God." Only with a complete trust in divine omnipotence, omniscience, and omnipresence can life be truly lived.

To have this trust and to build this life, all of the previous tools of Masonry can be used, but one tool above all else represents the power of the

**Trestle Board for the Master Mason Degree**

The imagery of the trestle board for the Third Degree centers on the coffin and the skull and crossbones, which symbolize death and mortality. The black border represents an open grave, while the acacia branch offers a symbol of immortality. Included on the coffin are the working tools of a Master Mason: a skirret (rope or cord on a reel), compass, and pencil at the top and a plumb, level, and setting maul (mallet) at the bottom. Also shown are an image of the Temple of Solomon and a cipher used to decode Masonic secrets.

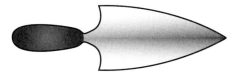

**The Trowel: A Master Mason's Tool to Spread Brotherly Love**

Master Mason: the trowel. Just as a trowel spreads cement to hold stone together, so the Master Mason spreads brotherly love in daily life, thereby helping to complete the building of the Temple.

In summary, the three degrees of Freemasonry instruct each member to:

1. Listen to those who have gone down the Path before him so that he may learn from their experience and tutelage.

2. Study the Seven Liberal Arts and Sciences so that through them he can improve his intellectual knowledge, understanding of creation, character, and spiritual life.

3. Search for the Lost Word, the seed of divinity within, the only true source of peace, power, and understanding. This is expressed in daily life through a broad and tolerant love of humanity. Just as the Grand Architect of the Universe is omniscient, omnipotent, and omnipresent, through our spiritual unfolding we can share and participate in that totality—but only through the power of love.

## A Mason in the World

This is interesting, because despite tradition, nowhere in the actual conferring of the degrees does it say that to be a Master Mason one must memorize the rituals, perform each act exactly as those before him without error, or even attend lodge meetings, for that matter. While it can be justifiably said that only through lodge contact and listening to those who have gone before us can we undertake those things, it is clear that to be a Master Mason, what goes on outside the lodge is more important than what goes on inside it.

To become better, we must leave the old self behind. The death of the little self—the ego—is encouraged through service: first to our family, then to our community, and finally to Masonry, each being an expression of our service to God as we understand it. This provides a unique framework wherein we have a yardstick with which to measure our actions and the fruits of our actions with one simple question: "Who does this serve?" In doing this, the Master Mason finds the Lost Word, the name of God invoked before any undertaking, within himself, his fellow human beings, and all aspects of life itself.

While hardly flashy by modern esoteric standards, it provides a means to make us think and reflect on what we are doing, why we are doing it, and what will come of our actions. In short, what kind of world are we building by doing such-and-such an action? Humility and egoless action are taught through service. In doing this, Masonry is one of the largest charitable organizations in the world and yet is heard of the least. Anonymous charity is true charity. Getting your picture in the paper or your name on a wall or having an auditorium or a building named after you is nice, but this is not charity from the heart—charity working as an "Unknown Superior" in the world. The true Mason does not draw attention to his actions, but rather helps others understand that helping the community, the religious organization, the philanthropic service, or a stranger in need is simply normal, everyday behavior and not something that needs to be rewarded with applause or special acknowledgment.

In the words of journeyman La Volonté de Vouvray:

> You can stay a simple workman and yet be a great workman. In this way, I have known some journeymen and some workmen who have not completed their tests, who were in my eyes masters and teachers of the trade, for they loved the trade with all their heart. They were also teachers of life, for they loved their fellow man, doubtless without even being aware of it. This is how they came to have the gift of teaching and handing on.[3]

---

3 Andre Nataf, *The Wordsworth Dictionary of the Occult* (Hertfordshire, UK: Wordsworth Editions, 1991), 67.

**The Pentagram: The Blazing Star of Freemasonry**

## The Pentagram

One of the more controversial and misunderstood symbols of Masonry is the pentagram. While Masons will state that the Blazing Star of Freemasonry represents the Five Points of Fellowship, the means whereby a Master Mason is raised as well as recognized, the occult aspects of the pentagram were well known by the time it was included in the ritual work of Masonry, as were many of the symbols presented. According to Cornelius Agrippa, the pentagram was the most important of all esoteric figures in that it represented the powers of the cosmos present in man or the microcosm. With it, the energies of the visible and invisible worlds could be contained and harmonized in the life of its possessor. The individual could raise himself from mere human status to cosmic peace and harmony with the Divine Mind—with God.

In his book *A New Encyclopedia of Freemasonry*, A. E. Waite gives ten Masonic explanations for the pentagram in its work: (1) the Star of the Magi; (2) Glory of Divine Presence; (3) Divine Providence; (4) a symbol of Beauty; (5) Light from God on the path; (6) Sign of a True Mason; (7) emblem of the Sacred Name of God, thus God Himself; (8) Sun as the Grand Luminary of Nature; (9) the Dog-Star of Anubis; and (10) Nature as "a volatile spirit animated by the Universal Spirit."[4] Pythagoras (c. 570–c. 495 BCE) considered the pentagram an important symbol of

---

4 Waite, *New Encyclopedia of Freemasonry*, 108–9.

mental and physical harmony. The brotherhood he founded used it as an identifying symbol, often with the Greek letters for "health" at each of the five points, and it was worn on a signet ring.

## Key Points

1. Membership in Freemasonry is a privilege and not a right. It can be requested but not demanded. With it comes responsibilities and obligations.

2. No one can be forced to become a Mason. Each candidate must come of his own free will.

3. Membership in a Masonic lodge is done by petition. Candidates for membership are interviewed by two or more members of the lodge; petitions are reviewed and voted on in the open body of the lodge that has petitioned. A single "black ball," or negative vote, is enough to deny membership.

4. Masonic membership is defined by having been accepted and initiated into all three degrees of the Craft, thereby making the member a Master Mason. All Master Masons are equal in their standing within the Masonry.

5. Initiation confers symbols, experiences, and knowledge that is distinct from religious worship. Initiation is the beginning of something new and has the potential to be a transforming event in the life of the candidate.

6. All Masonic activity begins with a prayer or invocation to the Grand Architect of the Universe.

7. Some Masonic rites use a preliminary chamber known as the Chamber of Reflection prior to initiation. This chamber has its origins in ancient initiatic rites and "Chambers of Art" prominent during the Renaissance.

8. The three degrees of Freemasonry are Entered Apprentice, Fellowcraft, and Master. Each has its own set of symbols and teachings

revealed on trestle boards. It is the duty and obligation of each Mason to study these symbols and find meaning in them for his life.

9. In the Entered Apprentice Degree, the candidate is counseled to listen to those who have gone down the path before him—to listen and to learn.

10. In the Fellowcraft Degree, the candidate studies the Seven Liberal Arts and Sciences to improve himself so that he may be of better service to his community, family, lodge, and God.

11. The Seven Liberal Arts and Sciences are divided into two sections: the trivium and quadrivium. The trivium consists of grammar, rhetoric, and logic, and the quadrivium consists of arithmetic, music, geometry, and astronomy (or astrology).

12. Masonry is concerned with how one acts in the world to make it a better place. All philosophic and mystical speculations must be put to the test of daily living to see if they are of value.

## Assignments for Chapter 3

1. Invoke the divine presence before undertaking any work. Ask others if they will do this with you. Notice their responses as well as the effect it has on the quality of the work resulting. Is there increased productivity? Creativity? Group harmony?

2. Copy the Entered Apprentice tracing board (page 52) on paper or, better still, on pavement with chalk. Examine your thoughts and feelings as you do this. Commit the symbols to memory and notice the effect such work has on your imaginative process, meditations, and dreams. Write down any ideas or inspirations that come to you as a result of this work.

3. Set aside a period of time each day for meditation and prayer, and, at the end of the day, reflect on what you have done and how you might have done it better. Commit yourself to this new course of

action, particularly if it affects others or has to do with improving your human relationships.

4. Create a sacred space within your home for meditation and prayer. Spend some time alone there, contemplating the nature of physical life, your personal mortality, and what it is you want to become or to accomplish, and who it will serve.

5. Begin a systematic study of the Seven Liberal Arts and Sciences and see how quickly your intellectual and spiritual life is enriched.

6. Each day, imagine that as you rise from sleep you have risen from death itself. Greet each day as something fresh, as a new opportunity. Spend time contemplating your mortality, what you have done with your life, and what you want to accomplish. What will be your legacy to your community, family, and self?

## Suggested Reading

*The Temple and the Lodge*, by Michael Baigent and Richard Leigh (Arcade Publishing)

*Turning the Hiram Key: Rituals of Freemasonry Revealed*, by Robert Lomas (Fair Winds Press)

*Hidden Wisdom: A Guide to the Western Inner Traditions*, by Richard Smoley and Jay Kinney (Penguin/Arkana)

*The History of Magic and the Occult*, by Kurt Seligmann (Gramercy Books)

*How to Think Like Leonardo da Vinci: Seven Steps to Genius Every Day*, by Michael J. Gelb (Delacorte Press)

*The Art & Practice of Creative Visualization*, by Ophiel (Weiser)

*The Masques of Solomon: The Origins of the Third Degree,* by C. Bruce Hunter (Macoy Publishing and Masonic Supply Company)

*Masonic Ritual: A Commentary on the Freemasonic Ritual,* by Dr. E. H. Cartwright (Lewis Masonic)

*Samuel Prichard's Masonry Dissected, 1730: An Analysis and Commentary,* by Harry Carr (The Masonic Book Club, vol. 8)

*English Masonic Exposures 1760–1769,* with full transcripts of *Three Distinct Knocks,* 1760; *Jachin and Boaz,* 1762; and *Shibboleth,* 1765, and commentaries by Brigadier A. C. F. Jackson, CVO, CBE (Lewis Masonic)

*Masonic Legends and Traditions,* by Dudley Wright (Rider and Company)

*Symbolism in Craft Masonry,* by Colin F. W. Dyer, PAGDC, Master of Quatuor Coronati Lodge (Ian Allan)

*The Symbols and Legends of Freemasonry,* by J. Finlay Finlayson (George Kenning)

# 4

# The Worldview of the Renaissance: The World Is Alive, and Magic Is Afoot

OVERVIEW
- *Natural Magic*
- *Angels Calling*
- *John Dee: An Archetype Come to Life*

> The occult philosophy in the Elizabethan age was no minor
> concern of a few adepts. It was the main philosophy of the age,
> stemming from John Dee and his movement.
>
> —FRANCES A. YATES

It is difficult for us to understand the nature of the Renaissance mind, let alone that of its magi. Their relationship to the world, Creator, and creation, in particular though the mediums of imagination, art, and symbols, which they called magic, is completely misunderstood in modern terms. As Hans Kayser points out in the preface to his 1921 anthology on Paracelsus, the world in which Paracelsus lived is "quite alien to our time, and only rarely comes into contact with it."[1] This is even more true at the dawn of the twenty-first century.

---

1 Quoted in Jolande Jacobi, ed., *Paracelsus: Selected Writings*, vol. 27, Bollingen Series (Princeton, NJ: Princeton University Press, 1951), xxviii.

While it is difficult to give a stereotypical profile of what the average Renaissance magician was like, they did hold many character traits in common. All were independent thinkers who looked both within and to the world for experience and knowledge. They sought to understand nature and didn't separate divinity from creation or its inhabitants, as did their medieval predecessors and their contemporary theologians. God was everywhere and in everything, and as such, divine power was literally in the hands and hearts of the magus who chose to use it. Plants, stones, the stars—all were a part of this divine power and creative expression, and all could be called upon by the magician to assist him in his redemptive work. This work was aimed at ultimately healing the soul—the rift of "the fall" in biblical terms—and it put the magician in a precarious situation in which he mediated between heaven and earth. A power desired by kings and popes, but also one that they could not have controlled except by sword and flame.

The greatest tool of the magician was, and still is, his creative imagination: the ability to create in the mind's eye images of reality not yet experienced or of an ephemeral, transcendental nature. Through the use of such images, the magician could enter into the etherial realms like Ezekiel in his chariot, control the destiny of nations, and command the very elements of creation itself. Through judicious use of imagination, will, and confidence in this inner power, the magus believed that anything was possible.

As he ascended in power and knowledge through the celestial spheres, the magus would enter into communion with beings of a highly specialized and sacred nature. Through them and the words they would convey to him, he could command the heavenly legions as well as spirits in the deepest bowels of the earth.[2] The Sacred Word (or Sacred Name), the first vibration of creation, was his tool to use, and in doing so, the magus identified himself with God. But power was not everything, often merely a byproduct of the mage's accomplishments. The true revelation came in realizing one's relationship to the godhead and in having direct commu-

---

2  For additional information, see "Bridging the Worlds: Modern Shamanic and Hermetic Practices," by Mark Stavish, at www.hermeticinstitute.org.

nication, free of interlopers and priests, with the Creator. This was done through love—a love so pure, etherial, and abstract that it was the veritable incarnation of the Platonic ideal of love. In this love, Creator and creation were one and could express and experience each other directly. This divine union, reminiscent of Gnostic, Hermetic, and even Buddhist and yogic doctrines, is best expressed by Johann Scheffler (1624–77) under the pen name Angelus Silesius:

> I know that without me
> God can no moment live;
> Were I to die, then He
> No longer survive.
>
> I am as great as God,
> And he is small like me;
> He cannot be above
> Nor I below Him be.
>
> In me God is fire
> And I in Him its glow;
> In common is our life,
> Apart we cannot grow.
>
> He is God and man to me,
> To Him I am both indeed;
> His thirst I satisfy,
> He helps me in my need.
>
> God is such as He is,
> I am what I must be;
> If you know one, in truth
> You know both him and me.
>
> I am the vine, which He
> Doth plant and cherish most;
> The fruit which grows from me.
> Is God the Holy Ghost.[3]

---

3 Quoted in Carl Jung, *Psychological Types*, vol. 6, *Collected Works of C. G. Jung* (Princeton, NJ: Princeton University Press, 1971), 256.

Theosophy via theurgy becomes the predominant focus of the Renaissance magus. This theurgy was different from its medieval predecessor, in that it stressed the individual's role in repairing the rift between humanity, creation, and the Creator. Ritual and invocations were no longer meant to summon evil spirits but instead to assist in human redemption. Magic became a kind of social sacred ceremony, a Mass in which all benefited but in which the magician was the sole participant. The tools of the magician combined with the love and compassion of the mystic, creating a synthesis greater than either could accomplish alone.[4]

It was because of this ability to successfully combine two seemingly opposing esoteric views in a climate that was at best lukewarm to the idea of their existence that many of the magi, such as Paracelsus, Cornelius Agrippa, and Giordano Bruno, were sought out by both Catholics and Protestants alike to heal the many rifts in Christianity—a function that Masonry would in part play in its nonsectarian approach to membership.

This love is borne out in the fact that despite the richness of their works, those who sponsored them (on occasion), and the never-ending stream of wealthy and poor seeking help, most of the prominent Renaissance magi died in poverty.

It is intriguing but also understandable to note that the majority of the great writers and practitioners of magic and alchemy in this period were either church-trained or active churchmen. The Roman Catholic Church in particular offered the easiest access to many of the "forbidden books" in its libraries, as well as the needed education and leisure time to read them. Some have made much of their apparent orthodox Christian calling or activity. In fact, until the end of the fourteenth century, *almost* anything was acceptable in Christian circles as long as the Holy Trinity was invoked and one considered himself a "Christian." Then the witch trials began to occur, thereby institutionalizing church intolerance and making it the norm.[5] With the Jews forcibly removed from Spain

---

4  See "Wisdom's Bliss: Developing Compassion in Western Esotericism," by Mark Stavish, at www.hermeticinstitute.org.

5  Valerie Flint, *The Rise of Magic in Early Medieval Europe* (Princeton, NJ: Princeton University Press, 1991).

the same year the last Arab stronghold in Europe fell (1492) and those remaining forced to convert or hide, Europe was essentially an officially "Christian" continent, albeit a heavily divided one.

The taking or even requesting of sacraments was in itself not enough to make "good Christians," either, for many sought not to remove Christ but to reinvigorate the church with pre-Christian classical wisdom and learning. The appreciation of Nature and observation of her truths is what drove them. The teachings of the church, the sacraments, and the rituals—these were merely the outer cloak that gave meaning and form to the magi's inner truths. God spoke to them through Nature, but the church gave the language of the day to express it. Since any title other than Christian would have brought a death sentence, it is an unanswerable question what they would have called themselves given the freedom to do so openly. Since "natural philosophy" is what united them, some chose to be called by the humble title "Philosophers of Nature."

> As such the magician operates in a manner wholly different from that of his precursor: where the one had a direct line to the god or gods of his tribe, the other (i.e. Renaissance magus) works with different techniques, different contacts, yet is always seeking to break through into the inner realm itself, to speak directly to God, as his ancestors (i.e., tribal shaman) had once been able to do. Thus, his magic is a practical extension of a philosophical/mystical underpinning, and without taking into account his dream of unity, however partial or superficial, with deity, is to mistake his whole purpose.[6]

And:

> Magic and ritual are microcosmic expressions of the macrocosm: man's tiny torch of desire uplifted to the fire of the stars. We plug into the universe though the enactment of ritual—beginning with . . . the propitiation of the elements and a desire to enter the womb of the world-mother. The Hermetic approach, as adopted by the magician, is more intellectually motivated, celestial rather than chthonic. The astrological calculations of "star-led wizards" of Milton's *Ode on the Morning of Christ's Nativity* are a

---

6 Caitlin and John Matthews, *The Western Way: A Practical Guide to the Western Mystery Tradition* (London: Arkana/Penguin Books, 1986), 290.

far cry from the instinctive actions of the tribal shaman—yet each in his way is motivated by the same needs and desires, only their methods have changed with the movement from tribal to individual consciousness. . . . The characteristic philosopher of the Elizabethan age was John Dee, whose mathematic preface to the English translation of Euclid (1570) begins with an invocation to the "Divine Plato" and quotes Henry Cornelius Agrippa on the three worlds. . . . His "mathematical" preface, and his teaching in general, were immensely influential in stimulating the Elizabethan scientific Renaissance.[7]

The word *nature* comes from "that which is born," or *nat–*, the root for *nativity, natal,* and *navel* (where the umbilical cord is cut). One's natal chart or horoscope is cast for the moment of birth to show the positions of the location of birth in relation to the heavenly spheres and thereby, through their relationships or angles that are formed, understand the cosmic influences that will influence the newborn's life. These angles are critical in the interpretation of a horoscope, and without them only the most basic of information can be understood.

Nature is born out of the cosmic night, the Ain Soph Aur of the Qabalists, the creative power of the Demiurge of the Gnostics, the primordial waters of the Egyptians. Nature is alive and filled with energy, matter, and intelligence. Like man, it has degrees of self-consciousness. What else explains why a rock is a rock and not a snake, or why one rock is a quartz and another a diamond or ruby? While modern science can explain the difference in terms of chemical compositions, these are simply another manner of stating that one stone vibrates at a different rate than the other. This "cosmic melody" of creation, this harmony of the spheres made concrete, is the essence of matter—of material form and life. It is even disingenuous to speak of energy and matter from the Hermetic and Renaissance perspective, for they are in fact one and the same—simply different perspectives of the same thing.

---

7 Ibid., 88.

## The World of Natural Magic

When we speak of "the world of natural magic," we are really speaking of the worldview of magic in which the energies of the invisible world impact the physical world—even creating it—and can be understood in a very impersonal manner. Spiritual laws exist, and the magician can understand as well as use these laws just as one can understand and use gravity. Everything is in contact and in sympathy with everything else, both visible and invisible, and it is only ignorance that keeps one from experiencing this fundamental unity directly.

This is no different than in Tibetan Tantra, in which, after taking various initiations, the physical world is viewed as a Buddha-field filled with enlightened beings and all objects are material reflections of pure light, wisdom, and energy. The magician does this in his ritual circle, the architect in the design of the temple or building. And in the Renaissance, the garden was a particularly unique expression of this kind of ideal, where heaven and earth were united and the designer saw himself not as the master, but as the "Handmaid of Nature."

## Angelic Magic

Angels have played an important role in the development of Western religious, mystical, and esoteric practices. While Freemasonry makes no specific reference to them in its rituals or symbols, the fundamental relationship Freemasonry shares with Middle Eastern traditions makes the link to angels an embedded idea. We often hear of the Genius of Freemasonry referred to as "she" and discussed in anthropomorphic terms—expressing human qualities, but on a perfected or archetypal level. This may be confusing to modern people, who often think of "genius" in terms of mental acuity rather than as an individual; however, the word *genius* is directly linked to the root for *genie*, or *jinni*. The jinn are considered to be beings of spiritual fire that Arabic magicians sought to control, and, as previously discussed, Solomon was considered the greatest magician of all time, building the Temple through the employment of fifty thousand jinn. With this in mind, consider the image of a woman sitting alone in a cell designed for contemplation wherein the mysteries are revealed, which is presented in the Closing Charge recited at that end of every lodge meeting. This symbol, then, takes on a deeper connection to both a literal spiritual force protecting Freemasonry and the Gnostic notions of the Divine Sophia, or Wisdom—the Bride of God.

## John Dee

To understand Freemasonry in the era before 1717, it is essential to understand two seminal figures: Elias Ashmole and John Dee. Ashmole's importance was to assist in linking Renaissance thought with the emerging era of the Enlightenment through the Royal Society and later existing Masonic institutions, which would in turn create the first Grand Lodge. However, to understand Ashmole and his role, it is essential to understand the Renaissance, and to do that, we must understand John Dee—for John Dee was the Renaissance incarnate.

Whereas we often think of Leonardo da Vinci as the seminal "Renaissance man," or polymath, in truth, despite da Vinci's genius, it was men like Dee who defined the cosmological milieu in which the architectural, artistic, literary, and scientific achievements of the Renaissance occurred.

### John Dee (1527–1608) and Edward Kelly (1555–97)

Of all the Renaissance magi, the most famous pair of angelic communicators are John Dee and Edward Kelly. At some times comic and other times tragic, this pair of celestial scryers are known to more modern practitioners of magic than all of their contemporaries combined. While that may say more about modern occultists than it does about the work of Dee and Kelly, the fact remains that Dee and Kelly have come to form the modern archetype of the Renaissance magus.

In their work on the Western tradition, Caitlin and John Matthews compare the magician to his ancient predecessor, the tribal shaman. In this context, the authors state:

> If Merlin is an inner resonator who generated the literature which gathered about his name, then Dr. John Dee must be considered almost his outer manifestation in the real world. He is probably the single most influential

aspect of the magician ever to have lived and a worthy successor to the Arthurian mage. Though his abilities have often been called into question, his influence has continued to be felt right up to the present time.[8]

Born in 1527, Dee rose to prominence in life quickly. His keen mind and brilliant intellect brought him fame while still a student, when he solidified his lifelong reputation as a sorcerer by building a mechanical beetle for a production of Aristiphanes' *Peace*. At twenty-three he was lecturing in Paris on mathematics, and a year later he was awarded a pension by Edward VI for skill in astronomy. When Mary Tudor ascended to the throne in 1553, Dee was received at court and invited to draw up her horoscope. Dee's love of learning prompted him to amass at least 2,500 books, one of the largest private collections at the time. Many of the manuscripts formerly in his collection now reside in the British Library.

When Elizabeth I succeeded Mary six years later, she asked Dee to choose her coronation date, which became January 14, as Dee saw it as astrologically auspicious. In 1564, Dee published *The Hieroglyphic Monad*, said to have been written in two weeks, and dedicated it to Emperor Maximilian II, king of Bohemia and Hungary. In addition to his occult studies, Dee was also sought out for his practical and mundane knowledge in such diverse topics as astronomy, navigation, geography, perspective, optics, and mathematics. Dee was also believed to have been a spy for Elizabeth, as well as possibly the tutor to a young Francis Bacon (1561–1626) and the prototype for Prospero in Shakespeare's *The Tempest*.[9]

Across his life, Dee was patronized by some of the most influential monarchs of his day; Count Albert Lasky of Poland, King Stephen of Poland, Count Rosenberg of Trebona, and even Sir Walter Raleigh sought his services. Dee's life moved on an almost fatal course after his meeting with Edward Kelly in 1581. Kelly, or Talbot, as he is also known, came into Dee's employ and became the source for the majority of the visions that make up the core of Enochian magic. While it is not clear whether Kelly and Talbot are the same or separate people, this is irrelevant, as

8  Ibid., 294.

9  Peter Dawkins, *Arcadia*, 5 vols. (Stratford-upon-Avon: Francis Bacon Research Trust, 1988).

the key portions of Dee's diaries are written during his association with "Kelly." The major problem we face with Kelly is not only his true identity, but also that we have only Dee's perspective of him. Many rumors are associated with Kelly—everything from forgery to necromancy. He is painted as a scoundrel preying on Dee's credulity. Despite their troubled relationship, they stayed together for seven years and experienced many adventures, and they have survived as a symbiotic pair—a sort of esoteric Siamese twins, or maybe Laurel and Hardy.

Systemically, the methods employed by the two were similar to what was typical in Renaissance magic, except for three things: Dee did not celebrate Holy Mass as part of the ritual; there is no ceremonial circle; and there is no license to depart. This is highly unusual, given the terrific fear of spirit obsession in the process of evocation and most ceremonial operations. For years, however, the two experimented, recorded, and rewrote the details of their sessions. Promises of long life, riches, and fame poured forth from the "angels" they communicated with. Kelly threatened to leave Dee on several occasions—but he always stayed.

Yet in the end, Dee's life was in shambles. His house was partially destroyed, along with the precious library he had worked so hard to build, by a peasant mob that had heard of his magical practices. Despite this, Dee continued to practice magic until the end of his life and was even willing to stand trial for witchcraft, certain that the courts of James I would see that his quest was an honest, Christian, and spiritual one. After splitting with Dee, Kelly boasted of possessing the Philosopher's Stone and was imprisoned for life for murdering a man in a rage. He died after falling from a tower while trying to escape and breaking his leg.

At least two plays have been written about Dee: one by Christopher Marlowe, *Doctor Faustus*, which put an end to Dee's influence at court, as it associated him and others doing similar practices with devil worship; and Shakespeare's *The Tempest*, where he is portrayed as the outcast and betrayed magus Prospero.[10]

---

10  Noel Cobb, *Prospero's Island: The Secret Alchemy at the Heart of the Tempest* (London: Coventure, 1984).

## The End of the Renaissance

Many postmodern critics have pointed out that it was not science that put an end to the magical operations of the Renaissance. The end of magic did not come from the rational replacing the "super-rational." Instead, it was the irrational. It was fear that put an end to the scientific explorations into the cosmos and consciousness that the Renaissance represented. Protestant witch hunts and the Inquisition of the Roman Catholic Church, and their desire to destroy anything that was not a mirror image of themselves, would deliver the crippling blows. Only with the establishment of the Royal Society at the end of the seventeenth century do we see official sanction for exploration and inquiry into creation, and with this official sanction, some protection. From this small coterie of scientists, inventors, and scholars of all types, this notion of freethinking is extended into Freemasonry and the formation of the Grand Lodge of England.

## Key Points

1. The metaphysical worldview of the Renaissance and the period leading up to the formation of the first Grand Lodge in 1717 is alien to our own; it is misunderstood by many scholars and ignored by contemporary Freemasonry.

2. Dame Frances Yates states it best: "The occult philosophy in the Elizabethan age was no minor concern of a few adepts. It was the main philosophy of the age, stemming from John Dee and his movement."[11]

3. This occult worldview was one in which a variety of nonhuman spiritual beings existed and could be contacted. The mind, imagination, symbols, and ritual action were all seen as having impact on the physical world. The arts, science, philosophy, religion, and so-called occult practices were seen as extensions of one another and not separate entities.

---

11 This quote, also the epigraph to this chapter, is from Francis Yates, *The Occult Philosophy in the Elizabethan Age* (London: Routledge, 2001), 88.

4. Within this world, the dominant religious organizations, primarily the Roman Catholic Church and various Protestant denominations, held sway over the intellectual, artistic, and spiritual practices and researches that were deemed acceptable. To step outside those bounds without powerful patronage was to risk death.

5. The primary occult practices of the age included the study of Jewish mysticism or Qabala, ritual magic, alchemy, and astrology.

6. These practices were often labeled the Hermetic arts and sciences and were connected to each other under the syncretistic umbrella of Renaissance Hermeticism.

7. These practices were often cast in the light of two schools of magic: natural and angelic.

8. Proponents of natural magic state that they are using the natural energy, cycles, and intelligence in nature and often physical objects. Proponents of angelic magic state that they converse only with the angels, or good and holy servants of God, and eschew demonic magic or sorcery as being counter to the will of the Creator.

9. Dr. John Dee, astrologer to Queen Elizabeth, ambassador, and spy, was the seminal Renaissance magus. He embodied the totality of the occult view, and for him, conversing with the angels of God was the highest form of magic and provided sources of information about material and spiritual realities.

10. Edward Kelly, Dee's assistant, was a man of peculiar talents and low scruples. He died after breaking his leg in a prison break.

11. John Dee died penniless, his life in shambles. At least two plays were written about him in his lifetime: Christopher Marlowe's *Doctor Faustus* and William Shakespeare's *The Tempest*.

12. Despite opposition to research into the possible validity of esoteric doctrines and associated occult practices by the Royal Society, it was not reason that put an end to the Renaissance worldview, but rather witch hunting.

## Assignments for Chapter 4

1.  Read one or more books from the Suggested Reading list.

2.  Spend time outside contemplating the power and presence of nature. Go a week without watching television or listening to recorded music or the radio. Limit your computer use to work-related activities only. Plan ahead so as to limit your automobile and mass transit use as well. Now imagine what it is like to live in a world in which nature is all-powerful, where everything you know is within walking distance and you have little information about the outside world. How does this make you feel? What are your concerns, and how can you address them?

3.  After having done the above assignment, imagine that the world you live in is alive, even populated with invisible beings of both good and evil natures. How does this affect your sense of security? Who or what can you turn to to get control over your life?

4.  Explore the nature of holism in modern education and health care. Is it really "holistic"? List ways you can begin to make your life more holistic and more in harmony with the forces around and inside of you while still living in a twenty-first-century environment.

## Suggested Reading

*Behind the Crystal Ball: Magic, Science and the Occult from Antiquity through the New Age*, by Anthony Aveni (University Press of Colorado)

*The Occult Philosophy in the Elizabethan Age*, by Frances A. Yates (Routledge)

*Giordano Bruno and the Hermetic Tradition*, by Frances A. Yates (University of Chicago Press)

*The Art of Memory*, by Frances A. Yates (University of Chicago Press)

*Eros and Magic in the Renaissance*, by Ioan P. Couliano (University of Chicago Press)

*Renaissance Thought and Its Sources*, by Paul Oskar Kristeller (Columbia University Press)

*Shakespeare and the Ideal of Love*, by Jill Line (Inner Traditions)

*Renaissance Magic and the Return of the Golden Age: The Occult Traditions and Marlowe, Jonson, and Shakespeare*, by John S. Mebane (University of Nebraska Press)

*Two Renaissance Mythmakers: Christopher Marlowe and Ben Jonson; Selected Papers from the English Institute, 1975–76*, edited by Alvin Kernan (Johns Hopkins University Press)

*Marlowe, Tamburlaine and Magic*, by James Robinson Howe (Ohio University Press)

*Prospero's Island: The Secret Alchemy at the Heart of* The Tempest, by Noel Cobb (Coventure, Ltd.)

*The Pope and the Heretic: The True Story of Giordano Bruno, the Man Who Dared to Defy the Roman Inquisition*, by Michael White (HarperCollins)

*The Magic Circle of Rudolf II: Alchemy and Astrology in Renaissance Prague*, by Peter Marshall (Walker & Company)

*The Planets Within: The Astrological Psychology of Marsilio Ficinio*, by Thomas Moore (Lindisfarne)

*Lake of Memory Rising: Return of the Five Ancient Truths at the Heart of Religion*, by William Fix (Council Oak Books)

*Freemasonry and the Birth of Modern Science*, by Robert Lomas (Fair Winds Press)

*The Magus of Freemasonry: The Mysterious Life of Elias Ashmole—Scientist, Alchemist, and Founder of the Royal Society*, by Tobias Churton (Inner Traditions)

*Restoring the Temple of Vision: Cabalistic Freemasonry and Stuart Culture*, by Marsha Keith Schuchard (Brill)

*The Genuine Secrets of Freemasonry Prior to AD 1717*, by W. Bro. Rev. F. de P. Castells (A. Lewis)

# 5

# Sacred Geometry, Gothic Cathedrals, and the Hermetic Arts in Stone

Numbers are the sources of form and energy in the world. They are dynamic and active even among themselves . . . almost human in their capacity for mutual influence.

—THEON OF SMYRNA

In many ways, attempting to understand Freemasonry from the viewpoint of the early twenty-first century is not unlike trying to understand lions by watching one in a zoo. While the lion is a lion, it most likely was born and raised in captivity, and despite having all of its natural instincts, walls forbid it to run free, to hunt game, to mate, and to raise its young. It is a lion, and truly a dangerous animal, but it has adapted to its world and, as can be seen in the eyes of so many lions in the zoo, suffers from the apathy that world creates. Freemasonry is little different. Modern Masons have much in common with their predecessors; however, many—Grand Lodge officers included—lack the critical worldview that dominated the intellectual landscape in which Masonry gestated and

**One of Masonry's Key Symbols: The Letter G**

flourished in the seventeenth and eighteenth centuries. As a result, much of contemporary Masonry has been reduced to fraternal and charitable activities, with philosophy being totally forgotten.

The most obvious aspect of this is in one of Masonry's key symbols: the use of the Roman letter G. So often it is asked, "What does the G mean?" To this, some less-informed Brethren will answer "God," not knowing that this would only work in English and other Germanic languages. If this were the answer, it would be the letter D in French, Italian, and Spanish lodges, with similar changes made elsewhere. (Even so, the appearance of the letter G is not universal in Freemasonry.)

However, G stands for geometry, the most critical field of learning for any educated person, particularly one who would be in the building trades.

*Geometry* means "the measure of the earth." The Greeks learned this science from the Egyptians, master builders of the Great Pyramid complex and thousands of temples and tombs great and small. Geometry is part of the Seven Liberal Arts and Sciences and is the cornerstone for them all, as through it the remaining are united. Through geometry, order, harmony, and synthesis are achieved, not in the abstract, but in the concrete and material world. Geometry is the study of archetypes and their physical manifestation in life.

The earliest form of sacred architecture in Western Europe during the High Middle Ages is Gothic building styles. It is in these structures—massive in size, with their wide open spaces, towering windows of stained glass, and impressive acoustical structures—that we see the growth of the building guilds that in part would give rise to Freemasonry. It is interesting to see images of Christ holding compasses to measure the world, symbolizing divine harmony at the heart of all things.

Just as Renaissance artists moved out of flat and two-dimensional representations into elegant, refined, and detailed use of perspective, we see the building trades, wherein the Master Mason was both architect and contractor, moving away from the small, squat, fortress-like structures of the Romanesque design into houses of worship that elevated the senses and, with them, spiritual consciousness.

Saint Bernard of Clairvaux, the advocate for the architectural style of the Cistercian Order, is said to have stated that there were to be no decorations in the designs, only the use of proportion to achieve visual, spatial, and acoustic harmony.

These buildings, many of which remain standing to this day, are in fact a living form of spiritual energy made concrete, no different than the popular methods of Chinese feng shui. Nor are the methods they use unavailable to the modern person or layman.

In *Sacred Art in East and West*, Titus Burckhardt points out that sacred art creates a vision of the cosmos that is holy, and that through its beauty it makes participation in the vision of holiness unconscious, even involuntary.

This ability to make human beings "participate naturally and almost involuntarily in the world of holiness,"[1] this subtle and unconscious pull into the divine, works to this day and is felt by nearly everyone who has entered into the realm of sacred art and architecture. Given that our ancestors were for the most part illiterate, the play of light and shadow, colors, and acoustical quality exercised a profound impact on the individual and collective imagination. This was not lost on the secular, ecclesiastical, or even heretical authorities of the day. Just as Albert Einstein is often quoted as saying that imagination is the most important tool we possess, we hear the same thought put even more forcefully by his Renaissance predecessor Paracelsus, the father of Western alchemy, who states:

---

1 Titus Burckhardt, *Sacred Art in East and West* (Louisville, KY: Fons Vitae, 2002).

Imagination is like the sun. The sun has a light which is not tangible; but which, nevertheless, may set a house on fire; but the imagination is like a sun in man acting in that place to which its light is directed.

Man is that what he thinks. If he thinks fire, he is fire; if he thinks war, then he will cause war; it all depends merely on that the whole of his imagination becomes an entire sun; i.e., that he wholly imagines that which he wills.

Man is a twofold being, having a divine and an animal nature. If he feels, and thinks, and acts as divine beings should act, he is a true man; if he feels and acts like an animal, he is then an animal, and the equal of those animals whose mental characteristics are manifested in him. An exalted imagination caused by a desire for the good raises him up; a low imagination caused by a desire for that which is low and vulgar drags him down and degrades him.[2]

In this context, the sights, sounds, and actions accompanying Masonic rituals, initiations in particular, take on a new significance. Everything is done to uplift the imagination and bring the full impact of symbols—in form and in action—into play, for symbols work in but one area of the human mind, and that is the subconscious. Masonic ritual, temples, and tools are designed to stimulate the subconscious minds of those exposed to them, thereby stimulating what Paracelsus calls our "divine nature" and "raise" us up.

In his *Three Books of Occult Philosophy*, Cornelius Agrippa writes:

The doctrines of mathematics are so necessary to, and have an affinity with magic, that they that do profess it without them, are quite out of the way, and labour in vain, and shall in no wise obtain their desired effect. For whatsoever things are, and are done in these inferior natural virtues, are all done, and governed by number, weight, measure, harmony, motion, and light.

And:

Hence a magician, expert in natural philosophy, and mathematics, and knowing the middle sciences consisting of both these, arithmetic, music,

---

2  Arthur Edward Waite, trans., *The Hermetic and Alchemical Writings of Paracelsus the Great* (London: James Elliott, 1894).

geometry, optics, astronomy, and such sciences that are of weights, measures, proportions, . . . knowing mechanical arts resulting from these, may . . . do many wonderful things, which the most prudent, and wise men may much admire.[3]

The most striking characteristic of Gothic architecture is the volume of stained-glass windows that are utilized. Chartres alone has over 6,500 square feet of glass. The method of creating stained glass likely originated in Muslim lands, where glass was affixed to plaster casings and reinforced with plant fibers. This technique appears to have been perfected in France, quickly spreading, with lead being used to hold the glass together as well as attach it to the surrounding iron framework.

The most famous windows in Gothic history are of course those of Chartres. The red and blue colors of Chartres have been the subject of much speculation, including that of modern alchemists who sought some metallic secret within their construction. The oldest windows date to 1150 and to an earlier building destroyed in 1194, yet nearly seven hundred years after their construction, the colors of the newer windows remain vibrant, particularly those where the red and blue colors are utilized.[4]

The most famous expositions on the esoteric symbolic meaning of the great cathedrals is found in the writings of the mysterious twentieth-century alchemist Fulcanelli. Little is actually known of who Fulcanelli was, although there has been and continues to be a great deal of speculation. Legends have grown up around him as well as *The Mystery of the Cathedrals*, the book attributed to him. First published in 1925, the book examines the sculptures of the major cathedrals in France, focusing on Notre Dame of Paris and Notre Dame of Amiens, and states that they represent the alchemical process as encoded and preserved in stone. The preface to the

---

3 Henry Cornelius Agrippa, *Three Books of Occult Philosophy*, ed. Donald Tyson, trans. James Freake (Saint Paul, MN: Llewellyn, 1993), 233.

4 It is a miracle that we even have Chartres today. The cathedral barely escaped demolition after the French Revolution and the anticlerical attitudes that followed. The city was occupied by Prussian troops for a brief period of time as a result of France's defeat in the Franco-Prussian War, but Chartres was undamaged, as it remained despite the destruction that would follow from 1914 to 1918. Some damage occurred to the city and minor damage to the cathedral during the Second World War, but the windows we so admire were removed in 1940 and put in storage to prevent their possible destruction.

second edition is most interesting, in that it refers to Fulcanelli as not yet having received the "Gift of God," or full Illumination, but being close, he kept with tradition and maintained anonymity in his writings so as not to attract the attention of the merely curious and the foolish.[5] Among those suggested as having been Fulcanelli is R. A. Schwaller de Lubicz, author of numerous books on Egyptian symbolism and temple architecture, and Jean-Julien Champagne, an erudite student of esotericism who fits the description given of Fulcanelli as a man who dressed and acted as if he were living in an earlier age.[6]

Regarding the Gothic cathedral, Fulcanelli writes:

> The Gothic cathedral, that sanctuary of the Tradition, Science and Art, should not be regarded as a work dedicated solely to the glory of Christianity, but rather as a vast concretion of the ideas, of tendencies, or popular beliefs; a prefect while, to which we can refer without fear, whenever we would penetrate the religious, secular, philosophic or social thoughts of our ancestors.
>
> The bold vaulting, the nobility of form, the grandeur of the proportions and the beauty of the execution combine to make a cathedral an original work of incomparable harmony; but not one, it seems, concerned entirely with religious observance.[7]

It is interesting to note that when the building phase occurred, many if not all of the great cathedrals, and to a fair extent the smaller ones as well, were dedicated to "Our Lady," or the Virgin Mary, the mother of Jesus Christ. Herein we see the material world giving birth or expression to divine ideals, taking them from the abstract and making them tangible, concrete, living.

---

5  Polite names for those we now refer to more accurately as "psychic vampires." They take and take for their own satisfaction and give nothing in return, nor are they awake enough to realize the fundamental degree of their selfishness.

6  Andre Vandenbroeck, *Al-Kemi: A Memoir; Hermetic, Occult, Political, and Private Aspects of R. A. Schwaller de Lubicz* (Great Barrington, MA: Lindisfarne, 1987) and Geneviève Dubois, *Fulcanelli and the Alchemical Revival: The Man Behind the Mystery of the Cathedrals* (Rochester, VT: Inner Traditions, 2006).

7  Mary Sworder, trans., *Fulcanelli: Master Alchemist; Le Mystère des Cathédrales* (Albuquerque, NM: Brotherhood of Life, 1984), 36–37.

It was pointed out in the previous chapter that this reverence for things feminine continues in Masonry, in which the Opening Charge, which is said at the beginning of each meeting, refers to the Genius of Freemasonry: "Wisdom seeks the secret shade and the lonely cell, designed for contemplation. There she sits, delivering her sacred oracles." This "Genius" is the guiding spirit of Freemasonry and every Mason who seeks to understand its mysteries. In an earlier age, one in which Masonry arose, this would be thought of as a real spiritual power and intelligence, not unlike a guardian angel, whose existence and influence was very real and not simply poetic license. Later esoteric groups would think of it in terms of an *egregore* of Freemasonry, or a collective consciousness that both gives to and receives from the actions of its members. Like "geometry" and "wisdom" in the form of Sophia before it, the tendency to turn abstract forces and ideals into anthropomorphic images, particularly of a feminine form, suggests pre-Christian sources in classical paganism.

One woodcut shows geometry personified as a beautiful woman, complete with the letter G and surrounded by the working tools of the building trade: "lewis" hoist for blocks, square, setting maul, measuring stick, and brick. She is even depicted using the compasses while two assistants nearby use astronomical equipment to survey the heavens depicted above. This form of personified expression is reminiscent of the Egyptians, who saw their gods, or *neters*, as powerful abstract forces who became accessible when transformed into the pantheon we know as the Egyptian gods. Given the relationship of geometry to Egypt, there may be some connection here to the ideals of geometry.

The importance of geometry cannot be understated, as it was an applied science among the ancients. Daily life was ruled out—literally in terms of measure as well as laws—according to perceptions of divine proportions. The Egyptian temples are among the finest examples of this. It is no surprise that the cornerstone of the Renaissance would rest upon the Hermetic arts and sciences for the revival of classical learning. Herein, the Emerald Tablet of Hermes, the Egyptian god of magic, wisdom, and learning, would reveal the entire secret in a few lines:

That which is above is as that which is below, and that which is below is as that which is above, for performing the miracle of the One Thing.[8]

For us, the key part to consider in relation to sacred geometry is the first: "That which is above is as that which is below, and that which is below is as that which is above." This illustrates the connected nature of the so-called material and spiritual dimensions. Here, in the hard reality of material life, the work of becoming a better person and creating an earthly paradise, a utopia like so many Renaissance dreamers wrote about, takes on true meaning only in the light of earthly inertia. To overcome the baseness of human nature—the sheer weight of habit, training, and cultural mores, be they beneficial or not—and to shape and form the world so that our conscious daily interaction with it and others is a reflection of divine laws is really the Masonic ideal as well as the Hermetic one. It is reflected in the words of Jesus, when he tells his disciples that they are to "become perfect as your father in heaven is perfect" (Matthew 5:48).

This interrelationship of worlds is also the cornerstone of natural magic, in which these relationships can be manipulated—be it in the building of a temple, the creation of a talisman, or the design of a garden, city, or political state.

It is through Mary that the Word is "made flesh" and through geometry that ideal becomes form. The Lost Word is what each Master Mason seeks, for he only receives a Substitute Word during his raising.

This notion of measure, building, numerology, creation, the feminine role in mortality and divinity, and earthly rulership is expressed in Edmund Spenser's *The Faerie Queene*. Spenser was in contact with the leading members of Dee's inner circle and sought to reform Hermetic philosophy to better suit his Puritan views. Despite this, his works are profoundly Neoplatonic and reflect the Hermetic philosophy of the period. Francis Yates calls *The Faerie Queene* "a great magical Renaissance poem, infused with the whitest of white magic, Christian Cabalist and Neoplatonic, haunted by a good magician [i.e., Dee]. . . . Spenserian

---

8  Frater Achad, *The Egyptian Revival; or, The Ever-Coming Son in the Light of the Tarot* (York Beach, ME: Weiser, 1974), chapter 8. Also available online at http://www.hermetic.com/browe -archive/achad/egyptian/egypt8.htm.

magic should be read not only as poetic metaphor . . . but also in relation to contemporary states of mind."[9]

> The frame thereof seemed partly circular,
> And part triangular, O work divine;
> Those two the first and the last proportions are,
> The one imperfect, moral, feminine:
> The other immortal, perfect, masculine,
> And twixt them both a quadrate was the base
> Proportioned equally by seven and nine:
> All which compacted made a goodly diapase.[10]

The metaphor of ancient philosophers was continued in the medieval and Renaissance eras—one in stone, in the construction of cathedrals, and the other in verse, in the language of poets and playwrights. Both are united in geometry, in the study of number, shape, form, and measure, but also on a more subtle level—that of numerology.

Fulcanelli states that there was a verbal Qabala based on, but distinct from, Jewish mysticism, in that it played on words in a phonetic manner whereas Qabala used an alphanumeric relationship between letters and numbers within words, sentences, and even paragraphs to suggest hidden meanings—again, pointing a Masonic student of these topics back to the idea of the Lost Word.

The world of the men and women of the classical world, the Middle Ages, and the Renaissance, up to and including the early period of the formation of the Grand Lodge, was significantly different from ours. This difference was not so much that of technology, environment, or even understanding, but one of perception and belief. While modern man worries much about the impermanence of human life and his fleeting mortality, the man or woman of earlier ages saw little difference between the material and spiritual dimensions. Physical bodies came and went, but *life* was eternal. The world was not a fixed and static place but one in which the elemental spiritual forces of nature, angelic beings of the celestial heavens,

---

9 Yates, *Occult Philosophy in the Elizabethan Age*, 127.

10 Edmund Spenser, *The Faerie Queene*, bk. 2, canto 9, stanza 22.

demons from the pits of hell, and even the dead could come forth and interact with the so-called living.

Referring to pre-Christian texts that permeated the medieval Christian era, Claude Lecouteux writes:

> What clearly emerges out of their study is that their authors were simply incapable of drawing a clear line between this world and the hereafter, between "life" and "death." This does not imply that they were indifferent to what must be called a change in condition or status, or that they did not conform to what is an obviated observation, that is . . . the "dead person," does not have the same type of reality as the . . . living person. . . . There is a mentality in which a dead person can come along at any moment and adopt the shape of the living, the living can animate the deceased, and surprising (for us) movement is established between the two realms.[11]

These themes are echoed throughout the Elizabethan era, particularly in the plays of Christopher Marlowe and William Shakespeare. Only at the end of the Renaissance, with an increasing emphasis on *humanism*, or the philosophy that places man as the measure of all things, does the magical worldview of millennia begin to fully unravel and become replaced by the god of Reason.

While these ideas are generally lost to the twenty-first-century reader, they were well known to the average literati during this period leading up to and well past the formation of the Grand Lodge of England in 1717. Esoteric and occult ideas based on the Renaissance magical and alchemical practices played a major role in popular folklore and even university education in Europe and the Colonies into the early decades of the nineteenth century.[12]

---

11  Claude Lecouteux, *Witches, Werewolves and Fairies: Shapeshifters and Astral Doubles in the Middle Ages* (Rochester, VT: Inner Traditions, 2003), vii–viii.

12  For a detailed exposition on this topic, see D. Michael Quinn, *Early Mormonism and the Magic World View* (Salt Lake City, UT: Signature Books, 1998).

## Temples, Talismans, and the Survival of the Stone

The notion of sacred geometry was applied on a grand scale to cathedrals, chapels, and private estates and even, some suggest, in the ground plans for the cities of Paris and Washington, D.C. However, even a landless individual, or one living in the cramped confines of a seventeenth- or eighteenth-century urban environment, could avail himself of the significance of symbols and proportions. This physical act of moving from the two-dimensional drawing of the trestle board to the three-dimensional expression of actual construction meant that the symbols of geometry came alive as Platonic solids.

One of the leading proponents of this kind of unified knowledge theory was Francesco Giorgi (1466–1540). Giorgi was a Franciscan friar whose main publications were *De Harmonia Mundi* (1525) and the *Problemata* (1536). Clearly influenced by Neoplatonism and the writing of Pico della Mirandola, he was also a Qabalist with access to Hebrew source material through the Jewish community in Venice, a community that expanded considerably after the Jewish expulsion from Spain in 1492 by the Catholic monarchs Isabella and Ferdinand. Like his predecessors in the Florentine Neoplatonic movement, Giorgi saw Qabala simultaneously as a means of proving the validity of Christianity and as a direct connection to the writings attributed to Hermes Trismegistus. In addition, Giorgi fully integrated Pythagorian-Platonic numerology, demonstrating the essential harmony of the world, and Vitruvian architectural theory, which he saw as being directly connected to the Temple of Solomon.

Giorgi further refines the angelic systems present in Pico and their essential harmonies, which allow man to climb to the font of creation itself. Number was the key to understanding Giorgi, for number was proportion and harmony. Through number, the unalterable cosmic principles of sacred geometry were revealed.

Platonic solids are the five basic shapes mentioned by Plato in *Timeaus* that are believed to have given rise to all known shapes and forms. These basic shapes are the tetrahedron, octahedron, cube, icosahedron, and dodecahedron. This was something that would have been clearly known to the early operative and speculative Masons, and not lost on them, as it forms part of the Seven Liberal Arts and Sciences. Johannes Kepler linked the five Platonic solids to the five planets that orbit the sun—Mercury, Venus, Mars, Jupiter, and Saturn—and, through them, to the classical elements of water, air, earth, fire, and ether.

The most significant aspect of Masonry for the non-Mason is the various regalia worn by Freemasons in their public and private ceremonies. Through the symbols that decorate the collar jewels and aprons of the officers, the tools of the work are revealed to the members present, and they represent the spiritual and moral function of the officers in the lodge.

Wearing of special objects, here referred to as "Masonic clothing," is nothing new and has been done since time immemorial to set the operations and proceedings apart from worldly or mundane affairs. In doing so, a special atmosphere is created and recognitions given to those participating by virtue of the particular jewel or emblem of the office they are wearing.

In the early days of the Craft, the symbols of initiation were drawn on the floor and wiped clean after the ceremony was completed. This gave way to the creation of special carpets or floor cloths that could be rolled out and easily transported and stored, known as trestle boards. By the mid eighteenth century, as Masonry moved out of rooms above taverns and into buildings exclusively dedicated to Masonic work, these cloths in turn became more or less elaborate paintings depicting Masonic initiation and were placed on easels for easier instruction.

These Masonic temples became living, three-dimensional representations of the ideas presented in the trestle boards and, in doing so, special places where the mystery of the Mason's Word literally became flesh in the laying of the first foundation stone and in the making of the candidates in the temple raised upon it. These were indeed special places, and everyone—both members and the general public—knew it. They were talismans of Masonic virtue.

*Talisman* comes from the Greek word *telesmata* and refers to the ancient art of making magical images designed to convey a particular power or energy. However, the word specifically refers to the act of consecration. Freemasons are regularly reminded that where they walk is "holy ground," that the place about the altar, the entire temple itself, is dedicated and consecrated to a specific act: that of making Freemasons and bringing Freemasons together for the act of mutual assistance and self-improvement.

Just as the cathedral can be seen as a giant, three-dimensional talisman, as described by Agrippa, so too can we see the same in a Masonic temple when a lodge of Masons is in session.

Amulets, often confused with talismans, are more of a general "good luck" piece and are not ritualistically created. If we look at the manner in which Freemasonry, or any similar organization for that matter, utilizes its ritual regalia, we see that the items used fall somewhere in between. While not magical in the classical sense of the word, they do create a psychological context that is more uplifting and formalized—and thereby special and of importance—than if they were not worn and lodge actions were performed in street clothes.

This emphasis on special "clothing" since the very inception of the first Grand Lodge and earlier is a link to the ancient mystery traditions that should not be dismissed or overlooked. The special clothing and jewels of the officers, as well as the simple aprons worn by attending members, all pertain to part of the legend of Hiram Abiff and the building trade. Even if we accept that the jewels were used earlier in the stonecutters' guilds for easier recognition by their members, the connection or similarity with even earlier traditions is not lost.

Masons wear special tools for the work they perform; that work has now become little more than learning and performing the basic rituals as the sum total of the Craft, whereas at one time it meant something else.

It is important to remember that in the worldview of the pre–Grand Lodge eras, to call upon God or any of the invisible beings said to inhabit the heavenly realms was considered a literal act—that is, call on them and they come—and not a formal but empty gesture. When a blessing was made, it was believed that an aspect of divinity was lit up within the person or persons receiving the blessing. When a building or structure was blessed, it was believed that an aspect of divinity, possibly even an angelic force, was made present and tangible in the structure.

When Freemasons ask for the blessing of God, the Grand Architect of the Universe, or the "Genius of Freemasonry who presides over all our actions," in the environment of the Renaissance this would have been seen as a literal invocation of divine power, no different than charging a dead battery with electric current. No explanation to the members would need to be given.

*The Fourth Book of Occult Philosophy*, attributed to Agrippa, states:

> Now we come to speak of the holy and sacred Pentacles and Sigils. Now these pentacles, are as it were certain holy signes preserving us from evil chances and events, and helping and assisting us to binde, exterminate, and drive away evil spirits, and alluring the good spirits, and reconciling them to us. And these pentacles do consist either of Characters of the good spirits of the superior order, or of pictures of holy letters or revelations, with apt and fit verses, which are composed either of Geometrical figures and holy names of God, according to the course and manner of many of them; or they are compounded of all of them, or very many of them mixt. . . . And if we draw about him any angular figure, according to the manner of his numbers, that also shall be lawful to be done.[13]

This emphasis on geometric shapes and forms is not unique to medieval and Renaissance European magic, but rather is also found in the earlier Middle Eastern practices upon which they drew, as well as in Eastern designs called *mandalas*, geometric images designed to present cosmological views in symbolic form. These mandalas were not limited to paper, stone, or cloth. Tibetan sand paintings, as well as the three-dimensional constructions of a *stupa* (similar in some ways to the old *herms*, or road markers, of the classical period), demonstrate the vital importance of putting archetypal patterns into material form to allow them to transform and enhance our lives.

Ancient civilizations symbolized the relationship between these pure ideas and the energies they directed through the function of the angle—or the fundamental relationship between two numbers. When personified, these ideas became the gods of Egypt as well as neighboring cultures. Thus,

---

13  Henry Cornelius Agrippa, *The Fourth Book of Occult Philosophy*, ed. with commentary by Stephen Skinner (Berwick, ME: Ibis Press, 2005), 34–35.

the angelic forces invoked in religious rites and esoteric practices are essential cosmic principles personified; they are, in their own manner, the creative word made concrete.

While the Temple of Solomon was a divine revelation, it was not a singular historical event, but was rather with cyclic regularity renewed, and in doing so, reinvigorated the world. The Temple was the key to understanding the laws of the universe: number, measurement, and harmony.

> That is why the Templars and other mystical idealists devoted lives to discovering the secrets of the Temple. It is like the philosopher's stone, a talisman that turns base metal into gold, that brings new light into the world and restores its natural condition as an earthly paradise.[14]

Given this context, it is peculiar that one of the most commonly known as well as commonly ignored symbols within Freemasonry is the Blazing Star, or pentagram. According to Agrippa, geometric figures are as powerful as the numbers they represent, with the number five belonging to the pentagram:

> A pentangle [pentagram] also, as with the virtue of the number five hath a very great command over evil spirits, so by its lineature, by which it hath within five obtuse angles, and without five acutes, five double triangles by which it is surrounded. The interior pentangle contains in it great mysteries, which also is to be inquired after.[15]

Elsewhere, Agrippa illustrates that man—the human body—is the perfect pentagram and that within the human body are energies that are in harmony with the invisible energies of the planets and the stars under the direction of divine providence.

Freemasons meet each other upon the Five Points of Fellowship, which is often the meaning given to the pentagram. While an important moral lesson, it robs this ancient symbol of its great power, both for the Fraternity as a whole and for each individual Mason. The average Mason remains

---

14 Michell, *Temple at Jerusalem*, 11.

15 Agrippa, *Three Books*, 330.

unaware of this ancient usage of the pentagram and its occult significance until the Twenty-eighth Degree of the Scottish Rite.

It is not until this degree, known as Knight of the Sun, Prince Adept, that we hear of the esoteric and practical importance of the pentagram:

> In the West, over the Warden, you behold the holy and mysterious pentagram, the sign of microcosm, or universe, called in the Gnostic schools "The Blazing Star," the sign of intellectual omnipotence and autocracy, which has been partially explained to you heretofore. It represents what is called in the Kabala microprosopos, being in some sort a human figure, with the four limbs, and a point representing the head. It is the universe contained with the Deity.
>
> It is a sign as ancient as history and more than history; and the complete understanding of it is the key of the two worlds [spiritual and material]. It is the absolute philosophy [Hermeticism] and natural science [alchemy].
>
> All the mysteries of Magism, all the symbols of the gnosis, all the figures of occult philosophy, all the kabalistic keys of prophesy, are summed up in the sign of the pentagram, the greatest and most potent of all signs.[16]

The reference to the ability of this symbol to keep evil spirits away is of significance to Masonry in particular, in that, as was mentioned earlier, King Solomon according to legend commanded fifty thousand spirits to build the Temple. Thus, in this simple image, we have an allusion to the great occult power of the Fraternity's traditional Grand Master and the Hermetic-Pythagorean-Qabalistic reference to number, harmony, and form, and finally, the idea that under the star of illumination, wherein the inspiration of God touches the members present, harmony is produced.

## The Forty-seventh Problem of Euclid: The Great Symbol of Masonry

Geometry is so important to Masonry and its understanding of the cosmos that the symbol of the forty-seventh problem of Euclid adorned the cover of Anderson's *Constitutions* when it was published in 1723.[17] While

---

16  Charles T. McClenachan, *The Book of the Ancient and Accepted Scottish Rite* (New York: Masonic Publishing Co., 1884), 412–13.

17  Euclid of Alexandria wrote what is considered the first textbook on geometry and published 465 axioms, equations, postulants, and theorems in his thirteen-volume *Elements*.

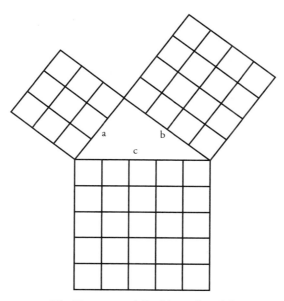

**The Forty-seventh Problem of Euclid**

this carries little meaning in an age of near-universal education when almost everyone learns the most rudimentary elements of algebra and geometry before high school, in the sixteenth century, geometry was the key to almost every conceivable art and science of material importance and was directly linked to the teachings of the Greek and Egyptian mystery schools—the sources of Hermetic knowledge—through Pythagoras. In addition, through the study of numbers, the secrets of the ancient texts, long suppressed by religious intolerance and secular power, could be understood using the Qabalistic systems of *gematria, notarikon,* and *temura.* These systems of letter-number substitution allowed for the creation of new words, connections, and magical devices. Numbers were the keys of heaven and earth, and through them, the locks that kept man in spiritual and intellectual ignorance could be opened.

On the level of Operative Masonry, the forty-seventh problem of Euclid is the most practical equation in construction. It states: "In right-angled triangles, the square on the side subtending the right angle is equal to the squares on the sides containing the right angle," or $a^2 + b^2 = c^2$. Through its application, it is possible to create perfectly squared angles, survey mountains (important for maps), calculate longitude and latitude (important for sailors at sea), and determine the distance of the sun, moon, and planets from Earth. Tunnels are built using it, allowing entrances to be started at both sides of a mountain and to meet exactly in the center. From a purely Speculative point of view, a symbolic image of the forty-seventh problem of Euclid is worn by Past Masters of a lodge to remind members to be lovers of the arts and sciences, thereby improving themselves, their communities, and their lives. It also reminds the more insightful that it is possible to start at very opposite places in life and arrive harmoniously at the center.

## Key Points

1. The use of the letter G in Masonic symbolism refers to geometry.

2. *Geometry* means "the measure of the earth" and was imported into Europe by the Greeks, who learned it from the Egyptians.

3. Through geometry, order, synthesis, and harmony are achieved in a concrete expression of archetypal ideas.

4. The earliest form of sacred architecture in Christendom is the Gothic style of architecture, which occurred in the High Middle Ages.

5. Saint Bernard of Clairvaux was the main advocate of this style of construction.

6. The idea behind sacred architecture is to allow observers to participate in the sense of holiness taking place around them.

7. Mathematics was linked to the occult arts and thereby during the Middle Ages the Roman Catholic Church forbid it to be studied. Agrippa, the most famous occultist of the Renaissance, states that the "doctrines of mathematics are so necessary to, and have an affinity with magic," that without them magic is in vain.

8. Mathematics is essential to geometry and architecture, thereby (for some) linking the great Gothic cathedrals to the Hermetic arts and sciences.

9. The mysterious twentieth-century alchemist Fulcanelli authored several books, of which *The Mystery of the Cathedrals* interprets the Chartres, Notre Dame, and others according to the alchemical practices of the Great Work.

10. Most of the great cathedrals were dedicated to *Notre Dame,* or "Our Lady," Mary, the mother of Jesus. The Black Madonna seen in several of these cathedrals has esoteric significance that is often overlooked but is well known in alchemy. It also links these structures to the Temple of Solomon, the presence of the Shekinah, and Solomon's purported worship of Astarte-Venus.

11. Washington, D.C., and Paris are reported to have been laid out according to the principles of sacred geometry, making each a giant talisman, or magical device.

12. The forty-seventh problem of Euclid is the great symbol of Freemasonry and is the most practical of all equations in material construction.

## Assignments for Chapter 5

1. Read one or more of the books from the Suggested Reading list. Research and collect images of the great temples, cathedrals, and buildings of the classical, medieval, and Renaissance periods. Place one or more of them in locations where you can be exposed to their beauty daily, even if subconsciously.

2. Obtain a picture or several images of one of the great cathedrals or temples and visualize yourself inside it. What is it like as you approach the doors? What do you see and feel? What is it like inside? Find a house of worship near where you live and, regardless of its simplicity or ornateness, approach it as if you were a pilgrim seeing it for first time after a long journey to pray there. What is the first thing that strikes your eye? What is your first impression of the building and its environment?

3. Obtain an inexpensive set of drafting tools and undertake a study of sacred geometry. Notice the effects it has on clarifying your thinking and creative process. Notice the importance of details and the amazing synthetic effects it has on consciousness.

4. Using your studies and meditations from the first and second assignment, along with the practical study from the third, plan your living space to the best of your ability with the notion of sacred geometry in mind.

## Suggested Reading

*Sacred Geometry: Philosophy and Practice*, by Robert Lawlor (Thames & Hudson)

*Math for Mystics: From the Fibonacci Sequence to Luna's Labyrinth to the Golden Section and Other Secrets of Sacred Geometry*, by Renna Shesso (Weiser)

*The Mystic Spiral: Journey of the Soul*, by Jill Purce (Thames & Hudson)

*Art and Architecture in Medieval France*, by Whitney S. Stoddard (Icons/Harper & Row)

*Gothic Europe*, by Sacheverell Sitwell (Holt, Rinehart, and Winston)

*Cathedral of the Black Madonna: The Druids and the Mysteries of Chartres*, by Jean Markale (Inner Traditions)

*Fulcanelli: Master Alchemist; Le Mystère des Cathédrales*, translated by Mary Sworder (Brotherhood of Life)

*The Dwellings of the Philosophers*, by Fulcanelli, translated by Brigitte Donvez and Lionel Perrin (Archive Press and Communications)

*A Compendium on the Rosicrucian Vault*, edited by Adam McLean (Hermetic Research Series)

*Temple of the Cosmos: The Ancient Egyptian Experience of the Sacred*, by Jeremy Naydler (Inner Traditions)

*The Temple of Man*, by R. A. Schwaller de Lubicz (Inner Traditions)

*The Pagan Dream of the Renaissance*, by Joscelyn Godwin (Phanes Press)

*The Survival of the Pagan Gods: The Mythological Tradition and Its Place in Renaissance Humanism and Art*, by Jean Seznec (Princeton University Press)

*Places of the Soul: Architecture and Environmental Design as a Healing Art*, by Christopher Day (Aquarian/Thorsons)

*The Art and Architecture of Freemasonry: An Introductory Study*, by James Stevens Curl (Overlook Press)

## 6

# The Lost Word
# and the Masonic Quest

OVERVIEW
- *In the Beginning Was the Word*
- *Sound, Number, and the Secrets of the Temple*
- *The Word: Masonic Light and the Holy Guardian Angel*

Architecture is frozen music.
—ARTHUR SCHOPENHAUER

## In the Beginning Was the Word

It is through Mary that the Word is "made flesh" and through geometry that ideal becomes form. The Lost Word that each Master Mason seeks—for he only receives a Substitute Word during his raising—is the power of creation itself. Mary is the Wisdom Seat, the foundation of all creation in the medieval mind, and the Word is her offspring. The power of creation is found in wisdom.

Harmony expressed in sound produces music, and in word, a certain rhythm, even a chant. This idea of words expressing power over their listeners is embedded in the word *enchanted*, or "to be chanted," which is derived from the Latin *incantare* (*in* means "against"; *cantare* means "chant").

Rhythm and rhyming have a particular effect on the consciousness of the listener as well as that of the speaker, and they are an effective memory device as well as tool of suggestion or hypnosis. It is no surprise that we see rhyme and rhythm playing an important part in magical incantations of the early homespun variety—known as witchcraft—and in the oaths and obligations of members of another craft: that of Freemasonry. Through peculiar wording and rhythm, extensive rituals are committed wholly to memory and passed on orally for centuries.

In Masonic initiation, the candidate would be blindfolded for the greater part of the ritual, and only through intense listening to the words of the lodge officers would he know what was happening. This detail may sound insignificant to anyone who has not undergone the experience, but for those who have, even decades after their initiations, entire lines from the ritual are memorable because of the concentration they had to give to what was happening around them.

Those who have found the Lost Word have heard the voice of God within and can truly be called Master Masons in both essence and form. The Lost Word has been recovered and is the True Word. The Substitute Word is no longer needed. The Master Hiram Abiff, who was slain by three fellows of the craft, represents the desire for humans to have power or privilege that is unearned. It is the false sense of self derived from identification with the material world that slays and cuts us off from communion with our true Inner Master, and as such, until we can humble ourselves at the porch of the temple, we cannot enter nor receive the Word. Until then, a Substitute Word is given. This substitute is religion.

*Religion* comes from the root *relig–*, meaning "to unite," and the goal of most religions is to unite the human consciousness with divinity in some fashion. However, most fall far short of this goal and instead are mediums of inculcating moral and ethical virtues into their adherents through the process of ritual and collective work. As such, true uniting can only occur on an individual level and in the privacy of one's own chamber, such as is used prior to the Entered Apprentice Degree and symbolized by Hiram's daily meditations in the porch of the Temple. Anyone who has truly understood the "plan" or lessons that are prepared for him, be it by predestination, chance, or karma, becomes like Hiram: unafraid in the face of certain death for failing to reveal a secret that cannot be revealed from man to man, but only from Self to self.

## Jewish Magic

Within Qabala, the possibilities of magic are clearly stated, particularly through the use of divine names. However, magic was considered to be a rare event, only performed by a pious person in times of emergency, and then at physical and spiritual risk to himself. While Qabalistic writings have warnings against the use of magic, there are no universal condemnations of it. This is further complicated by the distinction made between purely physical or material magic and inner or spiritual magic, when such distinctions in practice are not always clear-cut.

Spanish schools of Qabala made a distinction between schools of practice received from the Lurianic tradition using the Tree of Life and those perceived as being derived from magical practices based on the Name, or "Masters of the Name." It is on these practices of the Masters of the Name that much of medieval and later surviving magical practices are based, including German and Pennsylvania "Dutch" folk magic. These distinctions between "practical" or magical uses of Qabala—and at times reproach for the former—is historically significant, since it is like a child disowning its grandparents, as practical Qabala is older than the speculative or philosophic schools.

The practical application of spiritual knowledge is derived from magical practices of the Talmudic period through the Middle Ages. They are very distinct and separate from the philosophic schools that use the Tree of Life and in no way are dependent on them. Yet the use of power, even naturally forming power, can corrupt but the most ardent soul, which gave rise to nefarious or "black magical" practices in which the "unholy names" of the fallen angels were employed to do harm, effect personal gain at others' expense, and disrupt the natural order of creation. Within the widespread diffusion of Jews across Europe and North Africa, Jewish magic took on some of the practices of its neighbors, especially Arab demonology and German and Slavic witchcraft. In turn, the practices of these peoples were also affected by Jewish magical doctrines, as the efficacy of Jewish magic quickly became legendary. The idea of "the Jew" being a powerful magician capable of conjuring up angels and devils amplified others' awe of practical Qabala, as well as their anti-Semitic fears. The *ba'al Shem*, or

"Master of the Name," was the archetypal magus of the medieval period; many Christians sought to imitate this model, despite direct prohibitions by the Roman Catholic Church against magical practices.

## Magical Writing

The use of special alphabets attributed to angelic or divine sources is a cornerstone of phonetic Jewish magic. It also influences those practices in which talismans and magical drawings are also used, in that many of these images are composed of carefully crafted constructions made up of Hebrew letters.

The earliest of these so-called magical alphabets, or *kolmosin* ("angelic pens"), is attributed to Metatron, the archangel of the Countenance (or Throne of God). Additional alphabets exist and are attributed to other angelic and archangelic beings, such as Raphael, Michael, and Gabriel, in the same fashion that various magical texts are attributed to Hermes, Solomon, Moses, and other important figures. Several of these alphabets are similar to Babylonian cuneiform, while others more closely resemble early Hebrew and Samaritan scripts. These alphabets are often referred to as "eye writing" because they are composed of small dots and lines, which resemble the human eye. This manner of writing was occasionally used to write divine names in nonmagical texts, but it was mainly used in the creation of talismans. These magical images are descendent from Greek and Aramaic theurgical practices of the first century CE.

# Reuchlin and the Miraculous Name

## Johannes Reuchlin (1455–1522)

Reuchlin, born in Germany in the town of Pforzheim, received a doctorate in philosophy from the University of Basel in 1477 and a degree in law from Poitiers in 1481. He traveled to Rome as part of the diplomatic corps before settling in Stuttgart. In 1492, Reuchlin learned Hebrew at the age of forty-seven. This was a difficult year for Jews, as it marked the beginning of several pogroms. Under orders of the new Catholic king and queen, Ferdinand and Isabella, Jews were ordered to leave Spain, convert to Catholicism, or risk death. Neighboring Portugal would follow this example within two years.

Reuchlin's knowledge of Hebrew allowed him to study Qabala directly from the original texts, and within two years he had produced his principal work on the subject: *De Verbo Mirifico*. *De Verbo* became a sort of bible on what would eventually be called "Christian" Qabala. In it, Reuchlin claimed to have reconstructed the "true" name of Jesus in Hebrew by taking the Tetragrammaton, or "four-lettered name" of God in Hebrew—Yod-Heh-Vau-Heh, or YHVH—and inserting the letter Shin in the middle to get YHShVH.

Moshe Idel, professor of Kabbalah at Hebrew University in Jerusalem, states:

> The main subject of Reuchlin's first book on Kabbalah, *De Verbo Mirifico*, was to expose the miraculous powers of the hidden divine name, the Pentagrammaton, formed from the insertion of the letter *Sh,* in the middle of the Tetragrammaton; this name formed, according to Reuchlin and his source Pico della Mirandola, the secret name of Jesus. In the Jewish Kabbalah we can find formations of "divine" names that cannot be detected in classical Jewish texts, which are as bizarre as the form YHSVH [sic].[1]

This miraculous name was quickly adopted to show that the true mission of Jesus was that of savior, but it was also used to show that within Qabala there were many secrets that had been forgotten since the time of the first Christian churches. This attempt to "Christianize" Qabala made it a politically safer topic for Reuchlin and others to study.

However, Reuchlin did eventually end up before the tribunal of the Inquisition. The position of Jews in Christian Europe was always a precarious one. Not accepting the Christian faith was bad enough; being blamed as a people for the death of Christ, the Son of God, only made things worse. When Emperor Maximilian I ordered all books in Hebrew burned on August 15, 1509, few might have really been surprised. However, authorities did ask Reuchlin—in what might have been an effort at

---

1 Johann Reuchlin, *On the Art of the Kabbalah*, trans. Martin and Sarah Goodman (Lincoln, NE: University of Nebraska Press, 1983), xix.

entrapment for his Jewish-leaning sympathies—if he felt it admissible to burn all Jewish books, sparing only the Torah. Reuchlin answered no and was ordered to appear before the Grand Inquisitor in Mainz to defend himself against charges of heresy. Fortunately for Reuchlin, he was a well-liked man. Representatives from fifty-three towns in the province of Swabia spoke up on his behalf. To thank him for the great risk he took in their defense, the rabbis of the town of Pforzheim supplied him with the documents he would later use in writing *De Arte Cabalistica.*

*De Arte Cabalistica* quickly became the bible of Christian Qabala[2] after its publication in 1516. It was dedicated to Pope Leo X, who had an interest in Pythagorianism. The basic format of *De Arte Cabalistica* is that of a dialogue between a Pythagorean and a Muslim, which is mediated by a Jew who explains how Qabala contains the oldest of divine wisdom. This wisdom states that the sacred letters and names of things—in Hebrew, of course—are not just symbols, but rather carry the very spiritual essence of the thing they are related to. The same doctrine was held by the ancient Egyptians regarding hieroglyphs and their sacred writings. To substantiate his claims, Reuchlin references the Zohar and the magical text the *Sepher Raziel* (Book of Raziel), whose authorship has been attributed to the archangel Raziel. Raziel, whose name means "the secret of God," is the archangel of the sphere of Hokmah on the Tree of Life. This makes Raziel the guardian of the secret wisdom of God, the archangel that revealed the mysteries to Adam, Enoch, Noah, and King Solomon. The *Sepher Raziel* describes the "Fifty Gates of Wisdom," of which the great king and magus Solomon was able to penetrate only up to the forty-ninth, with the final "gate" being closed even to him.

### Distinctions Between Magic and Mysticism

While magic was seen as filled with dangers and used mainly for creating effects in the outer world, mysticism, which employed many of the same principles, was seen as a means of increasing one's personal holiness and relationship to God. Through prayer and meditation, it was believed that the

---

2  Spellings of *Qabala* vary; however, strictly Hebrew mysticism is increasingly spelled *Kabbalah*, Christian variations *Cabala*, and in Hermetic schools *Qabala.*

individual could ascend the celestial spheres and attain increasing knowledge, love, and wisdom. These spheres, or the biblical version of Jacob's Ladder, were patterned after the prophet Ezekiel's vision and its latter adaptation in Lurianic Qabala as the Tree of Life.

In *Kabbalah*, Gershom Scholem states:

> The Kabbalah regarded prayer as the ascent of man to the upper worlds, a spiritual peregrination among the supernal realms that sought to integrate itself into their hierarchical structure and to contribute its share toward restoring what had been flawed there. Its field of activity in kabbalistic thought is entirely in the inward worlds and in the connections between them. . . . The ontological hierarchy of the spiritual worlds reveals itself to the kabbalist in the times of prayer as one of the many Names of God. This unveiling mystical activity of the individual in prayer, who meditates or focuses his *kavvanah* (meditation) upon the particular name that belongs to the spiritual realm through which his prayer is passing. . . . Such "inward magic" is distinguished from sorcery in that its meditations or *kavvanot* are not meant to be pronounced. The Divine Names are not called upon, as they are in ordinary operational magic, but are aroused through meditative activity directed toward them.[3]

We see that for the pious Jew practicing Qabala, the so-called divine names were not a starting point or an end point, but something that was revealed from within during periods of prayer and meditation, acting as signposts along the way. They were not functional tools in and of themselves, nor were they meant to be. Only in later years did specifically Qabalistic prayers and meditations develop.

The end goal of these prayers and meditations was complete absorption into the godhead. In doing so, the breach between God and humanity, symbolized by "the fall," was repaired, and God became accessible once again. This often revealed itself in the form of ecstasy, sometimes even contagious to those around the one praying, and heightened states of awareness, such as prophesy, healing, and clairvoyance. These phenomena, however, were regarded as side effects of the state and not a goal in themselves. They were viewed as similar to Paul's advice on the charismas of the early Christians: a sign of grace, but not the act of grace.

---

3 Scholem, *Kabbalah*, 177 (see chap. 2, n. 14).

# Fludd and the Rosicrucian Connection

## Robert Fludd (1574–1637)

Robert Fludd, or Robert de Fluctibus, as he preferred to be called, left us a remarkable work on medical theory. Fludd, a physician and member of the Royal College of London, believed that the root cause of all diseases could be found in original sin. He believed that disease was caused by demons and was healed, or at least combated, by angelic forces. Thus, prayer was seen to be as effective as medicine in bringing health to patients.

Fludd was the son of a Kentish squire and traveled on the Continent in his youth, returning to study medicine at Oxford and graduating in 1605. Fludd probably met Michael Maier during his visit to England sometime after 1612. It is from this possible meeting that Fludd may have come into contact with the Rosicrucian stream of Hermeticism that was beginning to flourish abroad, especially in Central Europe. While the connection of Fludd to Rosicrucianism via Maier is clearly circumstantial, what is not is Fludd's publication of a defense of Rosicrucianism and the "Rosy Cross Brotherhood" in 1616: *Apologia Compendiaria Fraternitatem de Rosea Cruce*, or "A Compendium Apology for the Fraternity of the Rosy Cross" by its translated name.

Fludd published this, and all of his important works, abroad with a publisher who had exhibited occult interests. Fludd also may have been a Freemason, and thus responsible for introducing Rosicrucianism into the early formation of Freemasonry. The first written suggestion linking these two forms of Hermetic initiation—Rosicrucianism and Freemasonry—occurs one year after Fludd's death, in Henry Adamson's poem *The Muses Threnodie*:

> For what we do presage is not in gross,
> For we be brethren of the Rosie Cross:
> We have the Mason's word and the second sight,
> Things for to come we can fortell aright.[4]

---

4  Christopher McIntosh, *The Rosicrucians: The History, Mythology, and Rituals of an Esoteric Order* (York Beach, ME: Weiser, 1997), 40–41. This poem can also be found in the *Encyclopaedia Britannica* under "Rosicrucian."

## The Mason's Word

In several of the degrees in Scottish Rite and Royal Arch, also known as Capitulary Masonry or Capstone Masonry, the Secret Word is revealed to the Master Masons present. This "word," so long hidden, has also lost much of its significance despite the massive amount of clues given in the dramatic and symbolic material presented during the performance of the rituals.

Prior to this revelation of the Lost Word, the Master Mason is given a word known as the Substitute Word. Unfortunately, the long oral tradition of Masonry has meant that in the transmission of this important word of recognition, the pronunciation has become garbled, giving rise to two actual words in use. One is predominant in Continental Europe and the other in England, the United States, and other primarily English-speaking countries. According to Albert Mackey, the second word came into existence and use during the formation of the High Degrees and under the influence of the exiled Stuarts on Freemasonry. What is intriguing about this is that both words have come to have their own unique and specific meaning, making both still of value to the Mason on the path of Illumination and not simply a card carrier. This value in part comes from the essential Hebrew origin of both words; the other is from the simple meaning of a word or spoken phrase in Freemasonry as well as esotericism in general. However, in some instances this meaning must be injected into the word, or whichever word the sound most closely approximates, because so many Masons were ignorant of the ancient languages and the meanings and pronunciations of their words.

While some Masons will object to "revealing" the Master Mason's Word, it must be pointed out that these words are easily found on the Internet as well as in numerous books on Masonry. It is hoped that those objecting will realize this fact, as well as the certainty that without knowing the additional means of identification or which word belongs to which jurisdiction, simple knowledge of the sounds will not allow someone to pass himself off as a Master Mason.

Mackey states that the proper word has four syllables, not three, as those we are about to examine:

The correct word has been mutilated. Properly, it consists of four syllables, for the last syllable, as it is now pronounced, should be divided into two. These four syllables compose three Hebrew words, which constitute a perfect and grammatical phrase, appropriate to the occasion of their utterance. But to understand them, the scholar must seek the meaning in each syllable, and combine the whole. In the language of Apuleius, we must forbear to enlarge upon these holy mysteries.[5]

In *Morals and Dogma*, Albert Pike states:

The True Word of a Mason is to be found in the concealed and profound meaning of the Ineffable Name of Deity, communicated by God to Moses; and which meaning was long lost by the very precautions to conceal it. The true pronunciation of that name was in truth a secret, in which, however, was involved the more profound secret of its meaning. In that meaning is included all the truth that can be known by us, in regard to the nature of God.[6]

Even here, as with so many words in Freemasonry, nothing is ever simple. As stated, Masonry's emphasis on oral transmission over written instruction has resulted in there being not one but two forms of the Master Mason's Substitute Word. One variation of the word is of Hebrew origin and has been mangled almost beyond recognition. It refers to one who is a carpenter, joiner, or builder. In the literal sense, it is purely a verbal means of recognition, yet in the esoteric, it refers to each Mason as a craftsman of his own life and a builder in the temple of God, an ideal to which all Masons strive for.

A second version of the word has received a great deal of attention in some of the popular books pretending to be exposés on Freemasonry. These state that it is a synthetic three-part word referring to "Ja" (or Yod-Heh, the prefix of the Tetragrammaton), "Bal," and "On," thereby showing that Freemasons are in fact not good Christians, Jews, or Muslims, as many profess, but instead worshippers of strange deities. Even if there

---

5  Mackey and McClenachan, *Encyclopedia of Freemasonry*, 856.

6  Pike, Albert, *Morals and Dogma of the Ancient and Accepted Scottish Rite of Freemasonry* (Washington, D.C.: Supreme Council, 33°, Ancient and Accepted Scottish Rite of Freemasonry of the Southern Jurisdiction, n.d.), 697. *Morals and Dogma* was first published in 1871.

is some truth to the origin of the three parts of the threefold name, all it would demonstrate is that Masons see all gods as one, in that each Mason recognizes a supreme power. Collectively, they call it the Grand Architect of the Universe; individually, they call it by different names; and in their hearts, many see all gods as being a partial and imperfect human expression of the One True God. For the majority of Masons, even these versions of the Master Mason's Substitute Word are little more than means of recognition, no different than the words given to craftsmen for traveling purposes in the Middle Ages. For the mystically inclined Brother, they are the keys to self-awakening, to the construction of the Inner Temple that each must build in his own heart and therein hear the voice of the soul.

## The Substitute Word

The identification of the Master Mason's Word as the Substitute Word is of critical significance to the Freemason who is paying attention. The ancient religious, philosophical, and esoteric notion of "the Word" is that of divine truth, unquestionable and omnipotent power, and authority to create. Thus, if the Word is divine truth, then the Lost Word must be that truth either forgotten, ignored, or transformed in some manner during the act of its very expression—just as clay still remains clay but is modified when it is turned into a piece of pottery. The Substitute Word can be seen as twofold: either as a failure to find the truth, as the Fellowcraft who went in search of Hiram failed to find the Word, or as a temporary bridge to assist one on his search for divine truth. It is a comforter to aid him until the Word is found. The suggestion of a "Substitute Word" is found in various rituals of the eighteenth century but is not identified as such until later. If the Word is then divine truth, the search for this truth is the very reason for the existence of Freemasonry, and each Mason's obligation and work is to find that truth. While variations of the Word do not change its essential character, the idea of it is critical to the very existence of Masonry. Without the Word, Masonry is dead. "The letter of the Law killeth, but the spirit giveth life" (2 Corinthians 3:6).

## The Word

Each Mason is tasked with finding the Lost Word, lost when the Master Hiram was slain, just as twelve Fellowcraft Masons were tasked with going in search of his body and returning to tell of the first sound they heard, as that would act as a substitute for the Lost Word.

The symbolism here is particularly subtle, in that the Word is not heard without, only a substitute for it, just as the word of man is only a substitute for that Inner Word—the Word of God, of the Cosmic, of the Grand Architect of the Universe, which speaks to our heart. This inner voice of God within is the True Word. It is unfailing, ever-guiding, and life-affirming, not only in the symbolic sense, but also literally as the power of creation itself.

Ptah, the eldest god of the Memphis Triad, was known to the Egyptians as the great builder or architect of the world. It was he who spoke the word from which all of creation came into being.

The Egyptians had complete confidence in the divine origin and creative power of speech. All living beings and objects, of either the material or spiritual world, had their origin in the utterance of sound. The entire universe was understood to be under the control of men and gods who knew the sacred speech. For the Egyptians, material creation was sound made substantial. Every sound, verb, noun, and descriptive word had substance and life—creative power—when uttered properly. In sacred speech, there is complete harmony between the spoken and the incarnate, between the ideal and the material form. Iamblichus regarded the Egyptian language as closest to the original primordial language of the gods, even more so than his native Greek.

Thoth, also known as Hermes from the Greco-Egyptian period, wrote down the words Ptah spoke. They made up forty-two books, which were closely guarded. Through the spoken word, Thoth was the Lord of Wisdom, but also of writing and magic. It is from Thoth-Hermes that we derive the name for that body of ancient theosophy known as Hermeticism, of which Freemasonry is an expression.

It is important to note that the Egyptians had no word for *religion*, only *heku*, or, poorly translated, "magical or creative power." The more creative

**Tetragrammaton: The Unspeakable Name of God**

power one had, the closer he was to the gods, or divine principles. This creative power, as we have seen, was closely linked to speech and writing. Written words or hieroglyphs were seen as living things, not unlike an animal, plant, or human being. Defacing them was tantamount to defacing the message they contained. Given that few people in any primitive culture could read or write, it is easy to see why the written word was held to be sacred, for it was memory, wisdom, and direction for its people.

However, Thoth's real power comes from the spoken use of the words, not simply their static, engraved, fixed, or ritualistic use. Through the process of speech and the vibrations it creates, words gave power to men, nature, and the invisible worlds. The names of the gods were held in secret, and even two names were used: one in public, the other in private ceremonies.

This belief in the power of names and words is carried over into Judaism, with the sacred four-lettered name of God, often called the Tetragrammaton, being whispered from mouth to ear of the initiate. If it were pronounced aloud, all of creation could be undone. The *Encyclopedia of Freemasonry* states that the Lost Word is none other than the search for the true pronunciation of this name: Yod-Heh-Vau-Heh.[7]

Of course, this doctrine of sacred or esoteric speech finds some of its most sophisticated development in the works of the alchemists and Qabalists respectively, often referring to it as the "green language" or the "language of the birds," which Solomon was said to be able to understand. Given the symbolism of the color green for life and the well-known use of various birds in Egyptian and Eastern mystical schools (and even Christianity, as a symbol for the consciousness or soul), the term "language of the birds" can be easily understood to mean that Solomon understood the inner voice of his Being.

---

7  Mackey and McClenachan, *Encyclopedia of Freemasonry*, 856.

Farther east, India and Tibet had their practices of mantra yoga, *mantra* being a Sanskrit word that literally means "mind protector." In this, we see the use of sacred speech reach its pinnacle of development and application. It is possible that the proper use of the name of God as a meditative device was being suggested in these early Masonic revelations. If so, it would clearly link Masonry with several schools of Qabala in which meditation on the Tetragrammaton and its variations was the core practice.

By the time of the early Christian era, when the first line of the gospel of John was penned and we are told, "In principio erat Verbum," or "In the beginning was the Word," the idea of the creative power of the spoken word to affect all of nature, seen and unseen, was already highly developed across the Middle and Far East.

To understand this emphasis on speech, we need only look at ancient cultures and reflect on the following facts:

1. Words reflect our inner psychic as well as subconscious state.

2. Words trigger emotions and ideas that cannot be taken back once initiated.

3. Words, after sex, are our foremost means of creating, and it is no wonder that the thyroid is a secondary sexual organ and is considered among esotericists to be critical to effective communication with the divine.

This last point is important when we remember that in Hiram's murder, the first blow was to his throat. It is often said that this was so he could not cry out for help. But help from whom? More likely it was so that he could not utter the sacred words that would protect him from his attackers, for as Jesus said, "If I wished it, twelve legions of angels would come down to protect me" (Matthew 26:53).

By this time, the deed was done, and the Slain Master could not have communicated the Word even if he'd wanted to. Not only was he injured, but more importantly, the Word is something we must each discover within ourselves.

Why destroy their very chance of receiving the Word? Maybe because the one who struck the first blow realized that Hiram would not give them what they sought but could in fact use it against them. In the New Testament, we read that the sick approach Jesus and proclaim, "Say the Word, and I will be healed!" (Matthew 8:8). We also read of Jesus telling his closest disciples to go out among the multitudes and heal the sick, raise the dead, and perform what we in the modern world call miracles, all "in the Name of the Holy Spirit." Could it be that their first blow was struck to stop Hiram from calling on the angelic legions to protect him, just as Jesus said he could do, as well as his disciples?

Such notions are radically foreign to modern thinking but must be reconsidered if the esoteric aspects of Masonry are to be fully understood. It is a proven fact that the very miracles described in the Scriptures are possible. They have been done, can be done, and are being done today, and they are in harmony with the known laws of modern physics. Brother Jean Dubuis, a French alchemist and well-known esotericist, wrote:

> According to mystics, a long time ago, on earth, there used to be a unique language called the original language which is sought today as the "Lost Word."
>
> The true Verb (Word), the Verb (Word) of the Bible's "Fiat Lux!" is the energy which is ceaselessly radiated by the formless being. The Fiat Lux is simply the vibrations of this energy as they are subjected to the law which is dictated by The Being, the Harmony where Beings, the Elohim came from, and all those who use this energy to create the worlds, the bodies of men and light of the sun which is but a pale reflection of this energy. Putting order into this energy results in Time, form, space; without these operations there can be only the Void, the Non-Manifest. Our body, our flesh, our blood are but vibrations which are subject to the ultimate law of vibrations: Harmony. Harmony exists in all realms, but we can get a clear idea of it in the realm of music. We see that some notes, while different, seem to have analogies between them.
>
> Let's imagine a keyboard, extending to the infinite of space. Let us strike the note of G, and increasingly move upward in octaves. Each G is recognized as being similar to those that went before it, yet different, of a higher vibration. The number of vibrations per second for G is 384, and doubles with each increase in octave.

Given this increase in vibration, after the first six or seven Gs we go beyond the realm of human hearing—but the note G still exists and vibrates. If we could build a keyboard with these higher octaves we could strike a note that would disrupt radio, television, even radar. We could even produce heat, and after the forty-second G a red light would be generated. Then, neither sound or light. A C note would produce hydrogen, an A note produce oxygen, and a chord would generate physical water.

We see in the Old Testament the idea that Adam named the animals, but can clearly understand now, that the First Being, or Adam, did more than name them. Through speaking he actually brought them into existence. Moses as well knew the true name of water, and as such, brought it forth from the rock.[8]

This original language is all but lost, and it is the initiate's duty to restore it. Just as the twelve Fellowcraft went in search of the Word and found it not but brought back a Substitute Word, initiates also use a substitute language, or series of languages, until this inner Word can be re-established. Many mystics see several of the ancient languages as being closer to the original tongue, thereby making Hebrew, as well as its Egyptian cousin and in some instances Latin, the preferred means of prayer and invocation.

Given this meaning, the biblical story of the Tower of Babel and the idea of the Lost Word in Masonry are more easily understood. In many ways, the Tower of Babel is a fitting story for Masonic study, as it more closely fits the Masonic myth than does the Temple of Solomon, for the Temple was completed and destroyed twice. The Tower of Babel, however, to be built on the plains of Shinar, was not completed. Masons, like humanity after the collapse of the Tower of Babel, are confined to speak many languages and, as such, encounter difficulty in the world of matter. The unity that we originally had is a faint memory, and the desire to re-establish it is reflected in the desire for various forms of cultural, racial, and linguistic purity. Masonry even has an injunction against "babbling," or meaningless speech, both inside and outside the lodge.

---

8 Jean Dubuis, *The Fundamentals of Esoteric Knowledge* (Winfield, IL: Triad Publishing, 2000), 10–11. Sample lessons available online at http://www.triad-publishing.com/Course_eso.html.

The only way that this unity can be re-established is individually, in and through each of us. The working tool to rebuild this Tower of Babel is the same as for the Temple: the trowel, for it spreads the cement of brotherly love and affection.

Only love—the emotion of the heart, the true organ of human consciousness and spiritual perception—can allow us to unite the many bricks needed to rebuild the tower that reaches to heaven. Only love can open the door to the Inner Temple, the true Sanctum Sanctorum that each Freemason must complete and build for himself.

The original language, or Word, is a vibratory image of the divine plan. When one reintegrates his consciousness with the inner unity symbolized by the Pillar of Wisdom and the station of the Lodge Master in Freemasonry, this language becomes a reality.

One does not need to be a Freemason to begin the search for the Lost Word; the quest is most easily started by examining one's own use of language. Are our words meant to be beautiful and harmonious, or are they sarcastic and divisive? Do we employ clear, precise, and simple speech, or do we use excessive, vague, and complex phrases to hide our true meaning? Are we vulgar and profane, or cultured and inspiring?

Attitude is also a clue to where work must be done. A positive attitude is critical to successful work in the material as well as spiritual realms. Only by having a firm, steadfast, and unwavering conviction can we accomplish anything, and in the realm of our self-Becoming, this is even more important.

If upon reflection one finds himself complaining on a regular basis about troubles, illnesses, or problems (while not seeking a genuine solution), then given the power of our speech, how can he expect anything else from life?

Masonry teaches that it is imperative to focus on the beautiful, the strong, and the wise and to invoke the spirit of harmony into daily life. Through the teachings of "the Work," Masons learn that all things, no matter how difficult they may seem, are only passing, and that, as Shakespeare said, "There is nothing either good or bad, but thinking makes it so." Through our speech—the spoken expression of our inner convictions and our attitude toward life—we bind ourselves to happiness or sorrow, health or illness, success or failure. And as creators of that bond, we are the only ones who can change it. This is the ultimate purpose of the Genius of Freemasonry and the search for the Lost Word.

## Key Points

1. The Lost Word is what every Master Mason is charged with seeking. During his raising to the Third Degree, he receives only a Substitute Word.

2. Harmony expressed in sound is called music, and in a word, a song or chant. Words and sounds express a power over the listener, just as David calmed the angry King Saul.

3. Masonry uses peculiar wording and language in its rituals, which links it to an earlier historical period while exerting a positive influence over the psyche of those participating.

4. In Masonry, there are three words: the Lost Word, the Substitute Word, and the True Word. Each is a reflection of the others and represents stages in human spirituality. The Lost Word is ignorance, symbolized by the fall from grace in Genesis and the murder of Hiram. The Substitute Word is the use of religion, law, and authority to bring harmony and order to the human condition. The True Word is the direct revelation or personal experience of the divine, the God within.

5. The name of God known as the Tetragrammaton, or YHVH, plays an important role in Jewish mysticism and magic. During the Middle Ages, rabbis known as "Masters of the Name" were said to have been able to perform miracles through the use of this and other divine names.

6. Special writing and divine names are linked to each other as well as to the angelic cosmology of Judaism. Angelic alphabets are often attributed to Metatron, who is also identified with Enoch. Enoch plays an important role in Masonic lore.

7. Johannes Reuchlin's book *De Arte Cabalistica* demonstrated how the sacred letters and names of things in Hebrew are not just symbols but are thought also to carry the very spiritual essence of the thing they are related to. Knowledge of the letters and words gives the power to create.

8. Within Jewish mysticism, prayer is considered more important than magical acts or the use of divine names.

9. Robert Fludd, an apologist for the Rosicrucian movement, advocated the use of prayer in healing.

10. The Egyptian god Thoth is identified with Hermes Trismegistus, the founder of the Hermetic arts and sciences, and is the master of "the Word," or the creative power of magical speech.

11. A positive attitude is critical in all work, be it spiritual or material, and our words reflect our attitude.

12. Positive speech is essential to human harmony, spiritual well-being, and physical health.

## Assignments for Chapter 6

1. Read one or more of the books from the Suggested Reading list.

2. Research the nature of speech and its importance in religious, mystical, and esoteric doctrines and practices. How does your particular religious practice use speech?

3. Pay attention to your speech. Limit your speech to only what is essential for one week. Notice how often you are tempted to speak only to be heard or to say something meaningless, sarcastic, or simply unnecessary.

4. Pay attention to the quality of your speech. Do you use positive action words, or are they passive? Do you speak negatively and in terms of limitations, or positively in terms of possibilities? From this, assess whether your fundamental worldview is optimistic or pessimistic.

## Suggested Reading

*Access to Western Esotericism*, by Antoine Faivre (State University of New York)

*Encyclopedia of Freemasonry*, by Albert Mackey and Charles Mc-Clenachan, revised edition (Masonic History Company)

*Masonic Presentation Bible* (Heirloom Bible Publishers)

*The Meaning of Masonry*, by W. L. Wilmshurst (Barnes & Noble Books)

*Spagyrics: A Course in Plant Alchemy*, by Jean Dubuis, translated by Brigitte Donvez (Triad Publishing)

*Symbols of Freemasonry*, by Daniel Beresniak (Assouline)

*The Men's House: Masonic Papers and Addresses,* by Joseph Fort Newton, Litt.D. (Macoy Publishing)

*The Mystic Tie,* by Allen E. Roberts (Macoy Publishing)

*Family Masonic Education Workbook: Using Masonic Symbolism in Daily Life,* by Burt Prater (Source Publications)

*The Way of the Craftsman: A Search for the Spiritual Essence of Craft Freemasonry,* by W. Kirk Macnulty (Central Regalia Limited)

*The Temple Not Made with Hands,* by Walter C. Lanyon (John M. Watkins)

*The Spirit of Masonry,* by William Hutchinson, FAS, new edition by Rev. George Oliver, DD (Bell Publishing Company)

7

# Scottish Rite and the Rise of Esoteric Masonry

OVERVIEW
• *High Degree Masonry on the Continent*
• *Scottish Rite Is Born*
• *Pike's* Morals and Dogma

The Occult Science of the Ancient Magi was concealed under the shadows of the Ancient Mysteries: it was imperfectly revealed or rather disfigured by the Gnostics: it was guessed at under the obscurities that covered the pretended crimes of the Templars; and it is found enveloped in enigmas that seem impenetrable, in the Rites of the Highest Masonry.

—ALBERT PIKE, INTRODUCTION TO THE SUBLIME PRINCE OF THE ROYAL SECRET (MASTER OF THE ROYAL ART), XXXII, FROM *Morals and Dogma*

## Origins of Scottish Rite: The French Connection

Scotch Rite or Scottish Rite, as it is more commonly known, originated in France in the early eighteenth century. Its name in part is derived from the claim that Scottish Rite was established in France by Scots fleeing the English invasion and seeking asylum on the Continent. Claims are often made linking various Masonic rites through Scottish Rite to "Bonnie" Prince Charles of Scotland and his Jacobite supporters in exile. Like many things in Masonry, these claims are easy to make and almost impossible to prove, making them more legend than history. However, as Scottish political interests played a part in the creation of many of these various rites and degrees, attempts to establish a connection between the two reflects the social and political culture of Masonry in the eighteenth century.

Critical to the formation of many Continental lodges and Masonic rites was the assertion by Chevalier Andrew Michael Ramsay of Scotland that Freemasonry was a direct descendant of chivalric and mystical societies brought to Europe by returning crusaders. As a result, most of the Masonic rites that appeared in France after 1737 were founded on Ramsay's assertion, along with the added notion that Freemasonry was connected to the Knights Templar, who, it was claimed, had in part fled to Scotland after their persecution by King Philip IV of France. The French currently refer to these degrees as *Hauts Grades*, or "High Grades," rather than Scottish.

Scottish Rite came to the New World with the appointment of Etienne Morin in 1761 as "Grand Inspector to all parts of the New World." With a missionary zeal common to eighteenth-century Masonry, Morin established a Rite of Perfection, consisting of twenty-five degrees, in Santo Domingo, West Indies, in 1763. It was from this Caribbean foothold that the Rite of Perfection spread to North America and grew into the worldwide movement of Scottish Rite. The Rite of Perfection was established in New York in 1765 with the arrival of Henry Francken, an associate of Morin's and a resident of Jamaica. The Rite of Perfection was later established in Charleston, North Carolina, by Isaac De Costa, in 1783. It is here in North Carolina at the beginning of the nineteenth century, far away from the traditional Masonic strongholds in the metropolitan centers of Europe, that things began to get interesting.

The Rite of Perfection changed its name and appearance in 1801, when Dr. Frederick Dalco and John Mitchell arrived in Charleston with a document granting the bearer the right to establish new chapters, allegedly under the authority of King Frederick the Great. The constitution went on to add an additional eight degrees to the existing rite, as well as referring to it as the "Ancient and Accepted Scottish Rite." It was dated 1786, and it apparently had the desired effect, for on May 31, 1801, the

Mother Supreme Council of the Thirty-third Degree of the Ancient and Accepted Scottish Rite of Freemasonry was formed.

Scottish Rite grew rapidly across the South and quickly became a dominant force—at least for a while. In the North, York Rite, with its additional degrees and bodies, was dominant. In addition, existing Scottish Rite bodies were embroiled in bitter disputes as to authenticity and jurisdictional authority. This devastating weakness of Scottish Rite in the North would continue to exist until after the Civil War, when in 1867 the Northern Masonic Jurisdiction (NMJ) was founded with the recognized authority to offer the degrees in fifteen states.

## "Ordo Ab Chaos"

The motto of Scottish Rite is "Ordo Ab Chaos," or "Order Out of Chaos." Nothing could be a more fitting description. While it is difficult for someone living in the early twenty-first century to understand why all of these groups existed, with their various degrees and rites, it is important to recognize the profound cultural differences between eighteenth-century European and American life and what we experience today.

In a world in which it took two months to cross the Atlantic and two weeks to go from Philadelphia to New York City, social connections were critical to personal success in life. Belonging to an organization that provided instant contacts in distant cities was in itself a major benefit, despite the political and religious persecution that may have accompanied it at times. In addition, without today's vast network of colleges, adult education classes, and near-instant access to information via the Internet and mail-order delivery, Masonry and its degrees provided a form of personal improvement. It also allowed members to have a means of "prequalifying" or screening potential business, social, and even esoteric contacts through a network of established channels and signs of recognition. The world of the eighteenth and nineteenth centuries was slower, more distant, and more disconnected than it is today. Freemasonry served as a major vehicle in bringing these distant points together.

# The Degrees

Scottish Rite is the second largest rite, and like York Rite, it confers the three degrees of Symbolic Masonry in Blue Lodge. However, in the United States, the symbolic degrees are not conferred by the Northern or Southern Masonic Jurisdictions; they are given only by lodges duly and lawfully chartered by a Grand Lodge.

From there, however, the number of degrees expands considerably, up to and including the famous Thirty-third Degree, or the Sovereign Grand Inspector General, which is given by the Supreme Council and is the administrative head of the rite for the jurisdiction under its authority. Below the Thirty-third Degree are twenty-nine other degrees, which are divided into groups, each with its own governing body subservient to the Supreme Council. In general, these bodies are as follows: Fourth Degree through Fourteenth Degree are conferred in a Lodge of Perfection; Fifteenth and Sixteenth degrees are conferred in a Council of Princes of Jerusalem; Seventeenth and Eighteenth degrees are conferred in a Chapter of Rose-Croix; the Nineteenth through Thirtieth degrees are conferred in a Council of Kadosh; and finally, the Thirty-first and Thirty-second degrees are conferred in a Consistory of Princes of the Royal Secret. Of course, like all things Masonic, there is some variation in these assignments according to jurisdiction.

> **Lodge of Perfection**—These degrees elaborate on King Solomon's Temple and the search for the Lost Word or unspoken name of God. They are similar to Royal Arch Degrees in York Rite.
>
> **Council of Princes of Jerusalem**—These degrees consist of the rebuilding of the Temple of Solomon. This particular division does not exist in all Masonic jurisdictions, and these degrees are included in the Chapter of Rose-Croix.
>
> **Chapter of Rose-Croix**—While Christian in tone, these degrees contain alchemical symbolism and suggest a Rosicrucian influence in Masonic development.
>
> **Council of Kadosh**—This is a particular classification for governing the Nineteenth through Thirtieth degrees within the Southern Ma-

sonic Jurisdiction. *Kadosh* is Hebrew for "holy" or "consecrated to God" and denotes the nature of the philosophic instruction of these degrees. There is a Templar connection as well.

**Consistory**—This is an administrative designation and consists of the meeting of members of the Thirty-first and Thirty-second degrees for the Southern Masonic Jurisdiction and the Nineteenth through Thirty-second degrees for the Northern Masonic Jurisdiction. There is a distinct Templar association with the Thirty-first and Thirty-second degrees, and as such, it is clear why Council of Kadosh is included in Consistory in the Northern Masonic Jurisdiction to reduce this redundancy.

The size and scope of these degrees constitute small theatrical productions, becoming a form of initiation combined with a morality or teaching play. In the United States, these degrees are rarely given to a single member at a time but rather to groups of men, often in an auditorium or theater specially designed for the purpose of degrees. In Europe and elsewhere, the degrees are conferred on a smaller scale with less theatrics, but the fundamental nature, teaching, and lesson of the degrees are the same.

## Albert Pike and the Renewal of Scottish Rite

It would be impossible to discuss Scottish Rite without taking a look at the life and work of Albert Pike (1809–91), one of Masonry's most profound and controversial figures. Pike was born in Massachusetts, and as a child he demonstrated exceptional skill in school, learning Greek, Latin, and Hebrew before the age of twenty. He passed his entrance exams and was accepted to attend Harvard University, where he completed two years of his undergraduate program in one year, but as the son of an alcoholic shoemaker, he was unable to afford the remaining tuition. In 1831, he left Massachusetts and headed west, where he ended up in Fort Smith, Arkansas. There, his natural talents came to the forefront as he taught school, edited a newspaper, practiced law, and even became a state supreme court justice. Pike married Ann Hamilton in 1834 and, with his wife's financial backing, entered politics. His military career began in 1846, when he led a volunteer unit at the Battle of Buena Vista against the Mexican army. Pike was popular with the local native tribes and represented them in court against the United States government. He continued to practice law later in life as well, arguing several cases before the Supreme Court.

It was during Pike's stay in Arkansas that he became affiliated with Freemasonry, joining Star Lodge #2, Little Rock, in 1850. In 1852, he assisted in establishing Magnolia Lodge #60 with sixteen fellow Masons, serving as Master in 1853 and 1854. Pike took the ten York Rite degrees and again was active on a state level. In March of 1853, he traveled to Charleston, South Carolina, where he received the Fourth through Thirty-second degrees and was appointed as deputy inspector of Arkansas for the Scottish Rite.

At the time of his joining, Scottish Rite was among the smallest of the existing Masonic bodies, with membership records showing less than a thousand members in the United States. Pike's extensive training in the classics and his scholastic skill made him a natural candidate for the position that would soon define his life's work. The Supreme Council of Scottish Rite's Southern Jurisdiction established a five-man committee to revise the rituals as part of a plan to reinvigorate itself. This committee never met, but Pike took on the task himself. As part of the process for this massive undertaking, Pike immersed himself in Hermetic philosophy and esotericism, hand-copied all of the rituals on file and available to him, and completed his draft in 1859. With the resignation of Albert Mackey as supreme commander that same year, and with only six years of membership under his belt, Pike became the head of the Southern Jurisdiction of the Scottish Rite in January 1859, holding the office until his death in 1891.

In 1861, Jefferson Davis, president of the Confederacy, appointed Pike as commissioner of Indian affairs, investing him with the rank of brigadier general. In 1862, Pike resigned his post and commission and published a letter stating that the Confederate government was in violation of its treaty agreements and obligations. Pike was arrested and jailed, but he was released when the Confederate military in the West collapsed in late 1862.

Without friends or family, in danger from both Union and Confederate forces, and bankrupt, Pike went to the Ozark Mountains, where he remained in a cabin until 1868. Studying Qabala, alchemy, Hermeticism, Eastern scriptures, and philosophy, he revised the rituals of Scottish Rite even further than he had in his earlier draft, including a large part of the Western esoteric traditions while doing so. With his work completed, he left the Ozarks for Washington, D.C., where he remained for the rest of his life, living in a small apartment provided for him by the Supreme Council. He dedicated his entire life to the development of Scottish Rite and other Masonic bodies.

## *Morals and Dogma*: The Unofficial Bible of Scottish Rite

To those who are familiar with him, Albert Pike is best known for his massive tome *Morals and Dogma of the Ancient and Accepted Scottish Rite of Freemasonry*, or *Morals and Dogma* for short. Few books have been so widely read, skimmed, flipped through, misunderstood, and misquoted as *Morals and Dogma*. In fact, this book alone is often the single most misquoted source for those wishing to demonstrate something insidious and malefic about Freemasonry in general and Scottish Rite in particular. The reasons for this are simple: Pike was a scholar who understood the fundamental esoteric teachings present in Masonic symbolism, which either went unnoticed or were misunderstood by most of its members.

Using the existing literature of his period and drawing heavily on the early works of the French occult revival (1865–1914), Eliphas Levi's in particular, Pike sought to demonstrate that Masonry was more than just the gentlemen's social club it was morphing into; instead, he wanted to show that it was the inheritor of a secret tradition of human unfoldment that was thousands of years old. What came from his research was largely published in *Morals and Dogma* and was meant to be used as a series of lectures for each of the degrees, making it a textbook of sorts for the candidate. Among the works most heavily quoted by Pike in the creation of *Morals and Dogma* was Levi's *Dogma and Rituals of High Magic* (1855). Copies of *Morals and Dogma* are easily found in many used and second-hand bookshops, as it was given to almost every Thirty-second Degree member of the Southern Jurisdiction until 1974. Despite Pike's importance to Masonry and the Scottish Rite, his works are today not universally adopted nor appreciated by many both outside and within the Northern and Southern Jurisdictions in the United States.

## The Royal Art: Freemasonry and Human Evolution

Freemasonry often refers to itself as "the Royal Art." According to Mackey's *Encyclopedia of Freemasonry*, Anderson's *Constitutions* refers to Freemasonry as the Royal Art as early as 1723, suggesting that this was not new. Mackey further points out that Freemasonry was first called the Royal Art in 1693, when William III was initiated into the Craft. Mackey also spends two pages stating that Freemasonry differs from a handicraft in that the Freemason is no mere technician, but a genuine artist who understands all aspects of his chosen expression—this expression being the perfection of himself in relation to humanity and God, a perfection achieved through love. Quoting an 1800 German Masonic catechism from Prague, he states, "Every Freemason is a king, in whatsoever condition God may have placed him here, with rank equal to that of a king and with sentiments that become a king, for his kingdom is LOVE, the love of his fellow-man, a love which is long-suffering and kind, which beareth all things, believeth all things, hopeth all things, endureth all things."[1]

However, it is difficult to believe that in 1723, or even in Mackey's time, the identification of the Royal Art and its preoccupation with the Great Work of alchemy could have been missed. An earlier encyclopedia entry states, "Freemasonry and alchemy have sought the same results (the lesson of divine truth and the doctrine of immortal life), and they have both sought it by the same method of symbolism. It is not, therefore, strange that in the eighteenth century, and perhaps before, we find an incorporation of much of the science of alchemy in that of Freemasonry. Hermetic rites and Hermetic degrees were common. . . . The Twentieth-eighth Degree of Scottish Rite, or the Knight of the Sun, is entirely a Hermetic de-

---

1 Mackey and McClenachan, *Encyclopedia of Freemasonry*, 647.

gree, and claims its parentage in the title of 'Adept of Masonry,' by which it is sometimes known."[2]

Regarding the Knight of the Sun, Prince Adept, Albert Pike states:

Like all the Mysteries of Magism, the Secrets of "the Great Work" have a threefold signification: they are religious, philosophical, and natural. The philosophical gold, in religion, is the Absolute and Supreme Reason: in philosophy, it is the Truth; in visible nature, the Sun; in the subterranean and mineral world, the most perfect and pure gold. . . . The Great Work is, above all things, the creation of man by himself; that is to say, the full and entire conquest which he effects of his faculties and his future. It is, above all, the perfect emancipation of his will, which assures him the universal empire of Azoth, and the domain of magnetism, that is, complete power over the universal Magical agent. . . . So that the Great Work is more than a chemical operation; it is a real creation of the human word initiated into the power of the Word of God. The creation of gold in the Great Work is effected by transmutation and multiplication. . . . The Great Work of Hermes is, therefore, an operation essentially magical, and highest of all, for it supposes the Absolute in Science and in Will. There is light in gold, and gold in light, and light in all things.[3]

When we compare this to Eliphas Levi's writings, we see a clear and present influence there on the writings of Pike, to the point of Pike lifting entire passages from Levi for use in *Morals and Dogma*. Levi is often viewed as the father of the French occult revival of the nineteenth century, a period during which fringe Masonry and occultism intermingled full bloom. It is simply impossible to understand Pike and his great influence on Scottish Rite if we do not understand Levi, whose writings had this profound effect on Pike. Masonry's obsessive search for the Lost Word, for men like Pike, was seen as being fully explained in the writings of Levi.

Magic is contained in a word, and a word well pronounced is more powerful than the combined powers of the Heavens, Earth and Hell. Nature is commanded by a Name; in the same way we can conquer power over the

---

2 Ibid., 44.

3 Pike, *Morals and Dogma*, 775.

different kingdoms of Nature. The occult forces which compose the invisible Universe are submissive to whoever can pronounce, in full knowledge of the cause, non-communicable names.[4]

Serge Hutin would later write on alchemy:

The fire principle plays a predominant part in many alchemical treatises, for it is the soul of the Microcosm. The elemental atoms of this fire, certain alchemists tell us, pervade the universe in the form of currents; these produce light when they intersect in the heavens, and gold when they meet beneath the ground.

Light and gold are sometimes considered to be fire in its concrete state: to "materialize" this gold, which is sown profusely throughout the world, one need only condense widely scattered atoms.

Properly speaking, gold is not a metal—gold is light.[5]

It is no coincidence that the Emerald Tablet refers to the Great Work as "the Work of the Sun."

Levi further states:

There is in Nature a . . . Universal Agent, whose supreme law is balanced and whose command answers to the Great Arcana of Transcendental Magic. . . . When it radiates it is called light. . . . The will of intelligent beings acts directly on this light, and through it on all Nature which then undergoes the modifications of the intelligence. Through the direction of this agent, we can even change the sequences of the seasons, produce phenomena of the day during the night, instantly correspond from one point to the opposite end of the earth, heal at a distance, provide speech with universal results and consequences. To know how to master this agent, so as to take advantage of its force and direct its currents, is to accomplish the Great Work, to be the master of the world and the depository of God's power.[6]

While such claims may appear outlandish on first reading, we need only consider that among those interested in practical alchemy and magic

---

4 Eliphas Levi, as quoted in Jean Dubuis, *Qabala*, trans. Brigitte Donvez (Winfield, IL: Triad Publishing, 2000), lesson 61, 4.

5 Michel Caron and Serge Hutin, *The Alchemists*, trans. Helen R. Lane (New York: Grove Press, Inc., 1961).

6 Dubuis, *Qabala*, 4.

at the time and involved with the development of Freemasonry, particularly in the higher degrees, were some of the most prominent scientists of the day. Both early science and Freemasonry were obsessed with geometry and mathematics, as these allowed for the study of optics, which in turn allowed for the study of light. Modern physics, particularly quantum physics, has demonstrated that the state of mind of the scientist conducting an experiment on the subatomic level—the level of light—can and does affect the outcome of the experiment.

In his book *The God Theory*, Bernard Haisch describes this background of light on the subatomic level as "zero-point energy," or the fundamental energy that is the basis for everything:

> If we are right, the dictum "Let there be light" is indeed a very profound statement (as one might expect of its purported author). Inertia is the property of matter that gives it solidity; it's what gives things substance. The proposed connection between zero-point field and inertia, in effect, suggests that the solid, stable world of matter is sustained at every instant by this underlying sea of quantum light.[7]

Haisch goes on to quote from a Jewish legend in the *Haggadah* he came across in a book titled *The Other Bible*, which reads,

> The light created at the very beginning is not the same as the light emitted by the Sun, the Moon, and the stars, which appeared only on the fourth day. The light of the first day was of a sort that would have enabled man to see the world at a glance from one end to another. Anticipating the wickedness of the sinful generations of the deluge and the Tower of Babel, who were unworthy to enjoy the blessing of such light, God concealed it, but in the world to come it will appear to the pious in all its pristine glory.[8]

To become fully human in the Hermetic traditions is to become fully alive and awake—to exercise one's will to the point at which nature obeys one's command, and to do so knowing that each of us is the "Son of his Deeds" and that universal justice cannot be avoided. If there is only one God, one creative force, then each of us is this god in miniature, and we

---

7 Bernard Haisch, *The God Theory* (York Beach, ME: Weiser, 2006), 93.
8 Ibid., 98–99.

are self-created beings learning to live to our full potential. For Pike, this is the great secret of Freemasonry, clothed in the alchemical language of the Knight of the Sun.

## Key Points

1. Scottish Rite has its origins in eighteenth-century France and is linked to exiled Jacobite supporters of "Bonnie" Prince Charles.

2. Chevalier Andrew Michael Ramsay of Scotland asserted that Freemasonry was a direct descendant of chivalric and mystical societies brought to Europe by returning crusaders. Most Masonic rites that appeared in France after 1737 were founded upon Ramsay's assertion, along with the added notion that the Craft was connected to the Knights Templar, who were said to have in part fled to Scotland following their persecution. The French currently refer to these degrees as *Huats Grades*, or "High Grades," rather than Scottish.

3. Scottish Rite came to the New World with the appointment of Etienne Morin in 1761 as "Grand Inspector to all parts of the New World." Morin established a Rite of Perfection, consisting of twenty-five degrees, in Santo Domingo, West Indies, in 1763. It was from here that Scottish Rite spread to North America and grew into a worldwide rite.

4. Scottish Rite is the second largest rite, and like York Rite, it confers the three degrees of Symbolic Masonry in Blue Lodge.

5. Albert Pike is the single most important leader in American Scottish Rite and is responsible for its renewal in the nineteenth century. His work *Morals and Dogma* established an esoteric and occult interpretation for the degrees of Scottish Rite, similar to what had occurred in the previous century.

6. *Morals and Dogma* is the unofficial textbook of the Southern Jurisdiction. Not all jurisdictions agree with Pike or support his views on the meanings of the degrees.

7. Pike was a scholar who understood the fundamental esoteric teachings present in Masonic symbolism, which either went unnoticed or were misunderstood by most members.

8. Using the existing literature of his period and drawing heavily on the early works of the French occult revival, Eliphas Levi's in particular, Pike sought to demonstrate that Masonry was the inheritor of a secret tradition of human unfoldment that was thousands of years old—not just a gentlemen's social club.

9. Freemasonry often refers to itself as "the Royal Art." Anderson's *Constitutions* refers to Freemasonry as the Royal Art as early as 1723. Freemasonry was first called the Royal Art in 1693, when William III was initiated. The Royal Art is also a term used to describe alchemy, which would not have been lost on the earliest of Freemasons during the seventeenth and eighteenth centuries.

10. The purpose of both Freemasonry and alchemy is called the Great Work. The Twenty-eighth Degree, Knight of the Sun, Prince Adept, states that the Great Work is threefold in nature: religious, philosophical, and natural. Above all, the Great Work is the perfection of human capacity by an act of will of the individual upon himself and nature, and it is essentially magical in origin and function.

11. Levi and Pike point out that the ancient magi and alchemists believed in an underlying stratum of light that created and sustains the physical universe and that this layer can be affected by human thought, thereby giving proof to the mystical doctrines of the ancients.

12. Modern theoretical physics refers to this underlying stratum at the quantum level as zero-point energy existing in a zero-point field. It is described in similar terms in ancient alchemical and Qabalistic manuscripts to explain the nature and function of the "Universal Agent," or "astral light," as it is sometimes called.

## Assignments for Chapter 7

1. Imagine yourself in mid-eighteenth-century Colonial America. What would it be like to travel to various cities, make contact with Masonic lodges, and discuss with the members the establishment of a new rite or system?

2. Read an article or book on Albert Pike. Seek to understand what passion drove him to dedicate his life to explaining and expounding upon his interpretation of the teachings contained within Scottish Rite.

3. Examine a copy of *Morals and Dogma* to better understand the degree of erudition that was required to compile it.

4. Read one or more books or articles on quantum physics, light, and the nature of reality. Meditate on how different your life would be if you could consciously create and alter reality through the force of your mind, and what this would mean to you. What kind of person would you have to be before such knowledge were given to you so that you could direct such power?

## Suggested Reading

*A Glossary to* Morals and Dogma, by Dr. Rex R. Hutchens, 33° (Supreme Council, 33°, Ancient and Accepted Scottish Rite of Freemasonry of the Southern Jurisdiction)

*Morals and Dogma of the Ancient and Accepted Scottish Rite of Freemasonry,* by Albert Pike (Supreme Council, 33°, Ancient and Accepted Scottish Rite of Freemasonry of the Southern Jurisdiction)

*The Holographic Universe,* by Michael Talbot (HarperCollins)

*The God Theory: Universes, Zero-Point Fields, and What's Behind It All,* by Bernard Haisch (Weiser)

*The Spiritual Universe: One Physicist's Vision of Spirit, Soul, Matter, and Self,* by Fred Alan Wolf, PhD (Moment Point Press)

*Symbolism of the Blue Degrees of Freemasonry: Albert Pike's Esoterika,* transcribed and edited by Arturo De Hoyos, foreword by Ronald Seale (The Scottish Rite Research Society)

*The Book of the Words: Sephir H'Debarim,* by Albert Pike, introduction by Arturo DeHoyos (The Scottish Rite Research Society)

*The Secret Tradition in Freemasonry,* by Arthur Edward Waite (Rider and Company)

# 8

# Occult Masonry in the Eighteenth Century

OVERVIEW
- *Rosicrucianism and the Hermetic Degrees*
- *The Elus Cohen and Pasquales*
- *Cagliostro's Egyptian Masonry*

## Occult Masonry

Many modern anti-Masonic groups, primarily the Roman Catholic Church and various fundamentalist Protestant churches, have used the writings of Pike as proof of an esoteric tradition within Masonry that runs counter to their established teachings and therefore makes Masonry incompatible with being Christian (as well as Muslim, according to some Islamic statements). Some Masons who have read Pike and do not like his conclusions have also attempted to distance themselves from the man who single-handedly revived Scottish Rite in the United States. However, this lack of appreciation of Pike's erudition, as well as the general ignorance of the many who have achieved their Thirty-second or Thirty-third degree without having read him, is further betrayed by a profound ignorance of the various genuinely occult rites connected with Freemasonry in Europe in both the eighteenth and nineteenth centuries.

In the mid eighteenth century, an occult revival was under way in Europe. While focused mainly among the social elite, who had the means and leisure to pursue such topics, the ripple effect across society was clear, and it came mainly through Masonic and quasi-Masonic channels. The explosion of rite and grade creating that gave rise to High Grade Masonry in Europe was mainly centered around the promise of secret knowledge that these rituals and groups were said to contain. While swindlers, frauds, and opportunists abounded—just as they do today within the New Age movement and even conventional religious scenes—there was in all likelihood some genuine teachings and practices that were of value. Unfortunately, one person's truth is another's lie, and figuring out what was useful from what was trash is simply a matter of opinion. Clearly, Masons not interested in esotericism will find none of it of value, while others may see it as the only "true" form of Masonry.

Among the most important of these movements that both sprang from as well as affected Freemasonry during the eighteenth century were Rosicrucianism, the Elus Cohen, and Egyptian Masonry.

## Rosicrucianism

No other topic in Western esotericism has produced so much awe, mystification, confusion, and even outright lying as the subject of Christian Rosenkreutz, the society or fraternity he built, and the vault said to have contained his uncorrupted corpse. Manly P. Hall called Rosicrucianism "the most mysterious Secret Order of the modern world."[1]

### The Rosicrucian Myth

When we state that the Rosicrucians are a myth, we are not saying that they are a fabrication or something unreal. We are simply pointing out that to everything there is a history, an interpretation of history, and a belief that grows up around both of these. This belief can become more powerful than either of the previous two, and so constitutes a metaphysical structure for interpreting historical as well as personal experiences. It is this metaphysical structure that we are referring to when we say "myth."

---

1  Manly P. Hall, *The Riddle of the Rosicrucians* (Los Angeles: Philosophical Research Society, 1996). This essay was originally published in 1941.

Like all metaphysical constructs, a myth is a mix of history, belief, and wish fulfillment. It can neither be proved nor disproved, nor does it need to be, as its purpose for existing is not to report history, but rather to give meaning to it. This meaning is seen in the light of invisible spiritual forces that affect and direct humanity toward a desired end. The role of the Rosicrucians and their philosophy—Rosicrucianism—is clearly outlined in the *Fama Fraternitatis*.

### Rosicrucian History

The Rosicrucian society appears on the scene of European history in the early seventeenth century. Its principal means of introduction was the publication of two announcements: the *Fama Fraternitatis* and the *Confessio Fraternitatis*.[2] The *Fama* appeared in 1614, and the *Confessio* a year later. Both may have been circulated in manuscript form as early as 1610. Besides their anonymous authorship, what is most peculiar about these documents is that they use the term *Rosicrucian* for the first time.[3]

Supposedly written in five European languages, only original copies in German and Latin are known to exist. The English translation was made from a German original forty years after its publication. The issuing of the *Fama* in German was a significant statement, in that it occurred over sixty years before universities began to hold classes in German; thus, it marked a small step toward the mainstreaming of knowledge and not just reserving it for the educated and privileged classes.

The *Fama* relates the story of Christian Rosenkreutz, a youth of royal birth yet impoverished. At five years of age, he is sent away by his parents to live in a monastery. Ten years later, he travels to the Middle East, where he learns the wisdom of the Arabic and Egyptian sages. Returning to Europe, "Father CRC," as he is now called, gathers about himself a small

---

2  Copies of the *Fama* and *Confessio* can be found in *The Rosicrucian Enlightenment*, by Frances A. Yates; *The True and Invisible Order of the Rosy Cross*, by Paul Foster Case; and online at Adam McLean's Alchemy Web Site: http://www.levity.com/alchemy/fama.html and http://www.levity.com/alchemy/confessi.html. A link to the main site can be found at www.hermeticinstitute.org.

3  Lewis Spence states that the term *Rosicrucian* may have been around as early as 1598, or twelve to sixteen years before the circulation of the *Fama*. Lewis Spence, *An Encyclopaedia of Occultism* (New Hyde Park, NY: University Books, 1968), 340.

group of pious men to form the first "Society of the Rosy Cross." These events occurred during the first half of the fifteenth century.

The part of the *Fama* that seems to have had the greatest impact on occultists is the description of CRC's vault and the six rules of the order. The message of the *Confessio*, however, is that of "Worldwide Reformation."

### The "Invisible Brotherhood"

Much has been said about the "Brethren of the Rosy Cross," running the gamut from the ludicrous to the barely rational. However, the inspiration of the ideal of the Rosicrucian Brotherhood has had the greatest impact on Western esotericism and may have been a kind of self-fulfilling prophesy.

If we dismiss the documents outright as a sophomoric prank or the equivalent of a modern-day urban legend, then we have no further to go. If we seek to find behind them an established, international "invisible brotherhood" of perfected adepts guiding the development of humanity, then we will be equally as disappointed, if not outright deluded. Since the rules of the society state that "anyone who claims to be a Rosicrucian is not one," if the Rosicrucians actually exist, and you were to meet one, then either he would be recognized for who he was, or he would not.

As a result of the Rosicrucian manifestoes in the early years of the seventeenth century, hundreds of lodges, organizations, and groups seeking to fulfill some part of the Rosicrucian ideal have sprung up, borne fruit, and died. This energy added to the strength of future movements, and as a result, we stand at the pinnacle of the "Rosicrucian Movement" today. It is time that we stop looking for the Rosicrucians in Tibet, Europe, or the Andes and instead seek the "Rosicrucian Within" so that we might bring it into the world.

### Utopianism and the Principal Documents

While the core of the *Fama* dealt with the biography of CRC and the rediscovery of the lost wisdom represented by his burial vault, the *Confessio* presents us with an extension of this spiritual ideal in the material world— that of "Universal Reformation." As a result, many utopian ideals sprang up and many utopian tracts were published, presenting solutions to the many ills that plagued humanity and proposing what the ideal state would look like. Francis Bacon, himself claimed by many either to have been a Rosicrucian or at least to have been familiar with some form of Rosicrucian-inspired movement, authored the best known of these utopian treatises, *New Atlantis*, and a sort of companion work, *Novum Organum*.

Bacon's *New Atlantis* is often interpreted as being a veiled description of ancient esoteric schools thought to have existed since after the biblical deluge to the present day. Others see it as a description of a secret society or "college" that Bacon either founded or was the head of. His description of the "College of Six Days' Work" strongly resembles the "Pansophic University" of the Moravian alchemist Comenius. While Bacon's work stands apart from the other utopian works of the period, they all hold several points in common that are still relevant today.

Education is stressed, and children are instructed in the arts and sciences, practical crafts, religion, morality, ethics, and social consciousness. Families are self-supporting, with work being viewed as honorable and the social leech as an outcast. Order, cleanliness, and sanitation are valued, and each individual fulfills his or her obligations to society. Medicine is socialized, and war is rejected as a means of settling disputes.

How these ideals are implemented changes from author to author; some advocate what would be considerably liberal even by modern standards, while others are overly controlled and lacking in recognition of the individual. However, the basic ideas presented between four hundred fifty and three hundred years ago are still the object of much political action and speculation worldwide, particularly in industrialized nations.

Yet when we speak of "reformation," it is clear that the authors of the manifestoes were thinking about more than just political and religious changes, as dramatic as they have been even to this day, but also changes in consciousness. For without changes in how people think and feel, there can be no lasting evolution in society and culture.

The worldview of the period was one of intense selfishness by the ruling classes. Varying degrees of determinism shaped the majority of people's beliefs, with God being the scriptwriter for everyone's life. Much of one's life was seen as disconnected from "cause and effect" and as dictated more by

"God's will." Individuals sought simply to make their brief span on earth as comfortable as possible, and they wasted little or no time in attempting to push for reforms that would strip them of their birth rights, the fruits of which they would never live long enough to see, let alone share in.

Given this climate, the Rosicrucian manifestoes were truly revolutionary, as well as evolutionary, in their effect.

The nature and origin of Rosicrucianism is possibly the most opaque of topics in Western esotericism. While there is a fair amount of evidence to go on that the initial Rosicrucian manifestoes were a satire on political and social reform, they apparently spread out of control and grew into something far larger than their youthful authors had ever intended, giving rise to numerous movements claiming the Rosicrucian mantle over the last four hundred years. That is, what began as little more than a collegiate prank became a phenomenon.

The first mention of the existence of a mystical fraternity practicing the arcane arts and calling itself Rosicrucian appears in 1614 with the publication of *Universal and General Reformation of the Whole Wide World*. This small booklet with a huge title was published in Cassel, Germany, by Wilhelm Wessel and consisted of a German translation of a chapter from Traiano Boccalini's *Ragguagli di Parnass* (1612), which mocks the utopian ideals of the day, followed by the more famous *Fama Fraternitatis*, or "Announcement of the Fraternity," which states the existence of the secret society or fraternity of the Rosy Cross. Therein the life of the fraternity's founder, Christian Rosenkreutz, is detailed, along with the discovery of a seven-sided vault containing his uncorrupted corpse, magical and alchemical implements, a book containing the fraternity's teachings, and an invitation to contact it. Unfortunately, no mailing address is given, so those wishing to know the secrets of the universe are at a bit of a loss. The last item included in the booklet is a letter attempting to contact the order.

The *Confessio*, which followed in 1615, contained an essay on the magical philosophy found in John Dee's *Monas Hieroglyphica*, further linking, at least philosophically, Rosicrucianism with Dee and, as we saw earlier, Dee with pre-1717 Freemasonry via Elias Ashmole. These tangential links between the Hermetic defenders of Rosicrucianism and the defenders of

Dee would develop into the idea that Freemasonry, or at least its reorganization from 1717 onward, was in fact an action by "Rosicrucian" superiors to further their goals of worldwide reformation.

*The Chemical Wedding of Christian Rosenkreutz* was published in Strasburg in 1616 and is an alchemical allegory describing CRC's journey as an old man to the wedding of a king and queen and the trials he experiences along the way. The story climaxes with the death and resurrection of the bride and bridegroom, or the alchemical symbols for the mundane personality and the spiritual consciousness.

While it was the last of the Rosicrucian trilogy to be published, *The Chemical Wedding* was the first to be written. Its author was the young Lutheran seminarian Johann Valentine Andreae. Andreae was deeply involved in the Hermetic society existing at the University of Teubingen. In addition, both his father and brother were practicing alchemists. It is in his autobiography, written near the end of his life and remaining unpublished until 1799, that Andreae mentions having authored *The Chemical Wedding* along with the *Fama* as a joke or mockery of the ideas of social reform that were current at the time. The word he uses is *ludibrium*, meaning "joke, mockery, comedy, or play."

It appears, however, that the original play took on a life of its own, as Andreae also notes that the actors had changed and the play lived on.


## The Elus Cohen

Of all the quasi-Masonic orders of the eighteenth century, none better embodies the notion of a magical or operative occult lodge or system associated with Masonry than the Elus Cohen and Egyptian Masonry.

The *Elus Cohen*, or "Elect Priests," was the short name for the Order of the Knight Masons, Elect Priests of the Universe, an order established in 1767 by Martinez Pasquales (also spelled Pasqually). However, while this baroque-sounding Masonic title is typical, the roots of the Elus Cohen can be found in an earlier order also founded by Pasquales: the Scottish Judges (*Juges Ecossais*), which claimed a connection to Scottish Rite. The first lodge of the Scottish Judges was established in Montpellier in

1754; the first lodge of the Elus Cohen (or *Elus Coens*) was established six years later in Toulouse.

Like many would-be adepts, Pasquales presented himself to the Grand Lodge of France in an effort to convert them, or at least interest them, in his rite. Like many before and after his, the effort failed, and he continued on his way regardless. It was during his visit to the Grand Lodge of France that Pasquales met Jean-Baptiste Willermoz. Willermoz was from Lyon and was influential in Masonic circles. It was through his assistance that Pasquales was able to establish the Elus Cohen across France.

The Elus Cohen system contained four grades, the first three of which were the same as Blue Lodge: Apprentice, Companion, and Master. However, unlike in standard Freemasonry, initiates of these degrees were given instructions and spiritual exercises to undertake. The fourth degree, that of the Elus Cohen, or *Grand Profes*, contained the inner magical teachings of the order and its entire reason for being. Here, at select times of the year, with the equinoxes (when day and night are of equal length), extensive rituals were performed by the Elus Cohen in their private chambers. These rituals involved a plethora of magical circles and designs, many seen only within the Cohen system, and often lasted up to six hours in length. Invisible entities, angels, and beings were invoked and brought to both visible and audible appearance. If all went well, this would culminate in the presence of *La Chose*, or "The Thing." Here, balls of light might be seen to flash or arc across the room, sweeps or "passes" would be experienced, and the presence of the redeeming power of Christ would be felt.

While the Cohen placed a great deal of emphasis on the importance of these psychic phenomena and their reality, they were only signs and were considered secondary to La Chose. For the Cohen, the reintegration of his spiritual self into the cosmic, thereby correcting the errors and evils of the fall from grace, was paramount, and this could be accomplished only by La Chose. This emphasis on the appearance of the divine glory, of the very power and presence of Christ—the repaired Adam Kadmon itself—makes Elus Cohen rituals unique in their nature as well as clearly different from the Catholicism of the day and even Masonry.

The teachings of Pasquales were a complex mix of Roman Catholicism, Qabala, and Gnostic dualism within a Masonic framework, utilizing the popular obsession with Scottish Rite in France as its vehicle of promulgation. Pasquales's only written work was an esoteric depiction of the Book of Genesis titled *Treatise of the Reintegration of Beings*, which was published in 1769. Pasquales, said to have had poor command of written French, may have had assistance in compiling this book.

The key ideas of *Reintegration of Beings* are as follows: Like its Gnostic and at times Roman Catholic predecessors, the Cohen saw the material world as evil, its original purpose being to act as a prison for rebellious spirits. Adam Kadmon, the "First Man" or "Primordial Being," was placed on the earth to act as a warden to keep the evil spirits from escaping. However, Adam was tempted by his desire to create, just as God had created, and in turn he "fell." His first creation was Eve, with whom he bore Cain outside of divine blessing, thereby bringing evil into the world. The birth of Abel was blessed, but this son was only to be killed later by Cain. Humanity is seen by the Cohen as the descendants of Seth, the third child of Adam and Eve, who was given access to all knowledge and wisdom. It was the children of Seth who mated with the children of Cain, giving rise to the human race. A small group of these humans were individuals who remembered the divine teachings and occult arts and sought to attune themselves with divine will. They were called the "Friends of Wisdom," and Pasquales claimed to be the final heir of that wisdom. Members of the order followed strict dietary rules, similar to the Levites, and abstained from specific animal products to purify themselves of evil and demonic influences.

The grade system, rituals, and initiations of the Elus Cohen continually changed, evolved, and became more complex. Many of the initiations constituted a sort of ordination in the clerical sense, as advancing members of the Elus Cohen considered themselves to be priests in the line of the disciples of Christ and the patriarchs.

The first grouping shows four classes comprising a total of twelve degrees, and the second series of degrees are placed in four groups with a total of eleven degrees. Much of the symbolism of these degrees focuses around Zerubabel, who rebuilt the Temple of Solomon, as Masonic legend states, with a trowel in one hand and a sword in the other to defend himself against the threats of his idolatrous neighbors. In that much of the preliminary work of the Elus Cohen is concerned with cleansing the earth's aura of the influences of demonic and evil forces—traditional sources of human error and confusion—the identification with this archetypal figure of both the Hebrew Scriptures and High Degree Freemasonry is fitting. Many of the rituals are distinguished from typical magic of the period by the fact that no metal, ceremonial swords, or even wands are present, which may have been deeply influenced by the book *The Sacred Magic of Abramelin the Mage*.

Pasquales died in 1774 in Haiti, and with no heir apparent, the order he dedicated himself to blew apart. Some segments survived as Elus Cohen, others in Strict Observance Masonry, and some in the philosophical tenets of Louis Claude de Saint Martin. Through Willermoz and the Rite of Strict Observance, some of the rituals were absorbed into Scottish Rite Freemasonry and exist in the Holy Order of the Knights Beneficent of the Holy City (*Chevaliers Bienfaisants de la Cite Sainte*); these, as we will see, became associated with the Knights Templar and York Rite. Through Saint Martin, the mystical philosophy of Pasquales would survive and be revived in the late nineteenth century by Dr. Gerard Encausse and his Martinist Order. The Elus Cohen were revived and reorganized during the darkest days of World War II, and they continue to operate to this day.

## Egyptian Masonry

Just as the Elus Cohen were nearly inseparable from their founder, so is Egyptian Masonry intimately connected to the life and fate of its creator, the enigmatic Cagliostro. The two rites may even have been connected through an equally strange and enigmatic Irish Jesuit priest living in London: Father George Cofton, who is said to have been associated with the Elus Cohen. Cofton either copied the rituals of Egyptian Masonry or wrote them himself.

In Cagliostro's *Secret Ritual of Egyptian Rite Freemasonry*, originally published from a handwritten copy made in 1845 and later published

under the above title in English, we can see that within a generation after the formation of the Grand Lodge of France, the desire had become
intense to see more in Freemasonry than just a social club, fraternity, or
charitable organization.

After due preparation and revelation of the signs of recognition, the candidate is instructed in a Hermetic-alchemical understanding of Masonry:

> Seven are the passages to perfect the primal matter; seven are its colors.
> Seven are the effects required to complete the philosophical operations [i.e.,
> the Philosopher's Stone].[4]

Further on, it states:

Q: What do you mean by the Arcana [Secret] of Nature?

A: The recognition of that beautiful philosophy, both natural and super-
natural, of which I have conversed previously and of which you found
the principles confirmed in the emblems which represent the Order of
Masonry and the tableau [i.e, tracing board] which was placed before
your view in all the lodges.

Q: Is it possible for ordinary Masonry to furnish an idea of the sublime
mysteries? Although I have been a Mason for thirty-three years and have
passed through all the degrees during Although I have been a Mason for
thirty-three years and have passed through all the degrees during that
long space of time . . . I have never considered that Masonry was anything other than a society of people . . . who for better unity have adopted some signs and a peculiar language.

A: God inspire me and I will lift one of the corners of the veil which hid
the truth; I will start to instruct you in the origin of Masonry; I will
give you the philosophical explanation of the Masonic view and I shall
finish when you have learned all of the meaning of the sublime and
mystic aims of true Masonry.[5]

---

4 Cagliostro, Comte de, *Secret Ritual of Egyptian Rite Freemasonry* (Whitefish, MT: Kessinger
Publishing, n.d.).

5 Ibid.

## *Numbers, Angels, and the Arcana Arcanorum*

The number seven plays a particularly important role in Egyptian Masonry. It is often depicted as a seven-rayed star with the name Elohim written in the center and a Hebrew letter for each of the seven angels of the ancient planets in the apex of each of the points. The catechism states, "Helohym signifies, I wish and I order that my will be done, and that all shall be done accordingly."

Green—associated with the number seven as well as Venus, the plant alchemilla, the regenerative powers of alchemy, Eastern philosophy, and Hermes—is the color worn by a Master of the Egyptian rite, in this case, along with a red sash.

While the Elus Cohen were concerned with invoking the presence of the seven principal angelic powers and the reintegration of fallen humanity back into the perfect expression of divine will, Egyptian Masonry sought to contact the seven powers for the perfection of man while still on earth and in the flesh. This alchemical emphasis can be seen most clearly in the teachings of the Arcana Arcanorum, or "Secret of Secrets." These teachings are said to have been derived from several orders and societies, and while present in Cagliostro's rite, they found their way into the Rite of Misraim in the Eighty-seventh through Ninetieth degrees. In the modern era, the Order of Hermes Thrice-Magistus (OHTM), founded in 1927 by well-known European occultists and Freemasons, is also said to contain these teachings.

The Arcana Arcanorum is composed of three areas of interrelated work:

1. Invocation of the angelic hierarchy of the elements, the planets, the levels of the Tree of Life, the angelic guide of the age, and the guardian angel or higher self.

2. Mineral alchemy working with antimony.

3. Interior alchemy, in which the external symbols and work find their correlation in the human body, thereby turning it into the perfect alchemical vessel.

What is of interest to modern students of Masonry and esotericism is (1) the similarity, as well as direct connection, the specific practices of the Arcana Arcanorum have with Rosicrucianism, including the Hermetic-alchemical practices of the Pietists of Colonial Pennsylvania at Fairmount Park and later Ephrata and the need for a forty-day alchemical retreat for physical rejuvenation; (2) the creation of the Philosopher's Stone directly from the distilled blood of the adept;[6] (3) its connection to the enigmatic picture book known as *The Secret Symbols of the Rosicrucians of the 16th and 17th Centuries*, published in Altona, Germany, in 1785;[7] (4) and its connection to *The Sacred Magic of Abramelin the Mage*, the work of Agrippa, and that of Peter Abano, presumably the *Heptameron*, which is often bound with the *Fourth Book of Occult Philosophy*, attributed to Agrippa.[8]

## Adoptive Masonry

In addition to their unique catechisms and instruction in operative methods of occult exploration, the esoteric lodges of the eighteenth century tended to share a common Masonic "heresy": they initiated women. Known as "Adoptive Masonry," lodges of this nature were often separate from male lodges and run as parallel organizations for women. Within Cagliostro's rite, his wife, Seraphina, ran a lodge composed exclusively of wealthy upper-class women whom she initiated into the mysteries of Isis; in this lodge, she was the Grand Mistress of the mysteries. Other systems allowed men and women to sit in lodge together. While "regular" Masonry is known

6 Lesson 30 of Jean Dubuis's *Mineral Alchemy* contains a detailed description of this process. Jean Dubuis, *Mineral Alchemy*, 4 vols. (Winfield, IL: Triad Publishing, 1987).

7 Several editions exist that are of interest to this work: Manly P. Hall, ed., *Codex Rosae Crucis D.O.M.A.: A Rare & Curious Manuscript of Rosicrucian Interest* (Los Angeles: Philosophical Research Society, 1996); Franz Hartmann, *Cosmology* (Pomeroy, WA: Health Research, 1996), which contains color plates; and J. D. A. Eckhardt, ed., *Secret Symbols of the Rosicrucians of the 16th and 17th Centuries* (San Jose, CA: Supreme Grand Lodge of AMORC, n.d.).

8 Henry Cornelius Agrippa, *The Fourth Book of Occult Philosophy*, ed. with commentary by Stephen Skinner (Berwick, ME: Ibis Press, 2005). This edition states that it is now clear that Agrippa is indeed the author of the *Fourth Book* and that it is not, as previously claimed, a pseudepigraphical attribution.

to have had women members, often by default—they were caught over-hearing or intentionally spying on an initiation in progress and were "made Masons" to keep their obligations—it is not a common practice. While not all forms of Adoptive Masonry were or are esoteric, it is common, both historically and in the present, to see esoteric Masons and quasi-Masonic rites being adoptive in practice.

## Hermetic-Alchemical Rites and the Illuminati

According to Mackey, within the oldest Masonic records, Hermes Trismegistus is often called one of the founders of Freemasonry and is recognized as the father of Wisdom, who established two pillars of stone wherein were placed the arts and sciences to be preserved for future generations. We often see two Hermes occurring: Hermes the Thrice-Great, purported author of the Hermetic tracts, and Thoth-Hermes, also known as Hermes-Mercurius, the Egyptian god of magic and learning who so resembled his Greek and Roman counterparts that their names were simply combined. In truth, it is difficult to separate these figures from each other. Hermes the Thrice-Great has been associated with several historical priest-philosophers who lived in Egypt, and he has been seen as an incarnation of the gods themselves. As such, looking for a historical connection outside of the fact that literature attributed to him exists is meaningless. The Hermetic writings have been among the most influential in the Western world, yet their importance in Freemasonry has been overlooked by most Craft members over the last century.

The myth of Hermes is what is important, for as we have seen in most human spiritual pursuits, myth is often stronger and more important than history. Myth represents an ideal to be strived for—a truth yet to be attained. As such, myths guide us into the future rather than simply expound upon or shed light on the past. Within Masonry, reference to Hermes the Thrice-Great is found in the York Constitutions. The authors of this early document undoubtedly derived their knowledge of Hermes from popular legend and the philosophical but clearly occult writings of the period; chief among these, as far as Masonic interest is concerned, is the *Polycronycom*. Written by Ranulf Higden, a monk, and translated by

Trevisa from Latin, it was published by William Caxton in 1482, during the opening period of the Renaissance's "Hermetic renewal."

Hermes the Thrice Great, master of the magical and esoteric arts, of which alchemy is the crowning jewel, and author of the *Corpus Hermeticum*, is most prominent in the writings of the intellectual elite of Europe prior to and slightly after the formation of the Grand Lodge in 1717. However, this should not suggest that interest in Hermes, Hermetic philosophy, and the latter's practical application through magic was limited to the upper echelons of society. Dating back to the Middle Ages, we find extensive interest even on the common level in items pertaining to Hermes, who was often depicted as being a contemporary of Moses. Hermes was included in Christian churches and art of this period and into the Renaissance.

The appearance of purely Hermetic and alchemical rites appears in Freemasonry during the eighteenth century. Prior to the flourishing of High Degree Masonry on the Continent, there was no appearance of overt alchemical themes in Masonic rituals. Alchemical material shows up in those rituals and rites with a specific Hermetic or philosophical theme. (*Philosophical* was synonymous with *Hermetic* in the eighteenth century.) In 1785, the Grand Orient of France ordered that small vials of salt and sulphur should be placed in the Chamber of Reflection, clearly suggestive of the alchemical milieu in which the candidates lived and the interpretation they were to extract from their initiations. References to purifications by fire and water and to the elements (here, the four elements of classical alchemy: fire, air, water, and earth) are also made. In fact, the Chamber of Reflection is supposed to be underground, further suggesting pre-Christian initiations as well as the element of earth. With this infusion of alchemical symbols, the Supreme Council of the Ancient and Accepted Scottish Rite in France introduced new initiations with explicit alchemical symbolism for the first three degrees.[9]

Specific alchemical instruction in a Masonic setting is clearly seen in the writings of Antoine Joseph Pernety (1716–1800) and the Illuminati of Avignon. This is also one of the most familiar alchemical or Hermetic

---

9 Antoine Faivre and Jacob Needleman, eds., *Modern Esoteric Spirituality* (New York: Crossroad, 1992), 268–69.

rites. Pernety (also spelled Pernetii) was born in Roanne, France, in 1716 and while still young joined the Benedictine Congregation at Saint-Maur. After a period of time in the order, he, along with twenty-eight brethren, applied for dispensation from their monastic vows and left the order in 1765. Pernety then traveled to Berlin, where he became the librarian of Frederick the Great, king of Prussia. Shortly thereafter, he left for France, where the archbishop of Paris attempted to convince Pernety to return to the monastic life. It was around this time that Pernety encountered the writings and doctrines of Emmanuel Swedenborg, the Swedish Seer, and took a deep interest in his mystical speculations. He translated Swedenborg's *Wonders of Heaven and Hell* and retired to Avignon, where he formed the Masonic rite for which he is so well known.

This rite was instituted in Avignon in 1770 and moved to Montpellier in 1778 under a new name: Academy of True Masons.[10] This academy contained four degrees, with the fourth degree called True Mason, which incorporated instruction in Hermeticism, laboratory alchemy, and the teachings of Emmanuel Swedenborg. In *A New Encyclopedia of Freemasonry*, A. E. Waite states that Pernety was involved with "the investigation of future events by means of a peculiar Kabbalistic oracle" that directed the members of Pernety's rite to "follow the teachings of Emmanuel Swedenborg," and he quotes one Masonic authority placing the rite in existence as late as 1812.[11] Pernety created additional Masonic degrees; he is attributed with having authored the Knight of the Sun, Prince Adept (Twenty-eighth Degree), within Scottish Rite. Sections of this degree and the True Mason can be found in Martinism, which is the philosophic descendant of the Elus Cohen.

The degree of the Knight of the Sun, Prince Adept, contains within it angelic magic, theurgic operations, hints of operative alchemy, and clear similarities to the works of the Elus Cohen. In his work *The Book of the Ancient and Accepted Scottish Rite of Freemasonry*, Charles T. McClenachan,

---

10  Waite, *New Encyclopedia of Freemasonry*, 385. Waite states, "It has been referred erroneously to the year 1760 and alternatively to 1785" and seems to support its institution in or before 1785.

11  Ibid.

Thirty-third Degree Mason and Past Master of Ceremonies of the Supreme Council, writes:

> There is but one God, uncreated, eternal, infinite, and inaccessible: that the soul of man is immortal, and his existent life but a point in the center of eternity: that harmony is in equilibrium, and equilibrium subsists by the analogy of contraries: that analogy is the key of all secrets of nature, and the sole reason of being of all revelations: and, finally that the *Absolute* is REASON, which exists through itself: that evil, and wrong, and misery are the necessary discords that unite with the concords of the universe to make one great harmony forever. Such is the argument of this the last philosophical [Hermetic] degree of the Ancient and Accepted Scottish Rite; its doctrine is derived from the Kabala, and is the same as that of the Hermetic philosophers who wrote on Alchemy.[12]

Elsewhere he describes the necessary symbols for the degree as a pentagram with an eye in the center and a hexagram in black and white, black being uppermost, with an inverted Hebrew letter Shin in the center. This is peculiar, because normally white, the color of energy and purity, is uppermost, but here black, the color of matter, solidity, and physicality, is pointing upward, forming the active or "male" triangle. There is a single triangle with a black, white, and red side—the three principal colors of alchemy, symbolizing the three stages from dense matter (black) to purity (white) and finally to perfection (red)—and the letters Yod and Heh in the center.

In this degree, there is also a triangular apron of white lambskin and a pentagram in vermilion. Vermilion, made from cinnabar or mercury sulfide, is used in alchemy. Red is the color of energy, power, and action and symbolizes the Philosopher's Stone as well as original man, or Adam. Here, the Master is referred to as "Father Adam," and seven officers are present, each representing one of the seven ancient planets and their angels according to Masonic attribution. Other members wear a color with a vermilion pentagram and are referred to as "the Lions of God." Leo, the astrological sign who is ruled over by the Sun and whose metal is gold,

---

12 McClenachan, *Book of the Ancient and Accepted Scottish Rite of Freemasonry*, 400.

is represented by these members as having attained the end of the philosophers: the confection of the Philosopher's Stone. The same vermilion pentagram is found engraved on a piece of square white marble that is placed on the altar toward the north side.

Two pillars capped by a white dove and a black raven, the birds of initiation and alchemical work, are present; although their interpretation is in terms of the fourth and fifth Sephiroth of the Tree of Life, there is also a peculiarly Masonic interpretation of the dove being life and the raven being divine justice. Attributing the raven to death would be more appropriate, and it would fit in with the alchemical attribute of the raven as the *caput mortum,* or dead head, of the alchemical process.

A large image of Eliphas Levi's "Macrocosm," which contains the Hermetic axiom "As above, so below" in Latin, is to be placed in the north of the lodge. This image is particularly interesting: it shows a crowned and bearded king with his elbows raised and hands flat, with its mirror image below it; on closer examination, the arms of both figures taken together with their crowns form a hexagram.

References are made to Egyptian initiation and trial by the four elements of fire, air, water, and earth as found in classical magic and alchemy. In surviving these trials, the initiate was said to have mastered the elements and was raised to the status of an adept—the fifth point on the pentagram.

For Pike, McClenachan, and others, the symbolic meaning of alchemy within Masonry meant not the search for the Elixir of Life, potable gold, the panacea, or the Philosopher's Stone—as this would be "unreasonable" by nineteenth-century standards—but instead to live a moral, upright, and well-ordered life in which one was a respected and productive member of his community, lodge, and family.

Pernety's principal contribution to the advancement of alchemy was his work titled *Treatise on the Great Art: A System of Physics According to Hermetic Philosophy and Theory and Practice of the Magisterium,* which was first published in English in 1898 by the Occult Publishing Company, located in Boston. In his *Treatise,* Pernety synthesizes the great writings on alchemy and spagyrics (plant alchemy) and presents one of the most lucid descriptions of the Great Work ever given. For Pernety, alchemy was seen as "an operation of Nature, aided by art. It places in our hands the Key to Natural Magic or Physics, and renders us wonderful men, by elevating us above the masses."[13] This eighteenth-century idea of self-improvement and understanding the divine natural order of creation is in perfect harmony with the Masonic ideal expressed in "making good men better." Pernety was deeply influenced by classical mythology, and he dogmatically, as well as convincingly, interpreted the ancient myths from the perspective of them being variations on the Great Work.

In addition to his alchemical and Masonic interests, Pernety published numerous volumes on mythology, theology, philosophy, geography, the fine arts, translations from Latin, and mathematics, both theoretical and applied. He died at Valence, in Dauphiny, in 1800.

Many bodies smaller than Pernety's existed and may have worked operative alchemy as well, whereas for others, alchemical symbolism was used purely in a speculative sense to suggest a deeper meaning for the moral and ethical teachings of Masonry. One could look at it as a form of "Jungian alchemical psychotherapy" before its time. There also appears to have been a preoccupation in many of these rites with the Revelation of Saint John, or the Apocalypse, and its interpretation along initiatic, alchemical, and theurgic lines. It is the operative schools that are of the most interest, as they will demonstrate either an actual connection between Masonry, the stone builders, and the Hermetic adepts or simply a belief that such a connection existed. This theme will be taken up a century and a half later and will culminate in the writings of Isabel Cooper-Oakley and her work *Masonry & Medieval Mysticism*, then find its capstone in Fulcanelli's *The Mystery of the Cathedrals*. Here, the mysterious alchemical adept of the twentieth century takes the position that within the stone facades of the great Gothic cathedrals—Chartres and Notre Dame in particular—is the entire alchemical corpus preserved in stone.

---

13 Antoine Joseph Pernety, *Treatise on the Great Art: A System of Physics According to Hermetic Philosophy and Theory and Practice of the Magisterium*, ed. Edward Blitz (Boston: Occult Publishing Company, 1898). Reprinted as Antoine Joseph Pernety, *An Alchemical Treatise on the Great Art* (York Beach, ME: Weiser, 1995).

## Conclusion

Despite the brief lifespan of many of these occult Masonic or quasi-Masonic orders, many would find themselves reinvigorated a century later during the Belle Époque of the French occult revival. Some would even influence the British occult revival via the Societas Rosicruciana in Anglia (SRIA) and the formation of the Hermetic Order of the Golden Dawn. Yet despite claims of occult power and influence on affairs on the world stage, most would linger, die, and never be heard from again. Like a shooting star flashing across the night sky of the eighteenth century, the great occult rites attached to Scottish Rite Freemasonry would amuse, entertain, and distract many for an instant, only to fade into the cosmic darkness, out of sight and mind.

## Key Points

1. In the mid-eighteenth century, interest in occultism was widespread across Europe. While focused mainly within the social elite, it was also widely popular among the middle class and peasantry.

2. Many occult movements arose within and around Masonry, Scottish Rite in particular.

3. While many anti-Masons have misquoted Pike and many Masons have distanced themselves from him, he is more often than not simply not understood or even read. Masonry is essentially afraid of its esoteric and occult origins, and modern reactions to Pike within Masonry are proof of this fear.

4. Rosicrucianism is central to the development of esotericism from the early seventeenth century onward. Many of the rites and degrees that appeared in eighteenth-century Scottish Rite claim connection to or influence from Rosicrucian sources.

5. Rosicrucianism is focused around the story of Christian Rosenkreutz and his travels to the Middle East in search of wisdom, and the fraternity he established upon his return. The key document in Rosicrucianism is the *Fama Fraternitatis*, published in 1614.

6. Utopian principles can be found in the *Fama* and related documents. However, the documents themselves may be a farce, poking fun at utopianism rather than advocating it.

7. The Elus Cohen, established by Martinez Pasquales, are one of the most important Masonic-styled bodies of the eighteenth century, linking operative medieval ritual magic, Catholic piety, and Masonic ritual. Their survival can be seen in the Rite of Strict Observance, modern Martinism, and modern Elus Cohen organizations.

8. Cagliostro is among the most famous of eighteenth-century Masonic celebrities. Branded a swindler, pimp, and fraud, he is also highly regarded for his healing of the poor free of charge and his generosity. Cagliostro established a branch of Egyptian Masonry, only to be the last person recorded to die in the prisons of the Roman Catholic Church's Office of the Inquisition.

9. A critical part of Cagliostro's system is known as the Arcanum Arcanorum, which deals with alchemical rejuvenation, communication with the seven planetary angels, and the perfection of the human body as an alchemical vessel. It is said to be based in part on a book titled *The Secret Symbols of the Rosicrucians of the 16th and 17th Centuries*, published in 1785.

10. French Benedictine Antoine Joseph Pernety established the Illuminati of Avignon, one of the most well-known Hermetic Masonic rites. The rite was based on the visions of Emmanuel Swedenborg, practical alchemy, Hermeticism, and Qabala and was eventually absorbed into Scottish Rite, where its core ideas can be found in the Twenty-eighth Degree, Knight of the Sun, Prince Adept.

11. Pernety authored *Treatise on the Great Art: A System of Physics According to Hermetic Philosophy and Theory and Practice of the Magisterium*. It was first published in English in 1898 and included a foreword by Edward Blitz, the leading Martinist in America at the time.

## Assignments for Chapter 8

1. Read one or more of the books from the Suggested Reading list.

2. Research the importance of Rosicrucianism in the development of Western esotericism.

3. Research the role of angels in Judaism and the various Christian faiths.

4. Read a book about alchemy and its attendant practices.

5. If you could live for one hundred, one hundred fifty, or two hundred years in good health, would you? What would you do with that time?

## Suggested Reading

*Saint-Martin: Theosophic Correspondence (1792–1797)*, translated with preface by Edward Burton Penny (Theosophical University Press)

*The Unknown Philosopher: Louis Claude de St. Martin*, by A. E. Waite (Rudolph Steiner Publications)

*The Comte de Saint Germain: Last Scion of the House of Rakoczy*, by Jean Overton Fuller (East-West Publications)

*Comte de St. Germain*, by Isabel Cooper-Oakley (Theosophical Publishing House)

*Comte de Gabalis*, by Abbe de Montfaucon de Villars (The Brothers)

*Secret Societies: Illuminati, Freemasons and the French Revolution*, by Una Birch, edited, enlarged, and introduced by James Wasserman (Inner Traditions)

*Cagliostro*, by W. R. H. Trowbridge (University Books)

*The Last Alchemist: Count Cagliostro, Master of Magic in the Age of Reason*, by Iain McCalman (HarperCollins)

*The Most Holy Trinosophia of the Comte de St. Germain*, with introduction and commentary by Manly P. Hall (Philosophical Research Society)

*A New and Authentic History of the Rosicrucians*, by Frater Wittemans (Rider and Company)

*The Rosicrucian Enlightenment*, by Frances A. Yates (Routledge)

*The Rosicrucians: The History, Mythology and Rituals of an Esoteric Order*, by Christopher McIntosh, with foreword by Colin Wilson (Weiser)

*The Rose Cross and the Age of Reason: Eighteenth-Century Rosicrucianism in Central Europe and Its Relationship to the Enlightenment*, by Christopher McIntosh (E. J. Brill)

*The Brotherhood of the Rosy Cross*, by A. E. Waite (University Books)

# 9

# York Rite and the Survival of the Knights Templar

OVERVIEW
- *Royal Arch and the Capstone of British Masonry*
- *Survival of the Templars*
- *York Temple Degrees and the Mystery of the Temple*

The formation of York Rite, like Scottish Rite, requires that its members be Master Masons in good standing in Blue Lodge. Like the Scottish Rite degrees, the York Rite system is said to further elaborate on and explain, albeit symbolically, the material presented in the first three degrees. While Scottish Rite was forming and growing on the Continent, additional degrees were brought into England that eventually became known as York Rite. However, unlike Scottish Rite, York Rite is divided into three related groups that go under the banner name of York Rite. These are the Royal Arch, Cryptic, and Chivalric degrees, whose capstone is the Order of the Knights Templar. As can be discerned by now, the exact number of degrees and exactly which rituals are used varies among some jurisdictions, but the essential ideas remain the same.

Initially, only Royal Arch and Knights Templar degrees were given. By the late 1730s, however, additional degrees that further expanded the system began being conferred, each one elaborating on the basic theme of the Temple of Solomon, hidden treasure, and secrets long lost.

York Rite also diverges from typical Masonic protocol in that while any Mason may petition for membership in Capitulary (Royal Arch) and Cryptic Masonry, in theory, only Christians may become members of the Chivalric degrees; this is particularly true of the Knights of Malta and the Knights Templar, because of their distinct Christian orientation and emphasis. These degrees in part arose after the anti-Masonic period of the early eighteenth century in an effort to make Masonry appear less like the anti-establishment, quasi-revolutionary, esoteric organization Scottish Rite was becoming in Europe and more like a good, mainstream Christian organization.

## Royal Arch: Capstone of Masonry

Like many things bureaucratic, logic and the written word should be no obstacle to making something a fact in the eyes of the beholder. During the period of contention between the Antient and Modern Grand Lodges, the Antients considered the Royal Arch Degree the philosophical completion of the making of a Master Mason. This was tricky, because it was clear that there were only three degrees in Masonry, of which the Master Mason was the highest. However, in the eyes and ears of *tradition*, this did not matter, and the conferral of the Royal Arch Degree was a major sticking point during the unification of the Antient and Modern Grand Lodges in 1813.

To make matters worse, as time went on, Royal Arch went from being a single degree to its own administrative entity as part of the compromise, and it now has a total of four degrees it confers: Mark Master, Past Master, Most Excellent Master, and Royal Arch. Cryptic degrees include Royal Master, Select Master, and Super Excellent Master. Knights Templar degrees are Order of the Red Cross, Order of the Knights of Malta, and Order of the Knights Templar.

What makes these degrees fascinating, however, is not their convoluted and mind-numbing organizational concerns, but the messages they teach and the symbols they convey—the secrets of the Temple of Solomon.

## Cryptic Degrees and the Lost Word

The Cryptic degrees first appeared in Freemasonry between 1760 and 1780, and from appearances, they are among the best written and informative of Masonic degrees. The degrees that make up Cryptic Rite are based on the biblical narratives and oral traditions of Enoch the Patriarch. Enoch is a particularly interesting figure. In addition to being Noah's great-grandfather, he also "walked with God and was no more," being transfigured into the archangel Metatron by some accounts. Metatron is of particular importance in Jewish folk magic and Qabalistic practices.

In *A Dictionary of Angels*, Gustav Davidson writes:

> The patriarch Enoch, on his translation to Heaven (Genesis 5:24), became Metatron, one of the greatest of the hierarchs, "king over all the angels." *Cf.* the Assyrian legend in the *Epic of Izdubar*. On earth, as a mortal, Enoch is said to have composed 366 books (the Enoch literature). Legend has it that Enoch-Metatron is twin-brother to Sandalphon (*q.v.*); that when he was glorified he was given 365,000 eyes and 36 pairs of wings. . . . The spectacular mode of Elijah's conveyance to heaven, as reported in II Kings 2, had, it seems, an earlier parallel in the case of Enoch, for the latter was also whisked away "in a fiery chariot drawn by fiery chargers," as related in *The Legend of the Jews* I, 130; however, a few pages farther on (p. 138) it transpires that it wasn't a horse or a team of horses, but an angel (Anpiel) who transported the antediluvian patriarch from earth to Heaven. . . . To the Arabs, Enoch was Idris (Koran, *sura* 19, 56). In the *Pirke Rabbi Eliezer* the invention of astronomy and arithmetic is laid to Enoch. Legend connects Enoch-Metatron with Behemoth.[1]

The image of Metatron appears on the first talismanic image or pentacle of the Sun in the *Clavicula Salomonis*, where it is given the description "The Countenance of the Almighty, at whose aspect all creatures obey, and the Angelic Spirits do reverence on bended knees."

Given that Enoch was ascended to heaven and transfigured into Metatron, the twin of the angel Sandalphon, ruler of the earth, it is peculiar that Masonic legend has him excavating a total of nine underground chambers,

---

1 Gustav Davidson, *A Dictionary of Angels* (New York: The Free Press, 1967), 106.

each beneath the other, on the site where the Temple of Solomon would be built.

Each of these vaults or chambers contained a specific secret, culminating in the ultimate secret of all—the Ineffable Name of God, YHVH—in the ninth vault. Here, buried in the depths of matter, is the secret name. Here, in the most material of locations, is the truth each Mason seeks. Like the Secret Fire of the alchemists, the Lost Word is found in this world, not in the next. It is the key to our understanding and liberation from ignorance and suffering, and it is found within the rough rock of daily experience. God, it appears, is everywhere and is hidden in everything, rather than only residing in the starry heavens. It would appear from the Masonic teachings of the Cryptic degrees that before we can ascend and be transfigured into divine beings of light, we must first dig deep within the world of matter and unlock the holy secrets it holds.

**Royal Master**—This degree takes place before the completion of Solomon's Temple and provides the candidate with information about Hiram Abiff and his successor, Adoniram.

**Select Master**—This degree takes place between the first and second half of the previous degree. It is common for degrees to jump in periods of time and then have other degrees revert to the period not elaborated on earlier. The main focus here is on the secret vaults and their location and the depositing of secrets within them.

**Super-Excellent Master**—This degree takes place after the destruction of the Temple and the period of the Babylonian captivity.

The degree of the Thrice Illustrious Master is sometimes conferred to a select leadership position within Cryptic Rite. Hermeticists will note the similarity in the title to that of Hermes the Thrice Great, with Hermes and Enoch interchanged in some early Hermetic texts.

Enoch is also associated with the angelic magic of Dr. John Dee and Edward Kelly, practices well known to several early and prominent Freemasons, Elias Ashmole in particular. While unrelated, a curious script known as "Angelic Writing" or "Enochian" appears on eighteenth-century Masonic trestle boards. This script, however, is distinct from the so-called Enochian alphabet used by Dee and Kelly.

While of little importance to modern Masons, in the eighteenth century, a period when biblical references and magical culture were still present, these references to Enoch and their attached significance would not have gone unnoticed.

Belief in magic and various occult practices was widespread in eighteenth- and even nineteenth-century Europe and America, particularly during the period of Masonry's most prestigious growth. Harvard taught alchemy into the 1820s, and one of its presidents, Ezra Stiles (1778–95), explored alchemy and Qabala. Virginia aristocracy was well read in astrology and alchemical healing. Benjamin Franklin openly satirized the public's obsession with all things occult, and Thomas Jefferson put it on par with the common belief in miracles. In England, physicians were the force behind the occult revival of the 1780s.

Across Europe, books on the occult were readily available to the lower classes, as noted by D. Michael Quinn:

> Even by the early eighteenth century, at least one English clergyman complained that common people had widespread access to books promoting magic. Worse, he said, well-intentioned books condemning witchcraft and the occult actually provided enough details for readers to perform the forbidden rites: "These books and narratives are in tradesman's shops, and farmer's houses, and are read with eagerness, and are continually leavening the minds of the youth, who delight in such subjects." In Nineteenth Century France, magic handbooks "abounded in the countryside" and judicial trails for sorcery often found that peasants owned occult books that had been out-of-print for two or three hundred years. This refutes the assumption that the common people were indifferent to academic magic, and also challenges that poor farmers had no access to published works and rare books.[2]

The widespread desire for books on the occult in rural and urban areas across the eighteenth and mid nineteenth centuries is an established

---

2 D. Michael Quinn, *Early Mormonism and the Magical World View*, rev. and enlarged ed. (Salt Lake City, UT: Signature Books, 1998), 21.

fact. In America, the flood of books from Europe was endless, and itinerant rural book peddlers reported making enormous amounts of money from occult book sales. In 1809–10, one peddler's records showed that he sold $24,000 worth of books door to door in the South, primarily to farmers. Given that the average price of a leather book was seventy-five cents, forty-four cents for a new book, and pennies for chapbooks, this documents a phenomenal interest in all things occult—seemingly without concern for any possible conflict with the prevailing religious ideas of the period.

## Chivalric Degrees

The Chivalric degrees constitute the height of Masonic initiation and its confusing mix of history and myth. While no historical connection exists with these actual orders and their non-Masonic successors, their existence does indicate that despite the egalitarian nature of Masonry, the need to have "further advancement" in the form of titles, separate meetings, and secrets appears to be inherent to human nature. If the common laborer had degrees that he could identify with, then it does not seem unusual for the upper class to have degrees it could identify with and give the growing middle class a sense of belonging to something powerful and important.

> **Illustrious Order of the Red Cross**—The theme of this degree links the Cryptic degrees with the Chivalric degrees as well as the Jewish and Christian Scriptures. This degree is not conferred in all Templar systems. Some, like the British, only confer the degrees below.

> **Order of Malta**—Here, the candidate is conferred with a series of knightly titles, bundling together the Knights of Saint Paul, Knights of Malta, and Knights Hospitaller.

> **Order of the Temple**—In this degree, the candidate will encounter what for many is the single most impressive series of ritual experiences ever encountered in Masonry, as well as outside of it. In addition to the Chamber of Reflection, here, each candidate meets with his Brethren and shares the communal experience of the draught

of mortality. Clearly Christian in orientation, those who take this degree state their willingness to defend the Christian faith if called upon to do so.

## Origin of the Templars

The Knights Templar came into being in 1118 CE, when Hugues de Paynes, a minor noble, and eight fellow knights from northern France took oaths of poverty and obedience in connection with their military vows, thus creating the first warrior monks in Christendom. They took the name "Poor Fellows of the Knights of Christ" and chose as their symbol two poor knights sharing a horse. Their task was to protect pilgrims on the overland route from Jaffa to Jerusalem. Jerusalem had fallen to Christian armies in 1099, and the act of pilgrimage was extremely dangerous, as the roads were crawling with Muslim brigands and outlaws attacking both solitary travelers and armed caravans. Simply dying on the journey was enough in some instances to have one's sins remitted. Few in number, the Poor Fellows of the Knights of Christ could not hope to fulfill their mission without additional support.

In 1124, de Paynes returned to France to receive an official sanction by the Roman Catholic Church at the Council of Troyes. While papal approval gave the Templars legitimacy, it was the endorsement of Saint Bernard of Clairvaux that sealed their future and guaranteed extensive financial and political support. Within a generation, they would become the wealthiest and most powerful military force in history.

The name "Knights Templar" would come from the location of their quarters in the palace complex of King Baldwin II, a rundown section on the former site of King Solomon's temple. It is often stated that the area they were given as quarters was previously used as a stable. This location was added to their name, and they were recognized as the "Poor Fellow-Soldiers of Christ and the Temple of Solomon," or "Knights Templar" for short. In 1139, the Templars were given a power unknown by any other military order: they answered only to Pope Innocent II. No other ecclesiastical authority could question their actions. They were exempt from taxes and virtually all civil authorities. This, coupled with the ability to keep all wealth captured during their campaigns, as well as from the commercial activities in the lands and castles granted them, made them the wealthiest military order of the day—and possibly all of history.

While the Templars controlled large tracts of land in Palestine and Syria, their influence was not limited to the Holy Land. Holdings in Europe began in 1131, when, with the Knights Hospitaller and the Church of the Holy Sepluchre, the Templars were given the responsibility of defending Aragon of Spain, receiving its wealth as payment in return. Templar priory, or chapter houses, and churches built in a unique circular design (reminiscent of the Round Table and magical circles of medieval theurgy) were constructed across Europe and the Middle East. The Templars were a de facto state within the state of Catholic Europe.

## Fall of the Templars and Their Survival

Defeat at Acre, near Haifa, in 1291 marked the beginning of the fall of the Knights Templar. Under assault by Muslim forces numbering 160,000 with siege towers and catapults, the walls were breached, and Christian control began to collapse. After leaving the Holy Land, the Templars went to Cyprus to reorganize. With nothing left in the East, they turned their attention west, to Europe and the massive holdings they had accumulated there. With their network in place and their reputation for exchange well known, the Templars focused their energy on banking. Efforts to merge the Templars with the Hospitallers failed, which was a signal that Rome saw little use for them with Jerusalem under Muslim control. Kings who were indebted to them also had reasons to see the all-powerful and nearly untouchable Templars reined in once and for all.

Unfortunately for the Templars, they found their archenemy in a man they had once helped, a man who in turn would destroy them. King Philip IV of France, also known as Philip the Fair, was a scoundrel by all measures. He expelled the Jews from France in 1306 in order to steal their property, stole money from Italian bankers in 1311, and debased the national currency, thereby weakening it and increasing the national debt. Philip even attempted to kidnap Pope Boniface VIII. However, it was in 1306 that Philip's dream of owning Templar wealth may have been whetted beyond all expectations. During riots that year in Paris, Philip was given sanctuary and protection in the Templar preceptory. There, Philip would have seen just a fraction of the Templar wealth, and that was enough to set him scheming.

Two events took place that would eventually provide Philip with the opportunity he was seeking: accusations of sodomy, idolatry, and blasphemy by a former Templar named Esquiu de Floyrian, and the contentious election of Pope Clement V. It was Clement whose election and eventual moving of Church administration from Rome to Avignon that began the period known as the "Babylonian captivity." His election was not an easy affair, and it took a year to be concluded. To facilitate his election, Clement had arranged with Philip that upon his election as pope he would repeal previous laws passed by the Vatican against France. This was the beginning of a friendship between a weak pope and an avaricious king that would end with the destruction of the Knights Templar.

At sunrise on Friday, October 13, 1307, the Knights Templar were arrested in a series of coordinated raids across France. In all, two thousand members of the order were imprisoned. The coordination for this kind of large-scale arrest is astonishing given the period and the sheer manpower it required. Multiple arrest warrants, all copied by hand, had to be produced and delivered with official seals under Philip's authority. Men had to be organized and deployed. The fact that someone sympathetic to the Templars did not leak information to them so they could secure their safety is in itself telling of both the jealously they may have fostered and the fear of Church punishment should one be found guilty of assisting the doomed Knights of the Temple. Less than a year later, Clement V would authorize additional arrests wherever the Roman Catholic Church held authority.

Charges brought against the Templars included heresy, denying the divinity of Christ, spitting on the cross, sodomy and homosexuality (giving an anal kiss to one's initiator in the order), and the most famous of all, worshiping an idol in the shape of a strange head known as Baphomet. While *Baphomet* has taken on many peculiar meanings over the years, it is in all likelihood a misspelling of *Muhammad* in medieval French.

Trials and interrogations were a mockery of justice, as torture and confessions extracted under torture were routine. Leading questions were the order of the day. No evidence, outside of that extracted through torture, was ever produced to support the accusations brought against the Templars. No Baphomets were ever found. Yet, in the end, about sixty knights who were arrested either died under torture or were executed after a puppet trial. Fifty-four of them, for recanting their confessions, were burned at the stake in 1310 under the charge of being relapsed heretics. The methods established for the destruction of the Templars would be perfected a century later during the beginning of the "Burning Times," the persecution of those perceived as practicing witchcraft.

Among those to die was the order's Grand Master, Jacques de Molay. After being imprisoned for seven years, on March 18, 1314, de Molay was burned at the stake. Before his death, he predicted that both King Philip and Pope Clement would soon follow him. Within a year, both were dead.

After their trials, most of the Templars were released and either joined other orders or retired to civilian life. Outside of France, the arrests and persecutions were not as strong.

## Templars in York Rite Masonry

Just as Chevalier Ramsay's Templar mythology stirred the imagination of what would become Scottish Rite, it also planted the seeds for what would become York Rite. French and German obsessions with this purported connection were the most fabulous and productive in the creation and spawning of degrees and even entire rites. While there was no evidence to support the notion that the Templars had fled to Scotland along with either the esoteric wisdom gleaned from their stay in the Holy Land, their massive treasure, or both, this did nothing to slow the explosion of the myth of a Templar connection to Freemasonry. By 1769, Templar degrees were given in the American Colonies, and in England by 1778. However, a distinct difference, even at this stage, was apparent between American and British Templar rites and those of Germany and France, the Order of Strict Observance in particular. In Continental Europe, a clear and direct connection was made between Masonry, Templars in particular; esoteric studies; and occult practices such as alchemy, astrology, and Qabala. In Anglo-Saxon Templarism, this connection is absent, and in fact, Templar degrees are little more than an additional degree to be had on the ever-expanding Masonic ladder.

## Templars and the Occult

The notion that the Templars were heirs to an Eastern treasure that was of a spiritual and not material nature appears in Templar mytho-history with Strict Observance Masonry. While such an idea may have existed earlier, it is not until the development of the Masonic grades that it comes forth full-blown and in a coherent manner, complete with rituals, rites, and teachings that suggest a continuity reaching back to the Templars themselves.

The traditional history behind Strict Observance states that Pierre d'Aumont, Grand Marshal of the Knights Templar who succeeded Jacques de Molay as Grand Master, and seven knights fled to Scotland, disguising themselves as stonemasons. It further states, or claims, that there they established Freemasonry in its present form. However, like all traditional histories, facts to support these statements are lacking, and the "history" is better understood as a mythology or teaching story than an actual history. Unfortunately, traditional histories are positioned as being actual facts rather than suggestive. This has created a hornets' nest of confusion within Masonic circles and for Masonic research up to the present day.

Founded in Germany circa 1754 by Johann Gottlieb von Hund, the Rite of Strict Observance was based on von Hund's assertion that he was initiated into a Masonic Templar lodge twelve years earlier and entrusted with the mission of spreading this rite. In addition to this mysterious initiation was the statement that his authority and knowledge were derived from "Unknown Superiors" who required perfect obedience. While it is possible that von Hund was initiated into a Templar degree or rite, it is unlikely—or he may simply have been fooled. The notion of "Unknown Superiors," those invisible masters of human destiny found in the writings of Madame Blavatsky and throughout the occult revival of the nineteenth and early twentieth centuries, finds its origins in part in Strict Observance.

Unlike later reports of these unknown superbeings, von Hund would state that he received his investiture and was left to his own devices on how to proceed; thus, Strict Observance is a vehicle of his own creation. Later occultists and Masons with occult interests would pick up where von Hund left off and state that they were in continued, often telepathic contact with their invisible masters and tutors.

With only his word of honor to go on, von Hund and his rite languished and fell into disrepair. With his death, the Lodge of Philalethes absorbed much of the rite, and coincidentally, a disciple of Pasquales was influential enough to absorb not only Strict Observance but also the teachings of the Elus Cohen as well. What remained of Strict Observance, like most things Masonic, was destroyed or scattered by the French Revolution.

Among the most important of Strict Observance brethren was Jean Baptiste Willermoz (1730–1824). Willermoz was a well-known Mason from Lyon and a cofounder of the Rectified Scottish Rite. He was also an ardent disciple of Pasquales, and one of his two heirs: Saint Martin being his mystical son and Willermoz his magical one. The stage was set at the end of the eighteenth century for the Elus Cohen to be absorbed into the cross-fertilization of ideas and practices of High Grade Masonry and, through Strict Observance, connected to the myth of the Templars and their esoteric wisdom.

Despite Strict Observance rejecting Rosicrucianism and its Hermetic-alchemical philosophy in favor of the Elus Cohen and their theurgy in 1782, Willermoz had been responsible for establishing a chapter of the Black Eagle of the Rose-Croix nearly twenty years earlier.

## Key Points

1. Members of York Rite must be a Master Mason in good standing. Like Scottish Rite, York Rite is a system that elaborates on the first three degrees. York Rite consists of several related groups, each of which confers a specific set of degrees, culminating in the Order of the Knights Templar.

2. Initially, only Royal Arch and Knights Templar degrees were given. By 1730, additional degrees were conferred, each elaborating on the basic theme of Solomon's Temple, hidden treasure, and lost secrets.

3. For many, Royal Arch is considered the pinnacle of Masonic achievement.

4. Unlike Blue Lodge or Scottish Rite, York Rite is distinctly Christian in its tone and membership requirements.

5. The Cryptic degrees of York Rite first appeared between 1760 and 1780 and are based on the theme of nine crypts or vaults existing beneath the Temple of Solomon. In the lowest vault is the Lost Word, placed there by the patriarch Enoch, who is also identified with the archangel Metatron.

6. Enoch is a critical figure in Masonry as well as being heavily identified with ritual magic and Qabala through his association with—or rather transformation into—Metatron.

7. Chivalric degrees confer knightly titles, but there is no evidence they are not historically linked to the actual orders they represent.

8. The Chivalric degrees culminate in the Knights Templar. The Knights Templar were founded in 1118 CE when Hughes de Paynes, a minor noble, and eight fellow knights from France took vows of poverty and obedience in connection with their military vows. In doing so, they became the first warrior monks in Christendom.

9. These knights, known as the Poor Fellows of the Knights of Christ, were given residence in a dilapidated section of a palace in Jerusalem on the former site of the Temple of Solomon, and thereafter they changed their name, calling themselves the Knights Templar for short.

10. The self-appointed task of the Templars was to guard Christian pilgrims on the journey to the Holy Land. They quickly rose to become the most powerful military and economic entity in the region, reporting only to the pope.

11. The Templars were arrested and their leaders executed on trumped-up charges of heresy, sodomy, and worshipping an idol called Baphomet. Torture was widely used to extract confessions, and on March 18, 1314, after seven years in prison, Jacques de Molay, the last Grand Master of the Knights Templar, was burned at the stake.

12. Following the death of de Molay and Chevalier Ramsay's Templar mythology in the eighteenth century, extensive myth and lore grew up around the Templars over the following two centuries. Most of these stories link the Templars to ancient treasures or secret wisdom of an alchemical, Qabalistic, or Arabic nature.

## Assignments for Chapter 9

1. Read a book from the Suggested Reading list.

2. Research the idea of "the Lost Word," or the divine secret hidden in creation. What does this mean to you? How do you believe it can be experienced?

3. Research the role of Enoch and Metatron in angelology. What does this idea of Enoch becoming transformed into Metatron and being taken bodily into heaven suggest to you? What similar ideas exist in other faiths, philosophies, and esoteric traditions?

## Suggested Reading

*Born in Blood: The Lost Secrets of Freemasonry*, by John J. Robinson (M. Evans and Co.)

*Templars in America: From the Crusades to the New World*, by Tim Wallace-Murphy and Marilyn Hopkins (Barnes & Noble Books)

*The Templars and the Assassins: The Militia of Heaven*, by James Wasserman (Inner Traditions)

*An Illustrated History of the Knights Templar*, by James Wasserman (Inner Traditions)

*The Templars: Knights of God; The Rise and Fall of the Knights Templars,* by Edward Burman (Destiny Books)

*The Knights Templar and Their Myth,* by Peter Partner (Destiny Books)

## IO

# Freemasonry and the European Occult Revival

OVERVIEW
- *Fashion, Salons, and the New Rosicrucianism*
- *The Hermetic Order of the Golden Dawn*
- *Theosophy, Co-Masonry, and Invisible Masters*

Know then O Aspirant that the Mysteries of the Rose and the Cross have existed from time immemorial, and that the Rites were practiced, and the Wisdom taught, in Egypt, Eleusis, Samothrace, Persia, Chaldea and India, and far more ancient lands. The story of the introduction of these mysteries into medieval Europe has thus been handed down to us.

—FROM THE THIRD ADEPT'S LECTURE, ADEPTUS MINOR RITUAL, HERMETIC ORDER OF THE GOLDEN DAWN

By the end of the nineteenth century, fringe Masonic and Masonic-style groups had become the focal point of the occult revival. Even an organization such as the Theosophical Society incorporated Masonic elements into sections of its work, becoming, as we shall see, the principal champion for a mixed Masonic order known as Co-Masonry. This period of time is of considerable interest to students of esotericism as well as mainstream Masonry because of the rich field of personalities, rites, charters, claims (and counterclaims) to authenticity, lawsuits, outright hostility, and occasional violence that dominated movements based on the philosophical ideal of the brotherhood of man and spiritual values. The irony is not lost on anyone who explores this period and is in fact its main attraction for more than one author.

Despite this, from the compost pile of human endeavors gone awry, the core groups from this period continued to exert an influence on esotericism in the United States and Europe long after their fires had burned their brightest. The seeds they planted, just as the seeds their seventeenth- and eighteenth-century ancestors had, grew quietly, their fruits to be discovered by future generations long after the personalities involved had become footnotes in history.

In some respects, it is these fringe groups that demonstrate what is best and worst about Freemasonry, with its human ideals and its activities as a whole. Strong ideals require strong character. The temptation to sneak around, giving the devil his due, is a powerful one, even more so when the promises of titles and material and spiritual power are attached to it. While many people have benefited tremendously (this author included) from participation in some of the groups listed below, it is also clear that movements can become a lightning rod for those seeking fulfillment and satisfaction through so-called spirituality that they have failed to find in material life. If we look at traditional Masonry, membership was allowed only on or after the age of twenty-one—nearly middle age for the average person living in the eighteenth century. Traditionally, Qabala was permitted only for men of "the age of wisdom," or forty. Clearly, a firm grounding and establishment in material life was expected by these points in life, and this was to be brought into one's activities within the Fraternity. If there is a lesson to be learned from the following brief study of modern fringe Masonic groups, it is that human ideals, no matter how noble, still require the imperfect vehicle of humanity to carry them out. Perfection is an ideal strived for but possibly never attained.

## Co-Masonry and the Invisible Adepts Revisited

Co-Masonry, among the most recent of Masonic bodies, is the direct off-spring of the nineteenth-century occult revival. Founded in 1900, Co-Masonry claims its authority through a variety of Masonic entities that seceded from the Supreme Council of France in 1879. The first Co-Masonic lodge was opened in London in September 1902, with Dr. Annie Besant acting as Vice-President Grand Master of the Supreme Council and Deputy for Great Britain and its Dependencies.

What makes this of interest is that while Co-Masonry admitted women into its ranks (and still does, as it is alive and well) on an equal basis with men in an era in which the women's suffrage movement was beginning to take on tremendous force in Europe and America, its members saw in this nothing irregular.

1. The fundamental tenet of Co-Masonry is that women were admitted to the ancient mysteries prior to the ascent of the Christian era and, as such, admitting them into Freemasonry is a restoration of something that was lost.

2. From this, it is clear that Co-Masonry views Freemasonry as a whole as a continuation of the ancient Middle Eastern and Eastern mystery schools under the guise of a stonecutters' guild, rather than as a social entity.

3. The leadership and members of Co-Masonry, from its origin to this day, are in some fashion involved with Theosophy. They see Christianity as a dying religion that will be replaced by a single universal system of belief, and they believe that the world will be united under a single government and, from this, universal peace and brotherhood established—thereby completing the political expression of the esoteric mission of Freemasonry.

4. Behind the established movements of Theosophy and Co-Masonry stands the "Unknown Superiors," or invisible masters who guide humanity, leading it to its goal of unity under an enlightened leadership.

The rituals of Co-Masonry were eventually revised to reflect the perception that the original initiations and working degrees of the Craft contained esoteric wisdom that had been lost since their inception. These revisions were completed in 1916 and were based on English and Scottish rituals.

More ideas were introduced from French rituals, as were innovations peculiar to the leadership of the period, emphasizing esoteric ideas. Additional degrees were eventually modified over the years, allowing Co-Masonry to create its own unique understanding of Craft, Royal Arch, and Scottish Rite Freemasonry.

The most influential leaders in Co-Masonry were Annie Besant (1847–1933) and Charles Webster Leadbeater (1847–1934), both well known and established in the Theosophical community. Besant was a phenomenal woman who was involved in many of the most important social movements of the period, moving through atheism, socialism, feminism, Indian nationalism, and the promotion of birth control at a time when one in six women could die in childbirth and urban poverty in industrialized nations was rampant. Leadbeater was a clergyman in the Church of England whose interests in Theosophy caused him to eventually leave the church; even later in life, he publicly stated that he was a practicing Buddhist. He authored several important Theosophical books as well as two on the esoteric nature of Freemasonry: *The Hidden Life of Freemasonry* and *Glimpses of Masonic History*, whose weight rest upon Leadbeater's status as a Thirty-second Degree Mason and his reputed clairvoyant abilities. Leadbeater's life, however, was filled with controversy, and he was forced to resign from the Theosophical Society in disgrace after allegations of homosexual liaisons with young boys began to surface and then were substantiated. Various actions allowed him eventually to rejoin the Theosophical Society and lead its Indian section, until the old charges of pedophilia re-emerged. Leadbeater, forced from India, settled in Australia. Next to Madame Blavatsky, Leadbeater is the most controversial figure in the Theosophical movement.

Theosophy itself is a peculiar term meaning "knowledge of God," and while often applied to unique streams of European mystical and esoteric speculation from the Renaissance onward, it has become identified almost exclusively with the writings of Russian seer and adventurer Helena Petrova Blavatsky. Madame Blavatsky (1831–91) was born in the Ukraine to the daughter of a provincial official of German extraction and minor nobility. She was reared by her maternal grandparents, both nobles, and in this environment was exposed to many esoteric and philosophic ideas, including Freemasonry, Strict Observance, and the ideas of Pasquales and Saint Martin. At the age of seventeen she was married to General Nikifor Blavatsky, a man very much her senior, and ran off after a few months of marriage.

For the next decade, she traveled widely—travels that in turn would be part of the foundation story for the myths and legends that would arise, as well as be crafted, around her in later years. The official story from Theosophists is that she ventured to Tibet, where she lived with the *Mahatmas*, or "Great Souls," those enlightened beings who guide humanity on its spiritual quest. Evidence suggests that she was more of an adventurer, a sometime circus performer, a possible spy, and of course, typical for the period, a fraudulent medium. It is unclear if she had any children, and during her later years she refused to discuss her wanderings despite the great body of lore they had produced during her lifetime.

It is known that Blavatsky spent time in Egypt, something that played an important part in the development of Co-Masonry under Annie Besant. Blavatsky was always involved in some fashion with fringe Masonry, Hermetic and quasi-Hermetic groups, and Orientalism in all of its forms, always using these contacts to claim access to some form of secret or hidden wisdom—a theme that reappears in Co-Masonry. Blavatsky was among the survivors of the shipwreck of the vessel that was carrying her to Cairo in 1871. While in Cairo, she founded a Spiritualist organization, aided by Emma Coulomb. Blavatsky's relationship with Coulomb would be long-lasting and fateful, as Coulomb would become one of her bitterest critics. The organization, known as the Société Spirite, was based on the theories of Allen Kardec and was established for the investigation of spiritualistic phenomena. It lasted a short time, however, one report saying as little as two weeks; it ruptured under the usual charges of fraud and the embezzlement of funds from scammed patrons. Blavatsky left the group early and focused her attention on Hermeticism and its accompanying practices of magic, astrology, and Qabala. She traveled to Paris by way of Eastern Europe and arrived in Paris by the spring of 1873. Her travels would eventually take her to the United States.

Using her travels and writings as a guide, it is clear that Blavatsky's life has two distinct periods: one Western and Hermetic, the other Eastern and Buddhist. It is her Hermetic period that dominated the early years of the Theosophical Society from its inception in 1875, reaching its zenith with the publication of *Isis Unveiled* in 1877. With Blavatsky's journey to Bombay two years later, the philosophical direction of the Theosophical Society changed as well, and a strong Indo-Tibetan approach became the norm. It was during her Egyptian period that Blavatsky met and claimed membership in the Hermetic Brotherhood of Luxor, and she learned enough details of Masonic ritual and teachings to suitably impress Parisian Masonic authorities.

Madame Blavatsky's past would begin to haunt her during her Indian period. In 1884, while Blavatsky was in London with her longtime friend and supporter Colonel Henry Steel Olcott, two Theosophical Society staff members, Emma Coulomb and her husband, Alexis, stated that they had emphatically assisted Blavatsky in the perpetuation of fraudulent mediumistic séances. The resulting publicity of these accusations created a split between Blavatsky and Olcott. With Blavatsky's death in 1891, leadership of the Theosophical Society fell to Annie Besant, after which it began to suffer from a series of schisms. While Besant's personality and apparent lack of tact and diplomacy played no small role in stoking the fires of revolt, her desire to promote Co-Masonry was also at fault, as many Theosophists felt that Co-Masonry and Leadbeater's Liberal Catholic Church were not appropriate topics given the clearly Indo-Tibetan direction of the organization.

## Martinism and Rosicrucianism Reborn

The popularity of Eliphas Levi's works *Dogma and Ritual of High Magic* and *The History of Magic* can be seen as the seed for what would eventually be termed the "occult revival" of the nineteenth and early twentieth centuries. Not a single movement remained untouched by their contents, and in many ways they gave birth to entire occult orders—not least among them the modern rebirths of Martinism and Rosicrucianism and, as we have seen, Pike's interpretation of the degrees of Scottish Rite.

It is in this twilight milieu of the Belle Époque that we see the emergence, or re-emergence, of the doctrines of Louis Claude de Saint Martin, student and disciple of Martinez Pasquales, under the umbrella of Martinism. In 1884, Dr. Gerard Encausse (1865–1916) united with Pierre Augustin Chaboseau and founded the Martinist Order. Writing under the pen name Papus, Encausse emerged as one of the leading figures of European occultism, even venturing into the czar's court and becoming the spiritual archrival of Rasputin. Papus has often been called the "Balzac of occultism" because of the number of books he published—over two hundred. While many are short and of little scholarly value, they point to his pivotal role and the popular desire for such works; many of them are still available a century or more after they were written. Papus published his first book, *Elementary Treatise on Occult Science*, in 1888, and his most famous work, *The Tarot of the Bohemians*, the following year. Dozens of titles were to follow until his untimely death in 1916 while serving as a physician at the front of World War I.

Prior to his involvement in Martinism (and later the establishing of several Rosicrucian groups), Papus was active in the Parisian Theosophical scene, but like Rudolph Steiner, he left when it turned from Hermeticism toward Asiatic mysticism.

In 1891, the Supreme Council of the Martinist Order was established, and efforts were made to bring into the fold the many diverse groups, circles, and independent initiators and teachers that grew out of the work of Saint Martin, Pasquales, and Willermoz's Strict Observance. The Martinist Order was to be the vehicle for this and the continuation of "the initiation" of valid lines of succession and teaching. Four degrees were utilized, showing a similarity in structure to Freemasonry. The fourth degree, that of Independent Superior Inconnu ("Free Unknown Superior," later L.I. or Free Initiator), gave its holder the authority to initiate others and to form lodges composed of the lower three degrees of Associate, Mystic (also Brother), and Superior Inconnu ("Unknown Superior"). As a result, Martinism spread quickly, even far beyond the shores of Europe; such rapid growth gave rise to personal innovations and schisms. Several attempts were made by Papus and others to use Martinism as a means of returning Freemasonry to its esoteric roots. These overtures were firmly rejected by regular Masonic authorities, and many even incorrectly saw Martinism as a form of irregular or clandestine Masonry based on the superficial similarities of its degree structure. Like many of the occult orders of the day, the Martinist Order admitted women on equal footing with men, although later attempts to change this and force a Masonic requirement on Martinist members led to the formation of one of many schismatic Martinist bodies.

A natural organizer, Encausse joined up with numerous well-known personalities in Parisian occultism to form the Kabbalistic Order of the Rose+Cross. This order was in part the brainchild of Stanislaus de Guaita (1860–98). A flamboyant artist and poet, de Guaita made his mark by creating a sinister persona around himself, reveling in the decadence of the period. He slept during the day, worked at night, and destroyed his health through addiction to morphine and cocaine, dying at the age of thirty-eight of a drug overdose in a public urinal. Like many dreamers of all ages and periods, de Guaita saw art as the means of transforming the world, and he participated in well-attended salons with esoteric themes. Similar to the New Age movement of the late twentieth century, spirituality, occultism, and counterculture linked together in nineteenth-century Paris to form a fashionable narcissism wherein the elect could find illumination in the arms of their mistresses under the influence of drugs and justify it in the language of revolution. And like its New Age counterpart, its impact on society at large appears to be negligible.

However, like so many idealistic movements, the illuminati of the Paris brothels were unable to hold their dream together. In 1890, one of the founding members of the Kabbalistic Order of the Rose+Cross left to found the Catholic Order of the Rose+Cross, an attempt to reunite art, mysticism, and traditional Catholic theology under a single initiatic movement. A series of letter-writing campaigns ensued, known as the War of the Rose, in which each side attempted to justify its position while decrying the treason of the other.

Like so many things esoteric, with only a few rare exceptions this made little impact outside the limited circles in which it occurred: day-to-day life went on for the man on the street. The siege of Paris, Verdon, Saint-Mihiel, Sedan, Compaiegne, Ypres, and others too numerous to remember, along with death in the trenches, was only a generation away. By 1919, most of the founding members of these orders would be dead, too old, or simply too tired to care any longer. The ancient feuds of authenticity were seen for what they were then and are now: a convenient distraction born out of the luxury of both time and money. Invoking the shades of the dead went from fashionable to commonplace as mourners sought solace in the glimpse of a loved one in the darkened chamber of the spiritualist medium or reflected in the magic mirror of the magus. There was no longer a need to talk of the demons of the abyss in the abstract; they were now neighbors.

From the period of the French occult revival, with its glory and its decadence, a spirit would arise and give birth—even if more in inspiration than in direct substance—to the single most important initiatic mystical fraternity of the twentieth century: the Ancient Mystical Order Rosea Crucis (AMORC), better known as the Rosicrucian Order. Within AMORC, the ideal of a single unified international esoteric movement open to men and women of all races within a quasi-Masonic framework of initiation, ritual, and instruction would be realized. Drawing on the inspiration of his contemporaries as well as Cagliostro and Egyptian Masonry, Harvey Spencer Lewis (1883–1939) achieved through AMORC what many esoteric and occult movements had attempted but failed: permanence beyond the death of its founder, physical temples worldwide, and a profound impact on popular culture and its understanding of traditionally secret and highly veiled themes and ideas. At different periods and varying from jurisdiction to jurisdiction, members of AMORC were at times refused Masonic membership, as during its early years it was seen as a clandestine Masonic body. This never seems to have become a widespread notion, more of a local peculiarity. However, Lewis, the organization's founder, was refused initiation as a Master Mason by the Grand Lodge of New York after having completed his Entered Apprentice and Fellowcraft degrees. This appears to have been due in part to Lewis's lack of tact in the early promotion of his fledgling movement and to a personal grudge against him by a former

AMORC member who was also a member of the lodge where Lewis was being initiated.

## The Hermetic Order of the Golden Dawn

Martinism drew on Freemasonry for some of its members and even, if ever so briefly, sought to change the face of Freemasonry itself. Co-Masonry saw itself as the rightful esoteric heir of the occult truth within Masonic ritual and form. Yet it is the Hermetic Order of the Golden Dawn that has had the most impact on the twentieth-century occult scene and is most clearly connected to Masonic and semi-Masonic movements.

The two main founders of the Hermetic Order of the Golden Dawn were William Wynn Westcott (1848–1925) and Samuel Liddell MacGregor Mathers (1854–1918). Both men were deeply entrenched in the Masonic and esoteric world of Victorian England, and they brought with them connections and skills that would fuse together in the creation of the most important magical order in over a century.

While the actual origins of the Golden Dawn are murky at best, it is known that in 1886 Westcott found, received, or created a set of documents in a unique code or cipher. These became known as the "Cypher Manuscripts." The documents contained teachings and rituals in outline form for an organization calling itself the Hermetic Order of the Golden Dawn. The structure of the order was identical to the eighteenth-century quasi-Masonic and alchemical Orden der Gold und Rosenkreuz.

Westcott says that the Reverend A. F. A. Woodford (1821–87), a fellow Mason with occult interests, found the documents in a bookseller's stall—just as Cagliostro had claimed of his Egyptian Rite. This is not improbable, but neither can it be substantiated, which causes many to question the authenticity of the story, some going so far as to level claims of forgery. Accusations of forgery come mainly because of the fact that letters later produced by Westcott supposedly from a Fräulein Sprengel in Germany are clearly written by someone with a limited command of German. Westcott was no stranger to claims of succession without documentation to support them. As a member of the Societas Rosicruciana in Anglia (SRIA), or Rosicrucian Society of England, he investigated claims by the society's founder, Robert Wentworth Little, that the SRIA was founded on documents discovered in Freemasons' Hall in London; Westcott found nothing to support this claim. He rose quickly through the ranks of the SRIA after joining in 1880, becoming Supreme Magus in 1891. Mathers was also a member of the SRIA. The grade structure of the SRIA was identical to that used earlier by the Orden der Gold und Rosenkreuz and later by the Hermetic Order of the Golden Dawn.

Westcott formally established the Hermetic Order of the Golden Dawn in March 1888 with the assistance of Robert Woodman and Mathers—the two other Freemasons he'd recruited for the task. As was to be expected, the initial membership was made up of the associates of the founders; it would grow to around three hundred members and at least nine temples at its zenith: six in Britain, two in the United States, and one in Paris. The first public announcement came in the form of a reply from Westcott to a letter published in *Notes and Queries* in December 1888. The letter inquired about the continued existence of a Qabalistic society that included Eliphas Levi and Rabbi Falk among its members. Westcott stated in the affirmative, prompting additional questions and increasing the Golden Dawn's membership significantly.

As the Hermetic Order of the Golden Dawn grew, its members desired more practical material than was issued in the lower grades of Neophyte, Zelator, Theoricus, Practicus, and Philosophus, and under the skilled hand of Mathers they were obliged. With the creation of the Portal and the Adeptus Minor rituals, a second or inner order of the *Ordo Roseae Rubeae et Aureae Crucis* was formed. Additional grades were planned, but their completion is disputed as a result of the Golden Dawn's breakup in 1900.

It was here in the second order that the practical magical teachings for which the Golden Dawn would become famous were actually taught and practiced, and it is with the order's self-destruction in its twelfth year that these practices were cast to the winds of fortune. While several organizations were created to continue the teachings of the Golden Dawn, including Mathers's own Order of the Alpha et Omega, most of them dwindled and died or were succeeded by those of second-generation students, such as Dion Fortune's Fraternity of the Inner Light (later changing its name to the Society of the Inner Light) and Paul Foster Case's Builders of the Adytum, to name just two. Fortune's society originally used several grades derived from Co-Masonry for its Lesser Mysteries. This ended, however, in 1961, when the work was reduced to one degree and took on a distinctly Christian tone. Case's organization, often known only by its initials, BOTA, works the Golden Dawn rituals without the use of Enochian. The practical work of the Golden Dawn survived in most part because its rituals were published—first by Aleister Crowley, a former student and close associate of Mathers, and then again in several volumes by Crowley's student Israel Regardie between 1937 and 1940.

Oddly, some of the Golden Dawn material also found itself in the SRIA. When Westcott was forced to choose between resigning his membership in the Golden Dawn or his position as a public official, he chose to leave the Golden Dawn, but he retained his Masonic activities. In 1907, the American branch of the English SRIA (known as the Societas Rosicruciana in Civitatibus Foederatis) experienced a schism when a faction wished to remove the Masonic membership requirement. The schismatic body adopted the name Societas Rosicruciana in America (also SRIA) and was established by Sylvester C. Gould, who was succeeded two years later by Dr. George Winslow Plummer (1877–1944). It was under Plummer's leadership that the Societas Rosicruciana in America grew and, using the methods of the day, developed a correspondence course that contained much of the teachings of the Golden Dawn. Upon Plummer's death, leadership of the organization fell to his wife, Gladys Plummer, better known as Mother Serena, who was succeeded by Sister Lucia. The Societas Rosicruciana in America continues to offer courses of instruction and is run by Soror M.A.; its headquarters is located in Bayonne, New Jersey.

## Knights Templar Anew

One of the most controversial and influential figures in what could be called the "magical fringe Masonry" of the early twentieth century is Aleister Crowley (1875–1947). Born into a wealthy family that practiced an unusually severe form of Puritanism, the Plymouth Brethren, Crowley was reared with a small fortune, a first-rate education, and a significant amount of psychological baggage. He saw himself as the prophet of the New Aeon, a messiah come to liberate humanity from its moral and ethical constraints to find its own "True Will" through magic (which he spelled *magick*). Crowley turned to magic while at college, after finding a copy of A. E. Waite's *Book of Black Magic and of Pacts*. In 1898, he became a member of the Golden Dawn, taking on a leadership role under the direction of Mathers and playing an important role in the events surrounding the order's demise. Crowley, however, would turn his talents against both Waite (who, after the schism of 1900, established his own Fellowship of the Rosy Cross, which worked the Golden Dawn scheme in a purely mystical manner) and Mathers, engaging in vitriolic diatribes against them in his writings. At the feud's lowest point, Mathers and Crowley were engaged in a running magical war, sending astral vampires to attack each other!

It was during his Egyptian period, while in Cairo in 1904, that Crowley had a series of experiences that involved communications from an entity calling itself Aiwass. These messages were written down over three days in April 1904 and became known as the Book of the Law, which among other things proclaimed Crowley as the Antichrist, the Beast of the Book of Revelations. Using up what was left of his inheritance, he published *The Equinox*, a magazine through which he brought the teachings of the Golden Dawn to a wider occult public. Soon afterward, he joined the Ordo Templi Orientis (OTO), a Masonic-style group run by Theodor Reuss.

The Ordo Templi Orientis was established by Karl Kellner (1851–1905) and Theodor Reuss (1855–1923), both of whom were entrenched in the occult world and the fringe Masonic movements that dominated Central Europe prior to World War I. In 1902, the men contacted John Yarker and purchased a charter to establish a lodge of the Rite of Memphis and Misraim, a Masonic rite consisting of ninety-nine degrees. The following year, they published a prospectus for the establishment of the OTO. The order made little headway over the next few years and only began to grow significantly with Crowley's membership. Eventually, as with all things Crowley touched, he would have a falling out with Reuss, as it became clear that Crowley was reinventing the OTO in his own image.

Despite Reuss's questionable character, several well-known occultists of the period had brief encounters with the OTO, including Papus, Rudolph Steiner, and Harvey Spencer Lewis. It is Lewis's connection to Reuss that would be the fuel for another running legal battle for Crowley when he attempted to take over Lewis's AMORC in the 1930s—just as AMORC was established and prosperous and Crowley's own money had long been squandered on drugs, alcohol, sex, and vanities of the highest order.

Under Crowley's leadership, the OTO adopted the Book of the Law as its principal text, and its members—both men and women—undertook a series of initiations in which magical knowledge was imparted through sex magic, something both Kellner and Reuss were obsessed with. However, by the time of Crowley's death in 1947, the only active OTO body left in the world was located in California.

By 1969, however, this began to change, as Grady McMurtry (1918–85) announced that he was in possession of an OTO charter from Crowley, which he had received when visiting the Beast in London in 1943. Despite claims and counterclaims, the legal authority of McMurtry's charter was established in court, and trademarks and copyrights were awarded to his branch of the OTO. Under his leadership, the OTO reached a far larger audience than it ever had under either Reuss or Crowley, and it currently is one of the most influential, as well as controversial, fringe Masonic movements in existence.

## Key Points

1. By the end of the nineteenth and beginning of the twentieth centuries, Masonry and fringe Masonic and Masonic-style movements were the focal point of the occult revival.

2. Despite claims of promoting equality and fraternity, many of these groups were torn apart by schisms and personality conflicts.

3. Co-Masonry moved into prominence because of several of its leaders' connection to the Theosophical Society. Co-Masonry admitted women on the same grounds as men and promoted an esoteric understanding of Masonic ritual and initiation.

4. Co-Masonry saw Freemasonry as a continuation of the ancient mystery schools and medieval occultism. It saw Christianity as a dying religion that would be replaced by a single universal system of belief and affirmed that the world would be united under a single government, thereby promising universal peace.

5. It was believed that behind Co-Masonry and the Theosophical Society were perfect beings known as "Masters" or "Adepts" and that these beings guided the movements' leaders, making them nearly infallible.

6. Eliphas Levi's writings were the impetus for the French occult revival, and they directly as well as indirectly gave birth to several organizations, including the Rosicrucian and Martinist movements.

7. Gerard Encausse, better known by his pen name, Papus, was a central force in Parisian occultism. He was a prolific author and tireless organizer. He is responsible for modern Martinism and, to a lesser degree, Rosicrucianism.

8. The "War of the Roses" between two conflicting French Rosicrucian movements demonstrated the human weakness behind the ideals of the time. What internal squabbles did not destroy, the First and Second World Wars did, making many modern esoteric movements irrelevant in day-to-day life.

9. The Hermetic Order of the Golden Dawn is the single most influential modern magical order to have appeared during this period. It lasted only twelve years, but its influence is felt more strongly than ever. Several of its founders were High Degree Masons and members of a Masonic Rosicrucian group.

10. Aleister Crowley was among the most famous, or infamous, of the Golden Dawn's members. He played a pivotal role in the order's demise and eventually published its teachings in his journal, *The Equinox*, thereby bringing them to the attention of the broader occult public for the first time.

11. Crowley later became a leading member of Karl Kellner's Ordo Templi Orientis, a Knights Templar–styled initiatic order claiming Masonic status. The OTO practiced a variety of forms of sex magic. At the time of Crowley's death in 1947, there was only one functioning OTO lodge in the world.

12. Starting in 1969 under the leadership of Grady McMurtry, a student of Crowley's, the OTO underwent a renewal process that within three decades would make it one of the largest movements of its kind, with active lodges across the globe.

## Assignments for Chapter 10

1. If you were to organize a movement, be it esoteric, charitable, or educational, what would its core ideals be? What would the organizational structure be modeled after?

2. How would you address the problems that can arise from personalities and leadership responsibilities?

3. Based on your knowledge of fraternal and secret societies, what are the main problems that seem to arise within movements of these types, and how can they be avoided?

## Suggested Reading

*Gnostic Philosophy: From Ancient Persia to Modern Times*, by Tobias Churton (Inner Traditions)

*Freemasonry and Its Ancient Mystic Rites*, by C. W. Leadbeater (Gramercy Books)

*Fulcanelli and the Alchemical Revival: The Man Behind the Mystery of the Cathedrals*, by Geneviève Dubois (Inner Traditions)

*Al-Kemi: A Memoir; Hermetic, Occult, Political and Private Aspects of R. A. Schwaller de Lubicz*, by Andre Vandenbroeck (Lindisfarne)

*Occult Symbolism in France*, by Robert Pincus-Witten (Garland Publishing)

*Eliphas Levi and the French Occult Revival*, by Christopher McIntosh (Weiser)

*The Theosophical Enlightenment*, by Joscelyn Godwin (State University of New York)

*Masonic Orders of Fraternity*, by Manly P. Hall (Philosophical Research Society)

*The Arcana of Freemasonry: A History of Masonic Signs and Symbols*, by Albert Churchward (Weiser)

*Access to Western Esotericism*, by Antoine Faivre (State University of New York)

*Modern Esoteric Spirituality*, edited by Antoine Faivre and Jacob Needleman (Crossroad)

*Freemasonry of the Ancient Egyptians*, by Manly P. Hall (Philosophical Research Society)

*The Occult*, by Colin Wilson (Watkins Publishing)

*The Lost Keys of Freemasonry*, by Manly P. Hall (Philosophical Research Society)

*The Practice of the Ancient Turkish Freemasons: The Key to Understanding Alchemy*, by Baron Rudolph von Sebottendorf, translated by Stephen E. Flowers (Runa-Raven Press)

# Modern Masonry:
# Much Ado About Nothing,
# or the Revival of the Lost Word?

OVERVIEW
- *The Decline of the Craft*
- *The Future of the Craft*
- *The Craft and the New Age*

One of the more interesting observations about Freemasonry is that while it has a series of landmarks, traditions, and rituals that make it recognizable from age to age and across jurisdictions, it is in many ways a malleable entity, changing to meet the particular aspirations of its members. As we have seen, there has always been the idea since the inception of the first Grand Lodge that something was missing from Freemasonry—that it held the deepest of mystical secrets within its breast but could not find the key to unlocking them. Simultaneously, we see Freemasonry growing and expanding as a social entity, a leveler of class differences, and a vehicle for men of good will, regardless of social and economic status, to come together. Each candidate brings what he has to the door of the temple— not in money or status, as that will, at least temporarily, be stripped from him, but in terms of who he is and what he hopes to become. For some, this will express itself through charity; for others, social climbing; and for a small group, philosophical and even esoteric and occult speculations and practices. In the introduction to this book, it was stated that it becomes difficult to speak of Freemasonry as a monolithic subject, for there are as many variations of Freemasonry as there are Freemasons. Each chooses to make of it what he will, and in turn the Fraternity both shapes and is shaped by its members.

The world of the seventeenth and early eighteenth centuries from which Freemasonry emerged as a highly organized entity with a centralized Grand Lodge is not much different from our own. Many of the same ideas that flourished then are popular now: utopianism, Atlantis and lost continents, and the feeling that the world was in chaos—that the center had collapsed.

Religious sectarianism and violence had broken the morale of the population, decimated the economies, and all but destroyed cultures built up over hundreds of years or more. The Thirty Years War (1618–48) would set German unification back two hundred years; that is, it would take Germany two hundred years to rebuild its infrastructure as a result of the damage done. England would recover more quickly from the Catholic-Protestant divide, but only because of its limited size and geographic isolation. Severe dictatorships, both secular and sectarian, also assisted in getting things done much more quickly in the small piece of land that would become the seat of the British Empire, and of Freemasonry.

In our own lifetime, Freemasonry, like all civic organizations, has seen a constant and steady decline in membership for the last forty years. However, for Freemasonry, or more specifically regular Freemasonry, the impact has been harder and is more difficult to resolve. The Craft in many instances is finding itself confronted with culture shock—not unlike the rift between the Antients and Moderns in the early years of the first Grand Lodge. Today, many of the young men joining regular Freemasonry are finding that their expectations of encountering men of learning, culture, and self-improvement are not being met. Instead, they are greeted by members of twenty, thirty, and even fifty years for whom the Craft has provided a lifetime of fraternity, social contacts, and civic service but has not been a philosophical or particularly highbrow organization. Masonic education has consisted of generous and impressive amounts of memorization, particularly in the rituals, but nothing in terms of their symbolic meanings or possible origins, let alone an active study of the Seven Liberal Arts and Sciences. Esotericism is all but unknown to 90 percent of the Brethren. This emphasis on form over essence has meant that Freemasonry has lost one if not two generations of potential members. In many ways, this is ironic, as many of the most important works on the esoteric symbolism in the Craft were written by Freemasons during the first thirty or forty years of the twentieth century, with High Grade members of the order authoring many of the popular books on New Thought, psychic development, and early comparative religious studies during those years.

And yet, despite the downturn, many of the young men joining Masonry who are seeking those very things are working with other Brethren and bringing them into reality. Lodges of Research, Colleges of Ancient Rites, Traditional Observance lodges, and a host of printed and electronic resources mean that Freemasons are more connected to each other now, and exchanging more information on what Masonry means to them, than ever before. Esoteric Freemasonry does not exist in every lodge, but it does exist, and it is growing quickly among regular Freemasons who see the ideals of the eighteenth century as vital to the twenty-first century. In many jurisdictions, Traditional Observance lodges, or lodges in which members must prove intellectual and philosophical proficiency before they begin advancing to the next degree and wherein esotericism plays a primary or strong secondary role in the interpretation of the Craft's meaning, will be the norm and not the exception within ten years.

In addition, Co-Masonry, Droit Humaine, and a host of co-ed rites that are specifically, openly, and unequivocally esoteric in their orientation and that demand proof of a member's ability to advance to the next degree are finding their memberships increasing and their discussions with regular Masons flourishing.

In terms of membership, Masonry is at the same point it was in the first half of the eighteenth century, as the number of Freemasons is dropping and will continue to do so as the current generation dies off over the next five to ten years. However, the hundreds of billions of dollars of resources available to various Grand Lodges means that Masonry will never die, and its charitable work is guaranteed by its investments; this gives Masonry the opportunity to focus now on rebuilding the philosophical aspect of the Craft—if it is to be called an actual fraternity and not simply a social club. Freemasonry is shifting back into a small, socially connected, elite organization composed of men who have chosen to be there rather than members who are members simply because their fathers or grandfathers were Masons. This choice means that Freemasonry is being reshaped to meet the desires of the current and future generations for education, involvement, and personal growth along spiritual lines. Regular Freemasons who find these things stay in the Fraternity and support their lodges. Those who do not find what they are seeking leave and join organizations that provide it.

Despite this temporary change of direction in the Craft's orientation, it is amazing to see how Masons of all ages greet each other upon meeting, even for the first time. Anger has been softened to patience, hurried gruffness to an apologizing nod and a pause to exchange sincere pleasantries, and distracted self-absorption into selfless assistance and even sacrifice at the sight of a ring on a Brother's finger or pin on his lapel.

Just as men change Masonry, Masonry changes men. It is an organization whose ideals are eternal and are needed now more than ever.

# Afterword

In life's pilgrimage, we travel many highways and byways. You have now completed the reading of *Freemasonry,* whereby you have taken a detour on your journey and have ventured into a fascinating and intriguing world. This world of Freemasonry has as its goal self-improvement. Do not be disappointed if you feel confused or puzzled about Freemasonry. I have been an active member and student for over forty-five years and still find myself suddenly becoming aware of a new way of looking at a symbol or motif that gives me a new understanding. Some readers may dismiss this text as another reading that may have had some interest for them, and they will now move on to another novel. Some may be interested in the overall picture of Freemasonry and, having completed the lessons and readings, felt satisfied with their understanding of Masonry and its relationship to esoteric philosophy. Others may have been interested in Freemasonry as a Western magical tradition phenomenon, while some may be members of Freemasonry and now find a new way of thinking about the Fraternity. There may also be a small group who, having gone this far, may wish to fully understand the mysteries of the Craft by petitioning a Masonic lodge for membership.

In the last decade, more and more attention has been focused on the esoteric aspects of Freemasonry. While we do not expect to find any documents that would have existed in the formative years of symbolic Masonry that would attest to the use of esoteric symbolism and procedures in developing Masonic ritual, we may draw implications from a reasoned study of the historic periods and probable influences. There have been publications on the study of the degrees of the Masonic lodge and their interpretation of the Qabala's Tree of Life and various aspects of Hermeticism. Yet few authors have gone beneath the surface of the Masonic ritual and its motif and allegory to examine the hidden symbolism that points to a past centered around ritual magic, which can be traced back through the Age of Reason, the Enlightenment, and the Renaissance into early traditional mysticism. This book has turned the corner in presenting the esoteric roots of Freemasonry in a comprehensive and understandable manner.

Mark Stavish has taken a very complex subject and has presented it with a common viewpoint. He did not illustrate this using only "regular and official" Freemasonry, which would be made up of the traditional Grand Lodges with pedigrees from some other recognized grand authority, but rather used the overall picture of Masonry, which includes various origins, affiliations, and makeup. In this context, he examined the esoteric roots and their applications, looking back through the eighteenth century. *Freemasonry*'s study/workbook format gives the reader an opportunity to search out and come to his own understanding of the subject.

As you traveled this path of Freemasonry, you were taken to the period of the Operative craft—the builders of classical temples and Gothic cathedrals. You were informed of the spirituality seen in architecture and found additional mystery in the initiatic illustrations throughout your readings. You learned that there is a spiritual potential that may transform one's environment beyond time and space. When venturing into the cosmology of Freemasonry, one may find a world that some believe takes them nearer to God.

As you journeyed through the transition of Masonry from an Operative to a Speculative art, you were introduced to elements that reflected an esoteric origin. You may have asked if the hidden mystery of Freemasonry is to be found in Hermetic philosophy, alchemy, or the Qabala. That should become a personal quest, and through meditation and study, you may be better able to understand the nature of man and the improvement of self.

In this text, Stavish presented the popular mindset of various eras and built upon the magical and alchemical practices found there to project the development of Freemasonry for the reader's mental reception, for throughout one was given clues and guided in making an esoteric connection to the present.

Freemasonry has many facets and is already the focus of over seventy-five thousand books. The student who only reads about Freemasonry is at the same level of understanding as the member who only watches the ritual. The richness of Freemasonry is given an even greater assessment when one may develop a wider appreciation for its heritage through an inward journey, one that seeks understanding of its esoteric background and interpretation. Through this venture, the two-dimensional experience of words, signs, and motifs becomes multidimensional. The "Word," which is central to much of ritual, resonates with new vibration and meaning and yields a deeper and more personal experience. Freemasonry as it once existed in the past is given renewed vision. While the recognized secrets of Freemasonry are in the modes of recognition—signs, passwords, and handgrips—the *real* secret and esoteric meaning of Freemasonry is in the personal journey each member must take in reflecting upon his own self and his travel in the deeper cosmology of that mystical, timeless landscape. Here he must confront his own archetypes and become his own Operative Mason who will find the True Word in his collective unconscious.

Whatever path you take, the destination is the same: becoming a more polished living stone for "a house not made with hands, eternal in the heavens" (2 Corinthians 5:1).

Charles S. Canning, 33°, KYGCH
Director, Harry C. Trexler Masonic Library

# APPENDIX A

# Sacred Geometry and the Masonic Tradition

*by John Michael Greer*

The idea that Masonry and geometry have quite a bit to do with each other is a hard one to miss. Brothers who familiarize themselves with the rituals of our Fraternity, or simply attend the Fellowcraft degree more than a few times, will remember that geometry is there described as the first and noblest of sciences, and the basis on which the superstructure of Freemasonry is erected. Most of the use made of geometry in modern Masonry is moral and symbolic. Just as the lectures on the working tools draw a distinction between the practical use of those tools and the "more noble and glorious purposes" of moral allegory, the common attitude toward geometry among today's Speculative Masons seems to be that it is to be contemplated in the abstract rather than studied and practiced in any more concrete sense.

This is certainly one way to approach Masonry, and an entirely valid way on its own terms. Yet historical interest, at least, would suggest that if the entire edifice of Freemasonry is built on the basis of geometry, a look at the foundations may occasionally be in order. Furthermore, the idea that Operative Masonry is necessarily less noble and glorious than the speculative form of the institution may be questioned by anyone who has experienced the noble and glorious creations of ancient, medieval, and Renaissance architecture. Buildings such as the temples of ancient Greece and the Gothic cathedrals are as much works of mind and spirit as of stone and mortar. They were designed and built not merely for practical purposes, but to uplift the hearts and enrich the lives of those who worshipped in them. To give such beauty and such inspiration to the world was no small thing, and it involved more than merely physical labor. Our ritual reminds us that our ancient brethren wrought in both Operative and Speculative Masonry, but I'm not sure how many modern Masons realize that these two were not seen as two separate things. Rather, our ancient brethren wrought in both forms of Masonry at the same time and in the same actions.

It's rarely realized just how close company practical geometry and philosophy kept before the Scientific Revolution. In an important recent study, philosopher Robert Hahn has documented that the origins of Greek philosophy itself are closely woven together with early developments in the history of Greek architecture, in particular with the adoption of Egyptian architectural methods for the first Greek temples of stone.[1] Thales and Anaximander, the first Greek philosophers known to history, were also famous for their accomplishments in geometry, engineering, and the sciences; ancient testimonies name Thales as the man who first brought geometry from Egypt to Greece. Pythagoras, who invented the word *philosopher* and was arguably the first known historical figure in the development of the esoteric traditions of the West, is still remembered today for his theorem on the relationship among the sides of a right triangle—a theorem we will be exploring in some detail a little later on.

Thus, the art of sacred geometry needs to be understood in its proper context. It is certainly true, as a recent and useful article about sacred geometry in Masonry suggests, that the principles of sacred geometry are

---

1   Robert Hahn, *Anaximander and the Architects: The Contributions of Egyptian and Greek Architectural Technologies to the Origins of Greek Philosophy* (Albany, NY: State University of New York, 2001).

based on "profound meditations upon geometric space and form"[2] rather than the deductive logic of Euclid or, for that matter, of modern schoolroom geometry. Yet these meditations did not remain in the realms of abstract thought and mystical perception; they came down the planes, as modern occult terminology would put it, all the way to the plane of dense matter—the plane of Operative Masonry, of stone, timber, and mortar. Our ancient brethren, if we may call the master builders of ancient, medieval, and Renaissance times by that term, applied the principles of Strength, Wisdom, and Beauty to their work. A mastery of strength enabled them, despite what we might consider very simple technical means, to raise buildings, some of which still stand tall more than three thousand years after they were built. A mastery of beauty enabled them to design and ornament those buildings with an elegance and grace that still evokes wonder today. These two are obvious; less immediately visible, but just as central to the ancient achievement, is the presence of wisdom.

That wisdom was founded above all on a mastery of proportion. Plenty of factors contribute to making today's buildings as mindlessly ugly as they are, but one of the most important is that their parts and dimensions have no relation to one another; convenience and the whim of the architect govern all. The temples of pagan Greece, the cathedrals of the Middle Ages, and the palaces and paintings of the Renaissance were cast in a different mold. Vitruvius, whose textbook of architecture is the only classical work on that subject to survive the wreck of the ancient world, explains that the six essential principles of architecture are order, disposition, eurhythmy, symmetry, decorum, and economy.[3] Only the last deals with the practical concerns that now ride roughshod over all other issues in building. The next to last deals with issues of style and decoration, which occupy all the attention modern architects can spare from purely pragmatic issues. The other four deal with the missing dimension of modern architecture: proportion, relation, balance, and harmony, set out by geometry and woven into every detail of the building from the ground plan to the fine points of decoration.

---

2 Herbert P. Bangs, "The Geometry of the Visible Lodge," *Heredom* 7 (1998), 115.

3 Cited in Richard Padovan, *Proportion* (London: E & FN Spon, 1999), 158.

Formed in ancient Egypt and passed on to Greece and Rome, this fusion of what we would now call Operative and Speculative approaches to geometry continued without a break into the Middle Ages, reinforced by the patronage of the early and medieval Christian Church. The Church's hostility to esoteric traditions from the end of the Renaissance on has made it hard for modern scholars—and often, even harder for modern Masons—to recognize that this state of affairs was a new departure of the early modern period and that things had been different earlier on. Valerie Flint's study *The Rise of Magic in Early Medieval Europe* documents that the Church, far from being hostile to esoteric spirituality, played a crucial role in preserving, transmitting, and disseminating it in the centuries following the collapse of the Roman Empire.[4] So long as people invoked the Trinity rather than pagan gods and stayed clear of obvious moral difficulties, almost anything was acceptable. This easy tolerance remained part of medieval Christian culture until the first witch panics at the end of the fourteenth century and was not finally forced underground until the Scientific Revolution of the seventeenth century made the entire subject too hot to handle.

Thus, the sacred geometries of classical pagan temples, copied by the builders of early Christian churches, became part of the stock in trade of medieval Operative Masons and survived in poorly understood forms in the fabric of modern speculative Masonry. This connection can be shown readily enough, for specific details of modern Masonic symbolism can be linked back to medieval building practice and demonstrate an unexpected meaning in that context.

A parallel example from another tradition will help clarify this. In some modern Druid orders, initiates of a certain grade wear a rope belt divided by thirteen equally spaced knots. Very few of those who wear such a belt have any idea of the origins of this custom. The knotted belt has in turn been borrowed by other traditions outside of Druidry, some of which have evolved their own interpretations of the knots, explaining them by way of mythological and spiritual symbolism. Yet the actual meaning of the knotted rope is wholly practical, or as we would say Masonically, operative.

---

4  Valerie Flint, *The Rise of Magic in Early Medieval Europe* (Princeton, NJ: Princeton University Press, 1991).

Thirteen evenly spaced knots divide the rope into twelve equal sections. Given one of these rope belts, three wooden stakes, and no other equipment, it is possible to lay out an exact right angle on the ground by using the simplest whole-number Pythagorean triangle: three units for the short base, four for the long base, and five for the hypotenuse. According to Greek sources, the ancient Egyptians used exactly this method to lay out the foundations for their pyramids and temples, and it has been suggested by modern scholars that similar methods were used centuries earlier in Britain and Ireland to lay out the great stone circles such as Stonehenge and Avebury. These Druid orders, which curiously enough were founded about the same time as the Grand Lodge of England, almost certainly borrowed the idea for their knotted ropes from the same Greek sources—there is no reason whatever to think that the building methods used at Stonehenge were passed down intact to the present—but the transformation from operative tool to speculative emblem is worth noticing, for this same method of laying out right angles by way of Pythagorean triangles has left its mark on Masonry as well.

I'm sure that everyone will remember the place of the forty-seventh proposition of Euclid in the rituals of our Craft, presented in our Washington ritual as "a discovery of our ancient friend and Brother, the great Pythagoras." There are plenty of propositions in Euclid, and any of them could have been singled out and interpreted in the moral terms standard in modern Speculative Masonry. Yet this one alone has a place in the ritual. Why? I suggest that the reason for its inclusion is the role of this proposition in the practical geometry of our medieval Operative brethren.

We are not forced to speculate about the methods used by the medieval Masons; the testimony of archeologists and historians is ready to hand, and relevant. For example, in the year 1134, the monks of the newly founded Priory of Saint Bertelin at Norton, not far from Liverpool, commissioned a stone church and hired the Master Mason Hugh de Cathewik to design it and superintend the work. His design methods have been reconstructed by the archeologists who excavated the ruins of the priory in the 1970s and 1980s.[5] These methods were as elegant and exact as they were simple. First,

---

5  J. Patrick Greene, *Norton Priory: The Archaeology of a Medieval Religious House* (Cambridge: Cambridge University Press, 1989).

Hugh laid out a straight line from east-northeast to west-southwest, angling it so that the rising sun would shine straight down the nave of the church on Saint Bertelin's feast day. The alignment was probably laid out with the skirret, a Masonic working tool no longer included in our Washington ritual but still mentioned in some English rituals, which consists of a marked rope or chalk cord on a reel.[6] A skirret, two straight staves, a trained Apprentice or Fellowcraft, and a practiced eye are the only pieces of equipment needed. Such a carefully selected solar orientation was nearly universal in churches before the Reformation and has echoes in the symbolic orientation of Masonic lodges to the rising, noonday, and setting sun.

Next, Hugh measured out three Pythagorean triangles, again using the skirret. The first two, starting from the west, were 25 medieval feet on the short base, 60 feet on the long base, and 65 on the hypotenuse; the last, on the east, was 25 feet on the short base, 30 on the long base, and 39 on the hypotenuse. The 25-foot bases determined the width of the nave, made the walls of the church precisely parallel with each other, and allowed exact right angles to be marked out for the east and west walls, the pulpit screen, and the west end of the chancel. Two overlapping squares, which again could be traced out quickly with the skirret on the bare ground, defined the transepts to north and south and the dimensions of the choir. Once that was done, fine details could be put in at will using similar methods. The entire process could be completed in a few hours, and work on the foundation started on the same day.[7]

The entire process depends on a mastery of whole-number Pythagorean triangles. Surveying equipment of the modern sort did not exist when the church of Saint Bertelin was built, nor for many centuries thereafter, nor was there yet a source paper large enough to draw up building plans to a workable scale. The skillful application of practical geometry was the only option available to the medieval master builder, and Pythagorean triangles one of the few efficient answers to the problem of laying out exact right

---

6 See Stephen R. Greenberg, "The Ultimate Implement of Freemasonry," *Proceedings of the Illinois Lodge of Research* no. 10 (n.d.), and Bob J. Jensen, "The Missing Working Tools in American Masonry," *Walter F. Meier Lodge of Research Masonic Papers* vol. VI no. 12 (December 1992).

7 The description of the laying out of the Norton Priory church is from Greene, *Norton Priory*, 81–83.

angles and parallel lines. It seems unlikely to be accidental that the geometrical principle central to this method of laying out buildings remains the one piece of actual geometry in our current Masonic ritual.

These Pythagorean triangles did not make up the whole of the medieval Operative Mason's geometrical stock in trade. They formed one of the basic elements of the builder's art: an element suited, in fact, to Fellowcrafts who had not yet earned the rank of Master. More important were the subtle geometrical patterns by which those first four principles of Vitruvius—order, disposition, eurhythmy, and symmetry—were woven into the fabric of sacred and secular architecture alike. These patterns form the core of sacred geometry as known to its modern practitioners. Each had its special meaning. The square root of 2, derived geometrically from the relationship between the square and its diagonal, represented generation and the fourfold world of nature. The square root of 3, derived geometrically from the equilateral triangle, represented integration and the threefold world of the spirit.[8]

Two different systems of sacred architecture, the ad quadratum and ad triangulum systems, unfolded respectively from one or the other of these basic proportions, and there were quarrels—on occasion, descending to the level of fistfights—between the adherents of the two systems. Yet there was also a third proportion, the master proportion of all sacred geometry: the golden proportion or golden section. Its mathematical properties are fascinating, its geometry complex; experiments have shown that a majority of people instinctively find shapes based on it more beautiful than any other.[9] Researchers have traced it in the forms of the Parthenon, the great cathedrals, and many other masterpieces of the builders' art.

Contemporary documentation for the golden proportion's use as a design principle in ancient, medieval, and Renaissance architecture is all but absent, but this can be understood in more ways than one. Operative Masons in the Middle Ages and Renaissance are known to have kept

---

8 For a discussion of these proportions, see Robert Lawlor, *Sacred Geometry: Philosophy and Practice* (London: Thames & Hudson, 1982).

9 See Padovan, *Proportion*, 308–16, and Matila Ghyka, *The Geometry of Art and Life* (New York: Dover, 1977).

certain of their practical methods secret, passing them on only to qualified members of their guild, under oath, on the attainment of Master's
rank. For example, the Regensburg ordinances, a set of rules established
by an assembly of German Master Masons in 1459, forbade any Mason
from communicating their secret method of working out the elevation of
a structure from the ground plan to anyone but a qualified candidate for
mastership.[10] Medieval guilds of all kinds had secrets of this sort. Yet the
transmission of such secrets in the Middle Ages and Renaissance posed
problems unfamiliar from a modern perspective. Most medieval Masons
were illiterate—mason's marks, those elegant geometrical patterns that
mark the work of individual stoneworkers in the fabric of the great Gothic
cathedrals, came into use because their owners were not able to write their
own names. How could exacting methods of geometrical construction be
passed on to each newly made Master Mason in a way that was memorable
enough to preserve the crucial information intact over the generations?

One way of doing this, much practiced in the Middle Ages as in earlier periods, was to convert the details of a practical method into the
events of a narrative: a story in which the central incidents served as re-
minders to the trained memory. Such a narrative, I suggest, conceals an
operative secret at the core of Speculative Masonry: the legend of the
Master Mason Degree.

We can begin exploring this dimension of Masonic sacred geometry
with the familiar title "The Widow's Son." This has been interpreted in
many different ways by Masonic theorists and students of comparative
mythology, but as far as I know, it has not yet been noted that this famous
title has a straightforward geometrical interpretation.

As mentioned already, the square with its diagonal forms the geometrical
symbol of generation (Figure 1). A widow, as half of a married couple—
the human symbol of generation—might be represented by half a square,
divided by a vertical line rather than the diagonal from which the larger
square is generated (Figure 2). Yet for the widow to have her own son, she

---

10  See Nigel Hiscock, *The Wise Master Builder: Platonic Geometry in Plans of Medieval Abbeys and
Cathedrals* (Aldershot: Ashgate, 2000), 186–95.

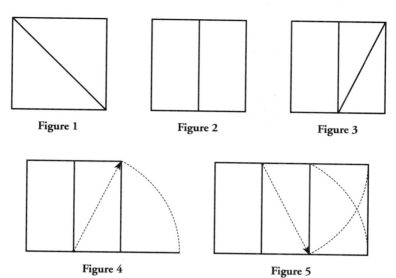

Figure 1      Figure 2      Figure 3

Figure 4      Figure 5

must have a diagonal of her own, so we draw a diagonal from the midpoint of the square to the opposite corner, as shown in the diagram (Figure 3).

For the widow to generate her son, the upper end of the diagonal then rotates downward until it lies on the same line as the bottom side of the square (Figure 4); in practice, this is done with a compass on paper, or with a skirret on the bare ground of a medieval building site. Next, the upper side of the square is extended the same distance, again using the compass or skirret. The ends of the two extended lines are then connected with a vertical line (Figure 5).

The result is a golden proportion rectangle (Figure 6). If the side of the original square is equal to 1, the long side of the new rectangle is the irrational number φ, equal to $(\sqrt{5} + 1)/2$ or approximately 1.618. The ratio 1:φ gives the golden proportion, the "precious jewel" of sacred geometry. If the argument presented here is correct, this proportion is also referred to Masonically as the Widow's Son, who sets out the patterns used by the workmen building the Holy Temple.

The construction just given is familiar to anyone with a good general knowledge of plane geometry. It has certain disadvantages for practical use in medieval architecture, however. The most important of these problems

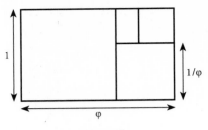

**Figure 6**

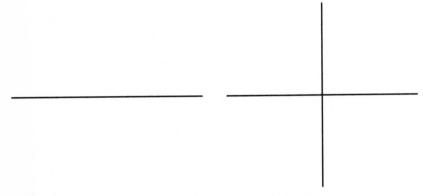

**Figure 7**                                    **Figure 8**

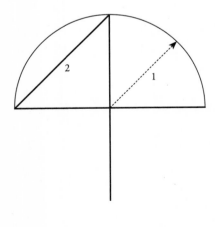

**Figure 9**                                    **Figure 10**

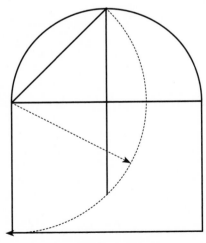

is that it starts with a smaller measurement and creates a larger one. In medieval practice, as shown in the design of the church of Saint Bertelin, the largest dimensions were usually set out first and all smaller dimensions produced as fractions of one or another of these primary measurements. Masonically, we can say that our Operative brethren were left in a quandary once these first measurements were traced out, for the Widow's Son was nowhere to be found, and without him the work could not go forward. The methods they used to search out this missing proportion will be familiar to any Master Mason.

The search for the Widow's Son begins with a line of any length (Figure 7), which is symbolically the empty work site, with no sign of the Widow's Son. The first step is to look for him in the four directions. This is done by drawing a second line of equal length perpendicular to the first and passing through its center (Figure 8).

Next, using compass or skirret, an arc is traced with the intersection of the two lines as the center, and the distance from the intersection to the end of the first line (that is, half the first line's length) as the radius (#1, Figure 9). This reveals the shape of a hill. It also resembles the upper part of a human face, and the medieval fondness for puns might suggest a term such as "the brow of a hill" for this diagram. Then a line is drawn from one end of the original line to the point where the curve intersects the perpendicular line (#2, Figure 9). This line, which will be removed to another place in the course of the construction, might be likened to the branch of some symbolically appropriate tree.

The branch is removed by setting the compass or skirret equal to its length and drawing a line of the same length perpendicularly from the end of the original line, using the square on paper or knotted ropes and Pythagorean triangles on the ground of a medieval building site. Another line of the same length is extended in the same way from the other end of the original line, and their ends connected with a straight line parallel to the original line, to form a rectangle (Figure 10). This rectangle might well be compared to a grave, particularly since the original line on the building site of a medieval church was usually lined up on the rising sun, as was the ground plan for the church of Saint Bertelin described above; the symbolic "grave" thus lies due east and west.

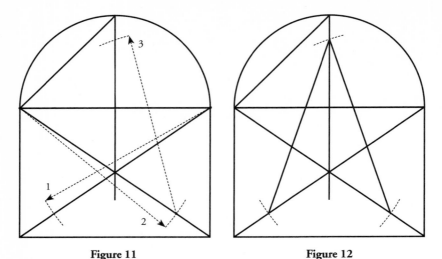

**Figure 11**                    **Figure 12**

Next comes the excavation of the grave, which is done by drawing diagonal lines connecting the opposite corners of the rectangle. But the Widow's Son hidden in the grave cannot be drawn out of it quite so simply. It takes three additional actions, which might be called three attempts, to do so. First, setting the compass or skirret to a radius equal to the original line and taking one end of the original line as the center, make a short arc on the diagonal line extending from the same end of the original line to the opposite corner of the rectangle, measuring the length of the original line onto the diagonal (#1, Figure 11). Next, with the compass or skirret set to the same measure, take the other end of the original line as the center and repeat the process along the other diagonal line (#2, Figure 11). Finally, using either of these two short arcs as center and with the compass or skirret still set to the same measure, make a third short arc on the perpendicular line drawn across the original line, as shown in the diagram (#3, Figure 11).

At this point, the Widow's Son can be drawn out of the grave. The two ends of the original line and the three short arcs mark out the points of a pentagram (Figure 12). The five points of this figure will readily remind any Master Mason of the five points by which he was raised from a similar state of concealment. It also forms a symbol that may be found in a position of honor in every Masonic lodge.

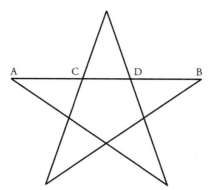

**Figure 12**

Geometrically, the pentagram divides the original line by the golden proportion in no fewer than six different ways, as shown in Figure 13. The ratio between AD and AB is 1:φ, and so is the ratio between CB and AB. Furthermore, the ratio between AC and CB and that between DB and AD are also equal to 1:φ, and so are the ratios between CD and AC, on the one hand, and CD and DB on the other. The remarkable geometrical properties of the golden proportion weave each of these relationships together by way of φ relationships as well; for example, the ratio between AC and AB is 1:φ², and that between CD and AB is 1:φ³. Thus the Operative Master Mason using this construction could produce a cascading series of φ-based proportions from a single initial measurement, such as the intended length of a building. To continue the same series of proportions down to even smaller scales, he could repeat the same construction using CD as the initial line, say, or do the same thing even more simply by connecting the five points of the pentagon at the center of the pentagram, creating a new pentagram with sides equal to AC or DB. Either process could be repeated as many times as necessary, so that everything down to the fine details of windows and string courses follows the same elegant system of proportion.

Can it be proven that this construction and its uses are what the narrative of the Third Degree was originally meant to conceal? Almost certainly, such a proof is beyond reach. As far as we know, among the Scottish or English Operative Masons from whose Craft modern Masonry descends, not one betrayed his trust and revealed the practical secrets of the Royal

Art. Barring such a disclosure, the diagrams and explanations I have presented are speculative—this time in the everyday sense of the word. Yet one point worth mentioning is that I have never encountered the construction just outlined in any ancient, medieval, or modern source. It is not in Euclid. I did not know of it when I began the investigation that led to this paper; it unfolded, step by step, as I tried to work out how the narrative of the Master Mason degree might make geometrical sense. It is also simpler, more elegant, and more practical for architectural uses than any alternate construction I have encountered for the same proportion.

It is also worth taking a moment to stress that even if this was the operative secret behind the story of the Widow's Son, that story is not limited to a purely geometric or architectural relevance. Its moral, philosophical, and spiritual meanings remain, and they were in all probability known to the same Operative Masons who also used it to remember a central secret of their practical art. As mentioned earlier in this paper, the art of the medieval Operative Masons was not simply a matter of piling up stones, and it took shape in a culture that still remembered that a symbol or a story can have many meanings.

Like the rest of medieval culture, and like the ancient cultures that came before, the Operative Masonry of our early brethren fused the physical and the metaphysical through the medium of a geometry that united matter and mind. It taught the building of both temples: that made with hands in the realm of time and change, and that made without hands, eternal in the heavens. We live in an age in which the very concept of such a unity of being is labeled an anachronism, in which a Berlin wall of the mind has been raised between the material and the spiritual sides of reality. Yet Freemasonry, among its many other virtues, is a time capsule that comes to us from an age before that wall was raised, and it suggests another and, perhaps, a better way of embracing reality. Like so many other spiritual traditions, it calls us to seek, as Socrates is said to have prayed, that the outward and the inward man may be as one.[11]

---

11  Plato *Phaedrus* 279b.

# APPENDIX B

# Symbols of the Tracing Boards and the Degrees

The various tracing boards of Freemasonry vary from period to period as well as between jurisdictions and rites. The following synopsis of the symbols and their basic meaning is given as a guide rather than a definitive list or set of interpretations. A careful study of the symbols and the boards they appear on, as well as actively drawing them with chalk or pencil, will help those of a more mystical orientation to understand how the mundane tools of the builder can be transformed into the inner teachings of morality and ethics—the foundation for all genuine spiritual unfoldment. From this newfound perspective, it becomes possible to transform any aspect of life into a spiritual teaching and allow us to see the divine in everything and everyone.

## Entered Apprentice Degree

**Apron**—The apron connects Masons to one another in the Fraternity and to the ancient building guilds of the past. It represents work, both material and spiritual, for the improvement of one's self and humanity.

**Ornaments of the Lodge**—These include the checkerboard floor or mosaic pavement, the Indented Tessel, and the Blazing Star. The checkerboard floor represents the duality of this world, or good and evil; the tessel border is fellowship and union; the Blazing Star is the divinity in man. These are not mentioned in the old rituals or in biblical references within Masonic rituals; as such, their origin in Masonic ritual is unclear.

**Burning Tapers**—Each lodge has three lights around the altar; these represent the light of the sun, which rules the day; the moon, which rules the night; and the Master, which rules the lodge.

**Three Jewels**—The square, level, and plumb are worn by the three stationed officers, or the Master, Senior Warden, and Junior Warden. They represent morality, equality, and personal integrity. They are called "Immovable Jewels," as these three officers must be present for a lodge to be opened.

**Movable Jewels**—The rough ashlar, perfect ashlar, and trestle (or tracing) board are called Movable Jewels, because they may be absent and a lodge still opened by the officers present. The rough ashlar is the crude and base nature of man yet unrefined. The perfect or smooth ashlar is the educated man who raises himself above the unthinking and common. He has done this through using the tools of the Entered Apprentice to smooth down the rough edges of his personality and character and refine it through the teachings of the liberal arts and sciences as instructed in the Fellowcraft Degree. The trestle board is the application of reason, planning, and foresight to one's life so that it may mirror the truths learned through Masonic fellowship.

**Holy Saints John**—Saint John the Baptist and Saint John the Evangelist are the two patron saints to whom Masonic lodges are dedicated. It is unclear why these were chosen over other saints, or even King Solomon; however, it may have to do with their feast days falling near the summer and winter solstices. Saint John the Baptist's day is June 24, and Saint John the Evangelist's is December 27. Both dates play important roles in Freemasonry.

**Point within a Circle**—The point within a circle boarded by two parallel lines (said to represent the Saints John) reminds Masons to keep their actions circumscribed and guided by the Volume of the Sacred Law, which rests above it. Building construction requires the ability to make a perfect square, which is tested by using the center point of the circle, a method that was considered a secret known only by Master Masons. Albert Mackey's *Encyclopedia of Freemasonry* also states that the point is the Will, the creative energy of God and the divine power in each person; the circle all that comes under its domain; and the parallel lines Wisdom and Power.[1]

**Working Tools of the Entered Apprentice**—The working tools explained to a newly made Entered Apprentice are the twenty-four-inch gauge and a common gavel. The gauge is representative of the hours in a day, the passing of time, and how we use it. The gavel is representative of power and its rightful and constructive use in life.

## Fellowcraft Degree

**Three Jewels**—In the Entered Apprentice Degree, the Three Immovable Jewels are present but not explained. In the Fellowcraft Degree, the meaning of the square, level, and plumb are given; these are the tools of a craftsman, a worker who must exhibit a finer level of skill than the laborer.

**Twin Pillars**—The pillar of Jachin is revealed to the Entered Apprentice, and the process is completed with the revealing of the pillar of Boaz to the Fellowcraft. Combined, they represent the Pillars of the Porch outside of the Temple of Solomon and mean, "I will establish (Jachin) in strength (Boaz)." This is in reference to the presence of divine power, the kingdom of God. By understanding the importance of power and control, or self-discipline, the Fellowcraft then encounters the Winding Staircase.

**Winding Staircase**—The Winding Staircase consists of fifteen steps, although some illustrations show seven. The first three steps represent the working tools of the Fellowcraft, the following five the five orders of architecture and the five senses, and the last seven the Seven Liberal Arts and Sciences. Combined, these lead the Fellowcraft to the Middle Chamber.

---

1 Mackey and McClenachan, *Encyclopedia of Freemasonry* (see chap. 3, n. 2).

**Orders of Architecture**—These are as follows: Tuscan, Doric, Ionic, Corinthian, and Composite.

**Liberal Arts**—The Seven Liberal Arts and Sciences are required if one is to be well rounded in his education as well as able to solve the practical problems of daily life. These consist of grammar, rhetoric, logic, arithmetic, geometry, music, and astronomy (or astrology).

**Middle Chamber**—The Middle Chamber represents the resulting reward for our labors. In life, Masons are told, we will receive exactly the payment we request. If we ask more from life, we will receive more; if we ask but little, we will receive but little. As the architect and builder of our own life, it is up to each of us to decide what we will get from it.

**Wages of the Fellowcraft**—Wine, corn, and oil are given as the wages of the Fellowcraft. Although corn was unknown to the ancients, as it belongs to the Americas, wheat is often used in its place and was more likely the actual foodstuff given in payment for work. Corn or wheat is abundance and represents the goddess Ceres; wine is refreshment after a day's work; and oil is joy and happiness in life.

**Tongue, Ear, and Heart**—These represent the need of the Fellowcraft to be attentive in his listening to instructions from the Master, constructive in his words to his fellows and those Entered Apprentices under his care, and faithful in his adherence to what he has received. For this reason, they are known as the Instructive Tongue, Attentive Ear, and Faithful Breast, further demonstrating the oral nature of Masonic ritual and instruction.

## Master Mason Degree

**The Square and Compass**—With these tools, the working tools of the Master Mason are tested by squaring the circle, or creating a firm and perfect foundation for building his inner spiritual life while being of service to his family and community. The compass draws the circle, whose point reminds us to be centered and balanced if we are to build successfully the life we want. The square provides us with the means of making a straight line, or firm decision, and the compass a means of testing its strength.

**The Trinity of Lights**—These form a triangle around the altar each Mason has passed and knelt before three times in his journey. It is the ancient symbol of deity and the divine inspiration each Freemason seeks.

**The Working Tools of the Master Mason**—These are all of the tools of Masonry combined, and the trowel in particular. The trowel spreads cement to bind the stones together, just as the Master Mason spreads brotherly love and affection to support and uphold his Brethren and maintain harmony in the lodge.

**Skull and Crossbones**—According to Jewish lore, all that is needed for physical resurrection are the skull and thighbones of a person. Here they represent the symbolic death of Hiram, as well as the selfishness and egotism that prevents each person from experiencing the mastery of life he seeks.

**Sprig of Acacia**—The "evergreen" or eternal life, immortality of the soul or consciousness of the Master Mason.

**Inner Chamber and Veil**—The temple built without hands, the deepest part of our selves and our connection to God.

# Excerpts from *Morals and Dogma* on the Three Degrees of Masonry

*The following excerpts are from Albert Pike's* Morals and Dogma *and can be found in many of the Bibles given to members of Scottish Rite. Additional sections are used to further illuminate the importance of the degrees of York and Scottish Rite and thereby to encourage study of the symbols presented. (The full text of* Morals and Dogma *can be found on Project Gutenberg's website at www.gutenberg.org/etext/19447 as well as at www.freemasons -freemasonry.com/apikefr.html.)*

## I. Apprentice

FORCE, unregulated or ill-regulated, is not only wasted in the void, like that of gunpowder burned in the open air, and steam unconfined by science; but, striking in the dark, and its blows meeting only the air, they recoil and bruise itself. It is destruction and ruin. It is the volcano, the earthquake, the cyclone—not growth and progress. It is Polyphemus blinded, striking at random, and falling headlong among the sharp rocks by the impetus of his own blows.

The blind Force of the people is a Force that must be economized, and also managed, as the blind Force of steam, lifting the ponderous iron arms and turning the large wheels, is made to bore and rifle the cannon and to weave the most delicate lace. It must be regulated by Intellect. Intellect is to the people and the people's Force, what the slender needle of the compass is to the ship—its soul, always counseling the huge mass of wood and iron, and always pointing to the north. To attack the citadels built up on all sides against the human race by superstitions, despotisms, and prejudices, the Force must have a brain and a law. Then its deeds of daring produce permanent results, and there is real progress. Then there are sublime conquests. Thought is a force, and philosophy should be an energy, finding its aim and its effects in the amelioration of mankind. The two great motors are Truth and Love. When all these Forces are combined, and guided by the Intellect, and regulated by the RULE of Right, and Justice, and of combined and systematic movement and effort, the great revolution prepared for by the ages will begin to march. The POWER of the Deity Himself is in equilibrium with His WISDOM. Hence the only results are HARMONY.

\* \* \*

Though Masonry neither usurps the place of, nor apes religion, prayer is an essential part of our ceremonies. It is the aspiration of the soul toward the Absolute and Infinite Intelligence, which is the One Supreme Deity, most feebly and misunderstandingly characterized as an "ARCHITECT." Certain faculties of man are directed toward the Unknown—thought, meditation, prayer. The unknown is an ocean, of which conscience is the compass. Thought, meditation, prayer, are the great mysterious pointings of the needle. It is a spiritual magnetism that thus connects the human soul with the Deity. These majestic irradiations of the soul pierce through the shadow toward the light.

\* \* \*

A "Lodge" is defined to be "an assemblage of Freemasons, duly congregated, having the sacred writings, square, and compass, and a charter, or warrant of constitution, authorizing them to work." The room or place in which they meet, representing some part of King Solomon's Temple, is also called the Lodge; and it is that we are now considering.

It is said to be supported by three great columns, WISDOM, FORCE or STRENGTH, and BEAUTY, represented by the Master, the Senior Warden, and the Junior Warden; and these are said to be the columns that support the Lodge. . . .

## II. The Fellow-Craft

In the Ancient Orient, all religion was more or less a mystery and there was no divorce from it of philosophy. The popular theology, taking the multitude of allegories and symbols for realities, degenerated into a worship of the celestial luminaries, of imaginary Deities with human feelings, passions, appetites, and lusts, of idols, stones, animals, reptiles. The Onion was sacred to the Egyptians, because its different layers were a symbol of the concentric heavenly spheres. Of course the popular religion could not satisfy the deeper longings and thoughts, the loftier aspirations of the Spirit, or the logic of reason. The first, therefore, was taught to the initiated in the Mysteries. There, also, it was taught by symbols. The vagueness of symbolism, capable of many interpretations, reached what the palpable and conventional creed could not. Its indefiniteness acknowledged the abstruseness of the subject: it treated that mysterious subject mystically: it endeavored to illustrate what it could not explain; to excite an appropriate feeling, if it could not develop an adequate idea; and to make the image a mere subordinate conveyance for the conception, which itself never became obvious or familiar.

Thus the knowledge now imparted by books and letters, was of old conveyed by symbols; and the priests invented or perpetuated a display of rites and exhibitions, which were not only more attractive to the eye than words, but often more suggestive and more pregnant with meaning to the mind.

Masonry, successor of the Mysteries, still follows the ancient manner of teaching. Her ceremonies are like the ancient mystic shows—not the reading of an essay, but the opening of a problem, requiring research, and constituting philosophy the arch-expounder. Her symbols are the instruction she gives. The lectures are endeavors, often partial and one-sided, to interpret these symbols. He who would become an accomplished Mason must not be content merely to hear, or even to understand, the lectures; he must, aided by them, and they having, as it were, marked out the way for him, study, interpret, and develop these symbols for himself.

* * *

Christianity taught the doctrine of FRATERNITY; but repudiated that of political EQUALITY, by continually inculcating obedience to Caesar, and to those lawfully in authority. Masonry was the first apostle of EQUALITY. In the Monastery there is fraternity and equality, but no liberty. Masonry added that also, and claimed for man the three-fold heritage, LIBERTY, EQUALITY, and FRATERNITY.

## III. The Master

To understand literally the symbols and allegories of Oriental books as to ante-historical matters, is willfully to close our eyes against the Light. To translate the symbols into the trivial and commonplace, is the blundering of mediocrity.

All religious expression is symbolism; since we can describe only what we see, and the true objects of religion are THE SEEN. The earliest instruments of education were symbols; and they and all other religious forms differed and still differ according to external circumstances and imagery, and according to differences of knowledge and mental cultivation. All language is symbolic, so far as it is applied to mental and spiritual phenomena and action. All words have, primarily, a material sense, however they may afterward get, for the ignorant, a spiritual non-sense. "To retract," for example, is to draw back, and when applied to a statement, is symbolic, as much so as a picture of an arm drawn back, to express the same thing, would be. The very word "spirit" means "breath," from the Latin verb *spiro*, breathe.

To present a visible symbol to the eye of another is not necessarily to inform him of the meaning which that symbol has to you. Hence the philosopher soon superadded to the symbols explanations addressed to the ear, susceptible of more precision, but less effective and impressive than the painted or sculptured forms which he endeavored to explain. Out of these explanations grew by degrees a variety of narrations, whose true object and meaning were gradually forgotten, or lost in contradictions and incongruities. And when these were abandoned, and Philosophy resorted to definitions and formulas, its language was but a more complicated symbolism, attempting in the dark to grapple with and picture ideas impossible to be expressed. For as with the visible symbol, so with the word: to utter it to you does not inform you of the exact meaning which it has to me; and thus religion and philosophy became to a great extent disputes as to the meaning of words. The most abstract expression for DEITY, which language can supply, is but a sign or symbol for an object beyond our comprehension, and not more truthful and adequate than the images of OSIRIS and VISHNU, or their names, except as being less sensuous and explicit. We avoid sensuousness only by resorting to simple negation. We come at last to define spirit by saying that it is not matter. Spirit is—spirit.

# Index

## To Write to the Author

If you wish to contact the author or would like more information about this book, please write to the author in care of Llewellyn Worldwide and we will forward your request. Both the author and publisher appreciate hearing from you and learning of your enjoyment of this book and how it has helped you. Llewellyn Worldwide cannot guarantee that every letter written to the author can be answered, but all will be forwarded. Please write to:

Mark Stavish
℅ Llewellyn Worldwide
2143 Wooddale Drive, Dept. 978-0-7387-1148-5
Woodbury, MN 55125-2989, U.S.A.
Please enclose a self-addressed stamped envelope for reply,
or $1.00 to cover costs. If outside U.S.A., enclose
international postal reply coupon.

Many of Llewellyn's authors have websites with additional information and resources. For more information, please visit our website at:
www.llewellyn.com